Jacques Derrida's Ghost

Jacques Derrida's Ghost
A Conjuration

David Appelbaum

State University of New York Press

Published by State University of New York Press, Albany

© 2009 State University of New York

All rights reserved

Printed in the United States of America

No part of this book may be used or reproduced in any manner whatsoever without written permission. No part of this book may be stored in a retrieval system or transmitted in any form or by any means including electronic, electrostatic, magnetic tape, mechanical, photocopying, recording, or otherwise without the prior permission in writing of the publisher.

For information, contact State University of New York Press, Albany, NY
www.sunypress.edu

Production by Ryan Morris
Marketing by Michael Campochiaro

Library of Congress Cataloging-in-Publication Data

Appelbaum, David.
   Jacques Derrida's ghost : a conjuration / David Appelbaum.
      p. cm.
   Includes bibliographical references and index.
   ISBN 978-0-7914-7607-9 (hardcover : alk. paper)
   1. Derrida, Jacques. I. Title.
   B2430.D484A66 2009
   194—dc22

2008003239

10 9 8 7 6 5 4 3 2 1

To Carl Lehmann-Haupt

The breakthrough toward radical otherness . . . always takes *within philosophy* the form of a posteriority or an empiricism. But this is an effect of the spectral nature of philosophical reflection, philosophy being incapable of inscribing (comprehending) what is outside it otherwise than through the appropriating assimilation of a negative image of it, and dissemination is written on the back—the *tain*—of that mirror. Not on its inverted specter.
—Jacques Derrida, "Outwork"

To filter fire? I have not given up doing so, only justifying or giving a reason for it.
—Jacques Derrida, *The Post Card*

Contents

Foreword	ix
Acknowledgments	xi
Exergue	xii
Introduction	1
Chapter 1 With the word I	5
Chapter 2 The book begins	15
Chapter 3 To be read	25
Chapter 4 With the voice	35
Chapter 5 Reading itself	43
Chapter 6 Words 'I' write	51
Chapter 7 A ghost	61
Chapter 8 Writing itself	71
Chapter 9 Into the Book	79
Speaking with the ghost	89
Notes	119
Bibliography	137
Index	141

Foreword

If a foreword for this work could be written, it would be on deconstruction. Such a foreword, Derrida warns, could never exist as a *foreword*, somehow distinct from the body-text. There is no '*hors de texte*,' outside of the text. The warning misleads in that there is nothing likewise *inside* of the text. Nothing through and through. But can one step back a little to ask what kind of 'apparatus' does Derrida have in order to assert this much? What is it for? Not simply, one hopes, to catch the unwary and naïve, or extol the true believer. Is it a gravitational field from which nothing can emerge, a perpetual womb, fecundity, its dizzying abyss, new births always at the expense of shibboleths, night, the black hole? Perhaps. But hearsay or idle chatter is always a lure for having the net of deconstruction drop on it. And, any foreword is hearsay, the author (or another) writing what the book "that you are about to read" is, textually speaking. What is at stake is the possibility of what has come to be called a metalanguage.

Still, to ask is to ask what is left *after* deconstruction wrecks the site to ruin. What is left after the pass over is a field of possibility, new beginning—interminability, in short. An other time, *autre temps*. Deconstruction opens the door to an other time, a temporal alterity. Here, the frame of the metalanguage is bent in the shape of the ethical: the command to risk the responsibility to face the open door. It is the deepest, most grave of responsibilities, to philosophy, discourse, and *ecriture*, writing. And, it antecedes the first word written, foreword or body-text.

A foreword on deconstruction, if it is even possible, would already be open to the ethical claim and want to repeat it 'at the beginning,' even if this isn't the 'real' beginning but a 'mere' repetition of one. Not that it would *posit* an ethical claim of any kind but that it would reiterate its tentative openness to responsibly face the interruption on the page—always casting an inquisitive eye on its recurrence in the text. If ethics lies in a concern for respect for recursive alterity, then deconstruction adheres to its principles by unprincipled displacements of favored positions. There are no principles immune to corruption. That there should be a foreword possible *on principle* does not preclude the work of corruption, an unworking or rendering inoperative, a *desoeuvrement*, that undoes *in practice* any such undertaking.

Does such a foreword, if possible, deal with 'out of the text'? Is it itself out of the text? Could one say it, the foreword at this very moment, provides a site for the advent whose disruption marks the text such that it becomes a 'sign' for the un-signed, the other-than-significative, non-significativity? For, the outside, Blanchot's night, first night, is incommensurate and holy to Levinas and Derrida, and is put into writing in but not of the text, whatever given form and content. The outside is unavoidably *in*. For that reason, the foreword, if possible, is already folded into the text, distinguishable only by closest examination—if then.

The very act of examining expresses the responsibility to which a foreword, if possible, is necessarily open. Such an act of interminability is how the foreword, as possible, expresses itself. The interminable insertion of the theme of any foreword, if any are possible, is the beginning that recommences each time that the theme reappears. Perhaps the call to responsibility and respect for the other as interruption is just that repetition.

To begin a foreword, if possible, with repetition is to expose the essence of the matter.

Acknowledgments

Acknowledgments are due to Roger Lipsey, for his skills at motivation, to Eugene Heath and Bruce Milem, for their skills at support, to Dee Nelson, for her educational assistance, and to Kate Hamilton, for her skills supreme.

Exergue

To learn to live: a strange watchword. Who would learn? From whom? To teach to live, but to whom? Will we ever know? Will we ever know how to live and first of all what "to learn to live" means? And why "finally"?

. . . A magisterial locution, all the same—or for that very reason. For from the lips of a master this watchword would always say something about violence. It vibrates like an arrow in the course of an irreversible and asymmetrical address . . .

But to learn to live, to learn it *from oneself and by oneself*, all alone, to teach *oneself* to live ("I would like to learn to live finally"), is that not impossible for a living being? Is it not what logic itself forbids? To live, by definition, is not something one learns. Not from oneself, it is not learned from life, taught by life. Only from the other and by death. In any case from the other at the edge of life. At the internal border or the external border, it is a heterodidactics between life and death.

—Jacques Derrida, *Specters of Marx*

Introduction

SOME MAPS DON'T fold neatly. This book is a case in point in that no sharp crease separates its scholarly concerns from those of 'life.' The presumption is that good philosophy serves a magisterial purpose, that its work lies with transmission, that it has access to a secret knowledge. The position is beyond the claim that philosophy teaches logical coherence and consistency in accord with its commitment to reason. To the contrary, a magisterial vocation must be knowingly assumed, not merely ascribed. There is an important corollary, namely, that the reader is an other, *tout autre*. Philosophy is cast into the role of a voice addressed to an other who, beyond the pale, would remain irrevocably silent were it not for philosophical discourse. In this regard, Jacques Derrida concurs with his dear friend Emmanuel Levinas, who writes, "What we are now exposing is addressed to those who shall wish to read it."[1] Not every reading voice can meet such a rigorous standard. Some other force, in the form of an exigency, must be brought to align text, author, and reader before transmission. The task of alignment and the response it entails constitutes a subtext of my study.

It may seem exasperatingly obtuse to take the words of "this prince of the interrogation mark"[2] in a magisterial vein. Ironic, eloquent, witty, critical, well read, yes, for it is he who hides behind blazing analysis and leaves a host of textual assumptions in disarray. Don't his own "deconstructive" propensities undo every intention of a magisterial sort? Perhaps. At the very least, a second look is required. For one, the estrangements of his writing are never toward debunking that work. Unlike other shibboleths demolished without mercy, its eminence forbids attack. For another, the naïve view that deconstruction unswervingly avows nihilism suffers from a means/ends confusion. The point is to reach an 'irreducible' stratum. There, where ineluctably, an "undeconstructible condition of any deconstruction" exists, the teleology must not be neglected.[3] Justice, a responsibility to the other, by necessity overrides any conceivable metaphysical commitment.[4] An extended analysis makes clear how *différance* is an ethical guarantor of respect for alterity. As with Levinas, Derrida's primacy of the ethical supports the magisterial enterprise. Both follow Kant in the manner in which practical reason reaches back farther than pure reason.

It, furthermore, needs to be said that the proposed 'syllabus' needs a safeguard. To prevent a superficial reading, where the magisterial is likely to misguide, is prudent. The teaching program is encoded. The secrecy of the secret is preserved by apophasis, hiding in disclosure, and a slew of other 'thaumaturgic' devices. Derrida acknowledges a reliance on the same apparatus as 'negative theology' while simultaneously simulating uneasiness with its aims. Why is it necessary, like the folktale, to bury the dog? Perhaps because ease of discovery ruins the transmission and destroys the lesson that is to-come. The result, if any; belongs to the future, the *a-venir*, and to an eventuality that is without precedence or prediction. Corollary to the claim, understanding itself is constituted by a movement of radical negation; it lies in shedding understandings, sloughing the dead skins of positionings and positivity in general. Consequently, the labyrinth of structures, metonymy of terms, and hierarchy of intelligences marshaled by deconstruction are excesses to still the mind with complexifying. There, its arrested intellectual pretensions may be transmuted into a new body of knowledge, one less fixed and presumptive. Could the revaluation be called transmission? However deeply the lesson is buried, there are clues left by the authors to the reader's special initiatory activity. By a magisterial intention, the work *survives* and is passed on, in spite of the necessary encryption.

It is interred in the trash heap of prejudices that would discard—in the name of reason—that which is deemed beyond belief. *Enter the ghost.*

Sophistication in thought would reject belief in ghosts, right? What is a ghost, really? The ghostly defiance of boundaries between life and death, presence and absence, truth and illusion, being and nonbeing likewise defies the *what* question, as well as the *why* and the *how*. Spectral ethereality gives ghosts escape velocity from the plane of reality, and challenges easy assumptions about substance, solidity, gravity, ground, and place. Such terms define a foundational reality to which philosophy as Western metaphysics is committed, a commitment expressed through grammar and semantics, logic and categories. But a close examination of the terms of discourse and affiliated termini raises the question, for Derrida, of closure. There unbounded, unbonded, and generally unloved, ghosts exert considerable force in his address to the reader who "shall wish to read it." Why? Primarily because "learning to live, finally" needs a relation with both life and death (presence and absence, truth and metaphor, etc.), not just one or the other. Neither Spinoza (meditate on life) nor Plato (prepare for death) hits the mark in this respect. Only a specter's knowledge of "between the two's," a gaze free of things substantial, like essence and existence, can help. To learn to live can only mean this: "to learn to live *with* ghosts, in the upkeep, the conversation, the company, or the companionship, in the commerce without commerce of ghosts. To live otherwise, and better. No, not better, but more justly. But *with them*."[5]

Another strange twist to the syllabus. Mastery of the life lesson is a gift of the phantom, one that teaches a phantom mastery through its necessary inadequacy, given the questions surrounding the enigma of mastery itself. A mastery that lacks mastery that, through the lack, teaches the undeconstructible 'subject,' justice. *What is owed the other by the one who desires to be taught.* The lesson is never forced but by a receptivity is accorded the standard of the voluntary act. Ghosts enter as soon as one acknowledges a responsibility beyond all living present (able to be present) that extends to others yet unborn as well as already dead—those absent or absented. This is a responsibility whose depth fissures the present and leaves it no longer coincident with itself—time out of phase, de-phased, asynchronous. One is then responsible for the phantom other, the other qua ghost, that other, though dead, that wanders among the living and calls into question the mastery of meaning and the meaning of mastery. Only a limited view would locate the specter in the past. More precisely, its roots lie in the future, the to-come. The paradox of the apparition thus is expressed: since in arrival, it comes back, the ghost is *revenant*, the returning one or the returning, period. Inherently, the life lesson of justice, taught by the ghost, would also be a *"politics* of memory, of inheritance, and of generations."[6] Thus one faces an already expanded syllabus.

These sparse thoughts can introduce the first untidy fold, the magisterial side of this doubly thick book. Doubtless, they leave out what the philosophy's "real" intentions might be and deal duplicitously with ones only imagined or imaginary. Perhaps there is no fault in the tack. Where the transcendental imagination is by necessity in play, some approach like this is natural. In what follows, some skewed lines of the 'third' situated perilously between the intelligible and the sensible realms (thought and 'the world'), will need to be traced. Regardless, the second fold, that of scholarship, now must be considered, first, in the form of a puzzle that asks after the work of ghosts. What is puzzling less concerns the machinery of the scholar (citations and endnotes, with their spectral intrigues) and more the clue that Derrida lets drop. There is the moment in Shakespeare, when Horatio, scholar, addresses the ghost of Hamlet's father, the dead king:

> It is quite possible that Marcellus had anticipated the coming of a *scholar of the future*, a scholar who, in the future and so as to conceive of the future, would dare to speak to the phantom. A scholar who would dare to admit that he knows how to speak *to* the phantom, even claiming that this not only neither contradicts nor limits his scholarship but will in truth have conditioned it, at the price of some still-inconceivable complication that may yet prove the other one, that is, the phantom, to be correct.[7]

What of scholarship of the future, scholarship's future as well as future scholarship? What would be the content of a scholarly study that could arise from speaking to the ghost? What is the work of the future scholar? Who will conduct it? In what economy and at what price, in light of a "still-inconceivable complication" that will prove the phantom correct?

As soon as scholarly activity is conditioned by the phantom, the themes of death and life, absence, sacrifice, responsibility, and mourning become passionate signifiers. The conventions of good scholarship are not therewith disbanded but moored to the phantomized 'subject.' Scholarship advances with the courage to let the ghost speak, and speak for itself. By disappropriation, thematic borders become tremulous in the double sense of unsteady demarcation and terrified responsiveness. Disinterest ceases to be an option. Under the phantom's spell, uncanniness pervades the research, which proceeds with a wary glance over the shoulder. Should the future of scholarship lie there, it is reasonable to assume that the rank of scholars would diminish in number.

The last point concerns to *which* ghost does the scholar speak—or rather, to *whom* do I as writer speak who step into the role of scholar? The answer is both obvious and intimidating. To the ghost one is prepared to conjure. The conjuration of Derrida's ghost, the present or present future entity of the author of the corpus signed by Jacques Derrida, would need to be accomplished in order to converse with it (him) on a specific matter: how to live life, finally, while undertaking the impossible work. The impossibility is not trivial. Levinas distinguishes a work (in contrast to games and calculation) in its "being-for-beyond-my-death."[8] A work must renounce the time of a personal immortality and through generosity, allow the triumph in a time *without me*. To abjure the result of the work is then a "passage to the time of the other."[9] Only this order of sacrifice permits, I suspect, the conjuration of and conversation with a phantom, the ghost of Jacques Derrida, to take place. Within or beyond the horizon of eternity.

With the word I

I WISH TO DO MORE than speak of conjuring. I wish to do a conjuring. I wish to conjure the ghost of Jacques Derrida.

At the start, the required know-how involves the performative aspect of philosophical discourse, the effectivity of putting it in writing.[1] To presume it can be accomplished out of respect for the ghost, in this case, of Jacques Derrida, is obligatory, an ethical directive. Interest in conjuration is focused on the ghost's part in putting the work in writing. Without the writing, no record of conjuration would exist, nor any conjuration nor anything to conjure. Since no formula or spell has been stated, it would be a surprise to discover his specter already haunting the writing, with its ghostly effulgence to alert the voice reading to its otherworldly supplementation. It must be avowed that the conjuring will not rely on trickery, sorcery, wizardry, or legerdemain, and will suppose no belief (or lack of it) in ghosts, the supernatural, or the occult—though there will be debt before a positive inheritance can be claimed. Although the scene won't rely on smoke and mirrors (dry ice and laser), it will provide an exhibition of Derrida's skill at thaumaturgy, although the proficiency conjures away the magician, leaving only a trace.[2] As far as magic is essential to conjuration, the ghost lives in it and is 'alive' in writing, for that is the site and situation in which conjuration currently is at work.[3]

A supplemental confession is needed on the part of the writer.[4] The avowal is connected with the work of writing, which must appear in any writing if it is to rescue meaning from oblivion. The confession has to do with telling the to-be-accomplished aim, which cannot be said before realized and cannot be realized if said. The supplementary concern will, by the law of contamination, be a contaminant in each segment of writing, a smudge of unruly energy or spirit across the page. The avowal is said in that movement, and to that degree, the work accomplished. The supplemental concern has a classical orientation in the search for a surviving element, a survivor, and looks for a guarantee of 'perpetual life' or immortality (as with the Greeks), where the writing outlives the writer. The writer retains a presence in it, as a presence to it, and thereby wins the continued privilege of presence by means of it. No event, it could be argued, more fully constitutes the writer's signature in writing than the living-on of the voice, listened to (modally) by the reader. The appointment of the proper name, given by the acoustic sign(al) of voice, shows the relation writing enjoys with ghosting. The voice (heard to whatever degree in the reading), whether absent, dead, unknown, or anonymous, addresses us to questions of 'Western metaphysics,' and the grammatics of philosophical discourse.[5] An incontestable ghostliness is put in writing as soon as the obverse of presence, absence, is resonant in the writer's present voice. Then the other, other-than-own, secretly voices a work 'behind the scenes' unpinning the logic as soon as it is articulated in philosophical discourse.[6] Thus, writing finds its vein of paradox, that is, thought's attraction to its other—the inconceivably absurd—familiar in Hegel, Kierkegaard, and differently, Heidegger. It is the voice writing in Derrida's extended meditation on philosophical work.[7]

A detour is as unavoidable at this point—and also the question of the detour. Is it the writer's predilection to detour, to go 'lateral,' or is a digression in reality an embedded preface ancillary to the design, but necessary to commence the text? Even as the first thought is put in writing, a supplement is added. It injects itself into discussion, presenting itself as an impasse *at the start*, (in the Greek) an *aporia*, that apparently cannot be circumvented by another route and requires beginning at a place other than the beginning. At the same time, a detour deceptively offers the impression that there is no way out, no way to bypass, skirt, or even prevent putting the detour in writing. The hidden appeal to the ubiquity of presence is worth noticing in the idea of an escape, what would void or avoid the possibility of no exit. Bracketing the beginning has the effect of the meaning of "impasse" in question, and of asking whether, through the non-passage or non-experience, the question of limits is correctly constituted. Already an occasion of profound irresolution, absolute indecision, and unsettled apprehension. The detour then initializes an interrogation of the idea of borders, boundaries, and ends.[8] One such limit or delimitation of great interest (returning to the original question), is whether and to what extent the work is the writer's own, and to what extent, Derrida's. Whose work speaks through this voice and whose voice voices this work in order to exert influence on the idea of limits?[9]

To return the focus to presence: presence is not merely the premier term of metaphysics, but a double genitive—metaphysics is a metaphysics of presence and the presence of metaphysics puts it in writing. Whether it is called "essence, existence, substance, subject, . . . , transcendentality, consciousness, God, man, and so forth," metaphysics enjoys a presence, invisible, behind the scenes, rarely recognized.[10] This means that writing of any genre, writing, period, is metaphysical in character. Metaphysics, or a similar term like (Western) philosophical discourse, owes its existence to the privilege accorded by thought to what presents itself, and in this special case, *in writing*. At the center of presence is the matter of identity. This or that thing, in the act of presenting itself (appropriating self-presence), comes necessarily to possess or appropriate a proper identity of its own.[11] Identity is the inalienable essence of a being, its proper name. A rose by any other name would smell as sweet; but if its proper name were known, its smell would be also. Derrida's inquiry will focus on the implications of appropriation, deploying a counter-strategy that will render "enigmatic what one thinks one understands by the words 'proximity,' 'immediacy,' 'presence' . . ."[12] The solid foundation afforded reality is cracked by the strategy as the underdetermined means of defining a well-defined boundary line disappear. Stage direction: enter the aporia. Its power to block passageways is far from obvious since whether it's an experience, a non-experience, or nothing at all remains moot. Such a result (anticipated consciously or unconsciously or not anticipated at all) implies a lack of rule, standard, or criterion by which to say decisively whether something is present, absent, in between, or in defiance of the categories in use. Aporia: opposite to presence, still not an absence or an absconding of presence, but an undecidable question.[13]

It is important to recall the themes of ghosts, ghost-writing, writing in general, and the writer of the works of Jacques Derrida.[14] The feature that unites the links of the chain lies with the voice. Voice refers to what puts it in writing, and at the same time to a supplementation to writing that is a voicification also engaged in *reading*. It has to do with that which ensures the readability of what is put in writing, that is, the possibility of reading. Whenever the identity of the writer of a work is in need of authentication—as the question of ghost-writing as raised—voice is implicated. The signature, putting the proper name in writing, is properly acoustic. At the same time an effacement of the mark is possible, and in Derrida's case, likely.[15] Along the search for authenticity lies a wreck of issues of contemporary import: plagiarism, the intellectual rights to works, and copyright laws. They will lure and divert the inquiry as it moves forward.

The question of putting what in writing authenticates these words as 'my own,' or what constitutes 'owning' these words, is important. They may belong to someone else, as in an act of ventriloquism, posthypnotic suggestion, dementia, or veiled coercion. The main problem lies in establishing an identity of the *who* that is writing "I am putting these words in writing."[16] To believe that the first-person pronoun has a meaning given it by the thought of a first-person is to revert to a 'private language argument.' Conversely, an exterior cannot provide authentication of the meaning, a science or other field of knowledge whose signification could be 'sublated' in a Hegelian fashion, with the belief in an I. The two, inside and outside, are what Derrida calls "undialectizable." There is no possibility in their otherness blending. The very theme of self-presence, the presence of the I, takes a decidedly vertiginous twist away from Heidegger's thinking. When Heidegger asks what is it to be? he urges that in the case of *Dasein* (whose essence is its existence and which isn't identical to the designation 'human being'), one needs to differentiate between the specific being (you, me, Jacques Derrida) and its Being (capitalization noted), the Being of the being. This, the ontological difference, tells, very roughly, that an inclusion in the headcount of objects excludes that from which this privilege of being counted among beings derives. They are not the same, eminently differentiated from each other. The second is the onto(theo)logical crux that, by Heidegger's argument, lies buried under a metaphysical amnesia since just after its pre-Socratic discovery and Platonic interment. To uncover it makes possible *the* possibility that authenticates self-presence. It allows presence to self *as self*, or more precisely (since *Dasein* 'is always mine'), as myself. With Heidegger, it could be said that to seize the possibility is the affirmation of supreme individuation unto singularity. Only then does one *own* the experience suffered or enjoyed, writing, speaking, or whatever.

The presence of the *who*, an epicenter of Derrida's thought, runs parallel to the writer's vocality, the containment of voice by putting it in writing: Derrida: "The question of the self, 'who am I' not in the sense of 'who am I' but rather 'Who is this "I" that can say 'who'"? What is the 'I' and what becomes of responsibility once the identity of the 'I' trembles in secret?"[17] By a deflection, substance is set in motion by a tremor and trembles in turn. The trembling of the 'I', the self's tremulation, is acoustically translated into voice. The trembling broadcasts itself as voice in writing. Jacques Derrida's self broadcasts the singular 'I' of Jacques Derrida, which gives voice to the reader who listens to the reading of what is put in writing. Ultimately, the trembling is in front of the mystery of existence (*mysterium tremendum*). Tremors of all kinds, the trembling of an ambiguous visual figure or the trembling in a difficult truth, have a reference in it.[18] The 'I' that trembles in seizure of its voice always speaks while in the throes of blockage, a passage denied—aporia. Aporia, a conflictful shadow of the mystery and cause of the trembling, afflicts identity with ambivalence, fuzziness, indeterminacy, or indistinctness, chasing Leibniz (and the principle of identity of indiscernibles) away and casting off the arrogance of a politics of self-presence.[19]

In the truth of the aporetic lies a possibility that the singular is the only actual, but as an actual that must remain a possibility. A strange possibility, that does not behave like the (Aristotelian version) possibility as a pre-stage of actuality, a preliminary, preface, or pretext. For the canonical variety, if the act is done, the possibility no longer exists; if it isn't, it has been voided. It is a bizarre (and Kantian) possibility that belongs to the transcendental, which Heidegger puts aphoristically as, "Every disclosure of being as the *transcendens* is *transcendental* knowledge."[20] The possibility haunts each and every disclosure of being-there, each and every moment and movement, purposeful, spontaneous, or unconscious, of the I. A being-there conjured with the haunting possibility of the very undergoing (suffering, enjoying) whatever, fashioned out of (the logic of) presence. The possibility of actual appropriation (*Ereignis*) takes the form of an *obsession* with an apparition of being. It adds a double to the I, a secret life, possibly lapsed, rarely cherished, mostly overlooked, and its ghostliness concealed in the thicket of egology. Affirmation of it and rejection of the presence of the present, which happen simultaneously, invite the uncanny (*unheimlich*). Connected with the latter as a link in a chain already mentioned is a second chain of terms: *aporia*, enigma, being-possible (*Seinmoglischkeit*), trembling, and apparition. Phenomenologically, the uncanny enters the scene from nowhere, disperses, and conjures a mood of homeliness, displacement, and impropriety. Any memoir of a phantom contains a full description of being-not-at-home.

The writing invites a double (*doppelgänger*), a loosely attached, neither audible nor sonorous, but trembling aura, signifying the possibility of singularity, and incorporating the mark of 'selfhood,' which is announced in the voice of the ghost. The acoustics present a possible seizure that frequents (like now) the performance of writing. As a result, voice grows more voicified and uncanny as a doubling that is represented by the division into reading and writing, writer and reader. (It is the word "and" that contests the meaning of the distinction.) The reading gives voice to the voice of the writer, which does not simply copy the reader's effort. The voice is put into writing and is in writing, and when the difference is 'differenced,' reading repeats the essence (what-being) of the writing (distinguished from its existence [there-being]) as voice. But vociferation—the giving of voice—is a ghost performance that refuses clarity and distinctness, revels in equivocity, and trembles in the intermittent seizure of owning itself qua itself. A correspondence with the tremor of the *mysterium* dwells in the ambiguity in the writing and with it an apprehension: fright at the ghost of voice. Put in writing, the phantom is inherently frightening; fright constitutes the basis of an avoidance whose deference requires a lengthy study.[21]

In this context, for Heidegger, the task of existence—*Ereignis*, appropriation or seizure of owning what takes place—is effectuated by an affiliation with death. The accomplishment results from resolute living in the face of "my death." The strain of avoidance is apparent in the quotation marks that mention but avoid use of the expression. The avoidance is further masked and recast as "the possibility of the impossibility" of *Dasein*. The work of putting it in writing must graze against the fact of mortality and its indeterminate meaning, and trembles under the scrutiny of the revealed invisibility.[22] From the start, such work belongs to mourning, and specifically, the burden that makes the writer's inheritance difficult. Of several questions, let us name just two: does the possibility of appropriation (i.e., of the writer's presence put in writing) cease with the admission of the ghost? Is 'impossibility' itself unleashed to haunt the rest of the writing with its apparitional quality? Both inquire again into the uncanny, revealed now in its affiliation with the impasse, aporia, paralysis, catatonics, and non-responsiveness. Using a discourse whose fundamental terms tremble in their places and grow distracted, the work—of putting it in writing, of mourning—is asked to embrace the undecipherable as a mark that exceeds its own marking to the degree of rendering it illegible. It is a work to put mourning in writing while in the dark.[23]

The possibility that ghosts (and hosts) the performance of writing is found at the fringe, near the margin, by the boundary, of the line. It produces a trembling in the identity of the I (that writes, that reads) that induces a loss of distinctness, a sacrifice of definition, and a surrender of determination. The end of the line. The line blurs and disappears in the inked granules of an eraser. The line is presence and where presence is lost, effaced, rubbed away, the 'natural' progression of dear and departed presence, dead presence, and ghost follows suit. There, at the end of the line, where the idea of limit is put into question, blurring enclosures, the meaning of "limit," and specifically, the limit of life, is left questionable. There, where the question "Is 'my death' the end?" comes to an end—aporia.

The possibility boils down to a spectral accompaniment to writing that enjoys a close affiliation with death and yet serves to authenticate writing. It isn't always there (like "my death") and not always not there. To speak about the trembling of its appearance (or nonappearance) seems to depend in part only on the seizure that makes presence present. The other aspect of dependence has to do with writing in the dark. To write then is never done with certainty, and even the encounter with incomprehensibility is indecisive. An appearance of tremor, beyond understanding, drawing on knowledge from the other side: putting it in writing *cannot* avoid the risk of misunderstanding. Flicker, shimmer, flutter, waver: this series designates the peculiar diaphanous effect of the specter put in writing. The words circumscribe the being/nonbeing's curious disrespect for limits and boundaries. Impassable borders in space-time fail to restrict its movements and do not serve to define its position. Much of the lore of ghosts follows from these facts. It is said that ghosts are said to be similars to entities in our dreams. They, as 'shades,' are believed to inhabit the 'land of the dead,' conceived as an afterlife realm of indeterminate location. Thinkers from Aristotle to Freud have composed treatises on the triangle whose apices are ghost, dream, death.

In "Literature and the Right to Death," Blanchot looks at a writer's work, the text, through an Orphic lens.[24] In itself, the text is situated in what he calls "night," signified by the trope of the land of the dead. To read is to be called thereto by those who dwell there. The act of reading is an echoic response to the ghost inhabitants whose 'vocalizations' make possible the acoustics of reading per se. It is the voiceless voice of what Blanchot calls "nothingness as being, the idling of being," which is related to Levinas's *il y a*.[25] Belonging to no person, the voice's recitation *sotto voce* relates to the spectral beings that inhabit the night and haunt the text. What are they, the haunts, and what do they want with the voice reading? The present scene of writing is hauntingly animated by words put in writing by Blanchot, Heidegger, and Derrida. At the end of the line as flesh-and-blood authors, banished to the night of the text (their own and others'), they reappear flickeringly in the acoustic interior of the haunted writing. That act of interiorization and memorialization comes to unsettle the proceedings that attempt to make it clear.

So, Jacques Derrida's ghost *might* be here if the interiorization were of sufficient force. The word "might" needs emphasis because of the trickiness of its presence (absence). The end, limit, boundary, or demarcation has faltered as a standard determination of the limn. This applies also to existence and the end to which 'my life' (quotation marks) will come, and an end interlaced with that with which Derrida's life came to an end, a mingling at least. He would go on to say that 'at the limit' is less an immovable barrier and more a chalk mark subject to blurring, effacement or erasure, flickering or wavering.[26] Insofar as it touches personal identity, that is, the *who*, the limit possesses built-in indetermination. The I trembles in the wake of the interminable misunderstanding of its terminus.

If to arrive at the limit is to arrive at a blur, the illegibility must condition each and every phase beforehand. The affliction of personal identity shows itself in a tremor. The condition provides the subject with no way to say with certainty whether the *who* is absent or present. If an identity, a self-identity, Derrida's, for instance, is to be situated in the tremulous play of being-there (or not), it's in neither nor both, but in a "something that escapes both being a something and not a something." The main point of deconstructive *force* is precisely the expression of the radical oscillation, alteration, and ambiguity of things, principles, positions, and arguments. The *play* between presence and absence is a 'product' of forces whose work lets them be different, 'produces' differentiation (*per saltum*), and provides the array of distinction that constitutes the world. This third 'sign' (in addition to plus and minus; Derrida likens to the middle voice)—*différance*—presents itself only in self-effacement, and thus safeguards its indetectibility. As a law of contamination (supplementation), *différance* ensures that absence is included in presence, that the 'integrity' of the I includes the not-I, and that the bearer of a proper name carries impropriety. Conversely, in simple form, to say that presence is a ghost of absence, or that life is a ghost of death, is a restatement of supplementarity. The question is not tangential to whether and to what degree the writer 'lives' in writing, and whether the reader partakes of the 'life.'

The argument that presence, properly a possibility, is ghostly follows from any discourse that propounds a transcendental philosophy. The reasoning lies at the heart of the canon of 'Western metaphysics,' which is an ungracious host to the ghost. When tradition asks about origin, it is on dangerous ground. Origin, ground, substance, principle, source, beginning; another chain of Derrida's. Each term plays on the concept of the *first* (as in Descartes' title, *Meditations on the* First *Philosophy*), which is necessary if philosophical discourse is to have foundational meaning. The beginning or *arche* functions as no more than a rule of exclusion that keeps other key notions out of play. The ghost can have no origin as long as the origin is held to be immune to mutation, indispensable, self-sufficient, incontrovertible, and pure—for the ghost is none of these. By contrast, the honorifics denote an elect precinct of thought that has been placed beyond further review. They constitute the 'inner' as opposed the other, 'outer' or exoteric ideas. As philosophical atoms, or philosophemes, they have acquired a level of privilege as prized building blocks of discourse lining the logically 'anterior' interior.

In a way, this is another attack on the meaning of class membership, the "is" of predication, and an empowering of the copula.[27] Any set logically excludes that which is exterior to it. And it is the same question about the line that separates member from nonmember as well as one from the other. This again is the flaw in the idea of a self-contained presence, that it can't be said without elaboration, articulation, deduction, construction, or representation of its meaning that supplements its existential 'perfection.' To erect an edifice on perfectly solid grounds (Descartes' trope) implies that the grounds themselves need building on, and in themselves, are inadequate to the task of underpinning. A need always incorporates an insufficiency, which defeats the alleged purity of the principle. As the process reiterates, the first is supplemented by a second, a third, and so on, implying its originarity was a phantom all along. If there is 'something' out of play, it would be the point, the *arche*, without supplementation, a mute and inaccessible point, Barthes' *punctum*. The muteness cannot be overemphasized.

How does a need for supplements ring in Jacques Derrida's ghost? The ghost is a non-acoustical replication of the voice put in writing that reading (out loud, 'silently') encounters, a sonic facsimile. Reintroduced in writing, the voice, eviscerated, depleted of its breath, and made a sub-vocal wraith duplicates the real exterior articulation of speech. Of course, no original exists to be replicated; there is only the existence of the iteration. Repetition without origin, the source infinitely removed. With destruction of an inside, separately constituted from outside, the thinking of foundations is void. If the ghost of reading is a copy (of a voice), it is a copy of a copy, not of an original. The identity of a voice that belongs uniquely to writing can no longer be conceived as that which the specter replicates—any more than the converse. The relation of ghost to voice, and voice to ghost, reaches an impasse. There, it is the aporia itself that opens what Derrida calls the "work of mourning."

The injection of a politics into a discussion of death is unavoidable. Once the grip of metaphysics on philosophical discourse loosens, the performative is again functional. That no presence, no substantial being, no life, no I, can be unequivocally signified leaves nothing to copy. Which makes everything a copy, in the sense of an audio reproduction. Within the sanctum of origin, the lack of ground threatens to disturb the 'sanctity' of life. But on the stage, in the scene, the pervasive uncanniness of the specter now bleeds to the edges of the page. Before, the meaning of the ghost seemed derivative: it was a second to the being that predated it. Now, with a refulgence of spectrality, the ghost, graced by Derrida with the French *revenant*, is one that comes back. The ghost lives in the aporia surrounding how the *revenant* can possibly begin by coming back. The mourning of the dead is the inheritance of putting it in writing as soon as the phantom is on the scene. And where a work of mourning exists, the dead lead the writing in interiorizing the voicification of life that was. In the domain of putting it in writing, the ghost always goes ahead and life follows, conjuringly. The ghost first, and the life it ghosts, second.

What is a work of mourning? To what extent is a conjuration of the dead a part of the work? The ghost of Jacques Derrida, which has 'always already' appeared, no longer a living personal entity/nonentity, the haunt of the French philosopher who died five years ago, appears to inaudibly mingle with the reading voice, a vibratory accompaniment to 'giving voice' to the writing. Even read aloud, the text is known both less and hauntingly more than assumed, leaving it undecidable what it would mean to say that the reader's voice belongs solely to the reader. The inclusion of another voice, Derrida's, in writing cannot be reduced to simple memory, but elevated through interiorization to commemoration of what he calls an "unbearable paradox of fidelity."[28] The ghost can be memorialized "only by exceeding, fracturing, wounding, injuring, traumatizing the interiority that it inhabits or that welcomes it through hospitality, love, or friendship."[29]

Conjuring. "Ghosts: the concept of the other in the same . . . the completely other, dead, living in me."[30]

The book begins

THERE IS PROPRIETY, at the opening of a scene, to ask what relation a new chapter could have to the preceding one. Is the first properly a preface, prequel, or introduction to the present one? questions Derrida raises about prefatory material in general.[1] Why should the *second* chapter (essay, partition, segment) be properly looked upon as following a first, as a second, a backup or additive, which exhausts its meaning? Is it a supplement to the first, therein behaving like a contaminant? If there is nothing exalted in the first, first essay, version, draft, document, exegesis, presentation—the first anyway—except perhaps in its future anteriority, then it may be a non-original. That it came into existence as a copy, one of a number of copies, each lacking an original. A fatherless copy, orphaned at birth, among siblings, that has come to existence to prefigure a certain work. (Fatherless, without gold, law, capital, logos, born to an economy of loss, destitute even in proper name—to tinker with another chain of Derrida's.) But a chapter (sequence, segment) deficient in ancestors could also mean a copy *sui generis*, to begin without benefit of a beginning, unprefaced, *sans introduction*, intrusively insistent to put it *in writing*, but avowing no *telos*, no agenda, just a simple replication as replication, which is to add an other as (to) the same. (Is replication simple?) The concept of replication succors and supports the conjuration of the ghost, as demonstrable by how multiple attempts to put the specter in writing produce an atmosphere of apparition.[2] As if "ghost" as a marginal concept were posited as the transcendental visitation of the very conditions of writing: that is, *the reading of the voice that gives the writing to be read*. Whether it suffices for proof of ghosting *in the reading of voice* is not a question of experience. By 'acoustic intuition,' listening directly to the voice, in contact with the inaudible audition, the indeterminate identity of the ghost is apprehended.[3] It lacks representation because there is nothing to represent, although it has a number of anthropological portraits. The very idea of demonstration here relies on distinctions called into question by specters. On the other hand, the voice of the ghost is neither a belief nor a transcendental event on the event-horizon; it can be heard even in disbelief or empiricism.

It isn't improper to ask about the nature of the ghost's presence put in writing, the apparition of the printed page. With regard to the sense of 'of,' is the page apparitional or is an apparition somehow included in the page? Deferring the question, there is evidence of a different haunting in the need to repeat the question that invokes the adventure and to do so beginning the second chapter (section, sector.) It is a phantom need, not opposed to the real, that desires recurrence, and it is drawn there by a need for the phantom of recurrence. A most primitive recurrence, a remembrance of repetition, its telos and destination, without which truth and the logos are not possible. Repeated in memory, the destination is to awaken the trace of another (the last) repetition, the other time the voice will have read the text, at the end of reading the last text, the end of its mute voice: the position takes on markings of truth. "Truth unveils the *eidos* or the *ontos on*, in other words, that which can be imitated, reproduced, repeated in its identity. But in the anamnesic movement of truth, what is repeated must present itself as such, as what it is, in repetition. The true is repeated; it is what is repeated in the repetition, what is represented and present in the representation."[4] The essence of truth is given in the gift of repetition, recovery, rediscovery. That the essence is given but through repetition has meaning for the conjuring act, namely that through repetition itself, a warrant of the ghost's arrival avails itself of writing, and is put in writing. Such that it be the ghost that might be that of Jacques Derrida whose voice unmistakable is sonically situated in the voice reading it.[5]

The recurrent conjuring, moreover, is not to be construed as mere polemic, a thesis resubmitted to drive the point home. In all instances of repetition, formulaic, procedural, arithmetic, an absence is iterated. In these cases, Derrida writes, "what is repeated is the repeater, the imitator, the signifier, the representative, in the absence, as it happens, of *the thing itself*, which these appear to reedit . . ."[6] The thing itself would be the self-same, the presence present in the present: the signified. It differs from the signifier or representative, which is transcendent and intelligible, in the Saussurean universe of discourse, in being phenomenal and sensible.[7] The den of the ghost lies within the cleavage, signifier, signified, phenomenal, transcendental, sensible, intelligible, empirical. Offer the difference on the altar of signification, and the signified comes back to endlessly haunt the signifier, an infinite debt incurred by the sacrificial rite. With infinite repeatability, the signifier retains the power to recall the former life of the signified—the motor of conjuration. The ghostly visitation (no longer visitor) arrives from the chasm, the Platonic divide, the 'two's,' from a middle no longer excluded, from a logic of contradiction, from a maw aporetic and full of stops. If it suffices for conjuration to iterate a signifier, nothing more performative would be necessary. In that case: *Enter, ghost. Enter, ghost.*[8]

The signifier, however, must be an adequate performative, not a second. Otherwise, an order (of priority, value, need, etc.) isn't established by the movement of opposition itself, and without the difference, there is no meaning to the apparition and no apparition of meaning. It is necessary to oppose presentation with re-presentation, to say that the first is that by virtue of ordination, before it is possible to put the ghost in writing. By virtue of the first's anteriority to the second, the spacing allows a phantom of the successor to appear in the predecessor, and conversely, a phantom of the predecessor to appear in the successor. In the double movement, the privilege of priority (a purity or inviolability) of the first with respect to the second is effaced; a privilege that appears in absconding. *This movement of opposition is fundamental to canonical philosophical discourse* (and it must remain open whether discourse could exist without it): visitation is guaranteed as an inherent (and inherited) trait of writing. The thing presented (first) is in need of a signifier if it is to be an identity, and cannot be complete, adequate, self-sufficient, total, or fully real without its nominative supplement, the representation (second). The supplement (through repetition) brings both meanings "add" and "replace" and they weave an antinomous web on strands of aporia. On one such aporetic radial, a reversal of opposites takes place and the representative "is" (in the sense of the copula) the one represented. The latter's place is left (un-)attended by the ghost of its former self. The doubling or duplicity is enacted fully in the scene of conjuration, and relies on Saussure's strategy of meaning conjuring voice, and voice in turn, meaning, at the site of signification. There, the signifier-conjurer draws immense power to the ghost conjured by voice, and voice, from the concept-meaning—a double truth of haunting and haunting of truth. The signifier-conjurer constitutes the 'living truth,' capable of "spellbinding powers of enchantment, mesmerizing fascination, and alchemical transformations, which make it kin to witchcraft and magic."[9] In the background, hear *sotto voce* Alcibiades' adulation of Socrates. Comparing the bizarre man's voice to a satyr's, Alcibiades says, "The only difference between you and Marsyas is that you need no instruments; you do exactly what he does, but with words alone."[10] Thaumaturgy at this point is successfully incorporated within philosophical discourse.

What is the ghost's proper work and why is it found disturbing? Taking the second first, philosophical discourse supposes that any problem, thought through 'to the end,' will terminate in a determinate manner, perhaps antinomously, as Kant shows. Terminus, arrest, finality, origin, basis. In light of how different grounding or founding series can be amplified *ad infinitum*, discourse invents a something impervious to mutation: "As center, it is the point at which the substitution of contents, elements, or terms is no longer possible. At the center, the permutation or the transformation of elements . . . is forbidden."[11] Being's essential repose is an exemplification for Heidegger of immutability, the always already. It is "an enchanted region where things return to themselves."[12] The concept of a grounding priority or anteriority (*die Fruhe*) falls under Kant's blade when he presents his antinomies of reason; and similarly whether limit or end have real meaning, regardless of the costs of eschatology and the messianic.[13] To think to 'the end' whether the end is meaningful is one way to prepare the ghost's return. It is at 'the end' that one encounters the ghost, the truth of the apparitional. But not only at the end but in each modulation or modification of voicing, spectral keys infiltrate classical ones with a prophetic voice. On prophecy, Derrida writes: "It had been stated that a 'logic' of the *beyond* or rather of the *step beyond* would come to overflow the logic of the position: without substituting itself for this logic, and above all without being opposed to it, opening another relation, a relation without relation, or without a basis of comparison, a relation with what it crosses over via its step or with what it frees itself from at a stroke."[14] Of a disturbance that insinuates itself without ever exposing its 'rules,' kept secret, it provides the platform from which the ghost works ghost-works. If it rubs out ground lines ('deconstruction'), then the voice reading must exhibit symptoms of vertigo, queasiness, spookiness—the uncanny. They stem from the contagion of another 'logic' that is radically nonexclusive, embraces contradiction, and offers no safe houses, citadels, or DMZ's. The center that can no longer remain an impeccable identity, the thing itself, the *an sich*: self-presence or the same, grows susceptible.[15] Such a logic no longer provides containment for the monad, closed and autonomous rules, but also a heteronomous logic, mutable and instable alogicality, visits itself upon 'traditional' logic and, without voiding the latter's formalism, opens the gates. The visitation is transcendental, and like the ghost, a matrix of possibility, in the hollowing out of solidity, spirits away the body, and leaves behind the 'visibility of the invisible.' This part of the work ends at the gateway to an abyssal experience enclosed by philosophical discourse, a troubling node of the empirical, or empiricism at bay.

The particular disturbance by spectral logic has meaning as a basic feeling (*Urfuhl*), an affectivity proper to the groundless and anarchic.

Derrida: "Such an apparition doubtless upsets the appeasing order of representation. However, it does so not by reducing double-effects but on the contrary by expanding them, by expanding the effect of duplicity without an original, which perhaps is what the diabolical consists of, in its very inconsistency."[16] The absolute indetermination of the intervention, upon arrival, diabolically enforces a vulnerability, a susceptibility to apprehension. That the phantom appears qua phantom in the guise of apprehension (angst) recovers psychoanalytic thought of the return of traumatism. There, the phantom's arrival is a coming-back in two senses. First, ontologically being-there, in Heidegger's sense, the apparition 'always already' awaits disclosure proper to it. The voice is 'always already' there, waiting to be read, yet reading it does not postdate the voice. Second, the specter behaves as though it has been there before, the *revenant*. *Revenant*, "the returning one," 'begins by coming back.'[17] By aporias and other circumstantial contradictions, its visitation is newly announced yet not the premier. The return, the double, the duplicitous: the movement of the chain is unsettled and ghostly. To where does the *revenant* return and when was it there before? A good question since once it is ego, subject, consciousness, substance, life, the presences are proscribed by their own logic. A forbidden, the *revenant* enters the scene again and returns to where it was before forbidden to repeat repetition per se: a circumstance that closes on itself, and in closure, closes the crypt of meaning. Isn't the *revenant* a restructured Kierkegaardian spirit that relates to the relation and therefore its ghost, namely, because it relates to itself and is "that in the relating that relates to itself," it finds the ghost of itself, itself's ghost? For the sake of ipseity, the dead come back to haunt the living, and the living live haunted by the dead. First and second do a round dance in the exchange of vows.

Whence the strange effect of apparition that casts a pall over the real, and spells the corruption of the determinate. Is the ghost simulation or simulacrum? The phantom returns and intrudes to open a fissure in thought that divides replication from itself. No simple presence is allowed to repeat without its ghost. The first trait to be phantomized, the synchrony of time present, would have gathered the constituents of a moment into a totality. When ghost time is plugged in, asynchronous time grows disjointed or "out of joint" disperses or disseminates them. When the ghost infiltrates living time, cleaving it from itself, dissociating ipseity, the voice reading resembles the voice on mute, with the volume up. Into that the *revenant* comes, a noncoincident that trembles to itself in duplicity. The emotional basis for apprehension: the return of traumatic guilt.

And what of the *revenant*'s itinerate travels? Blanchot's Orphic hermeneutics has the strange perception that the reader is conjured simultaneous to the voice of writing: the reading voice is the voice reading it put into writing. The reader is the haunted site of voice and the ghost-voice, the haunting projection. Conjuration is the ghost risen from encryption in writing. Blanchot presumes that in rising from the dead and returning to the living, the ghost must not look back, toward the hellsmouth, the maw of the abyss, if it is not to 'fall back in.' If it does, does the voice entombed in the text fail to accomplish the conjuration, and leave the writing in the night? Only an effort to put it in writing, repeated constantly, prevents the conjuration from failing. At limit strength flags and putting the ghost in writing falls into voicelessness: the death of the dead.[18] Suspended, it awaits an opportunity for a next visitation to the living, which is determined by a principle of 'deferred obedience.' The ghost is wound in the disjoints of time, ready to spring from a coded 'archive,' a thanotopic memory crypt into which the *revenant* was consigned and records effaced.

One can suppose that the ghost might be an Orphic figure whose return is the conjuration of the voice reading. Its ectoplasmic 'essence' would be acoustic, its signature melodic and rhythmic, marked by a tempo. Blanchot's adaptation relies on the alchemical trope in which an encrypted being 'comes back' transmuted, androgynous, belonging to neither life nor death. Entombment (secret archive, address rubbed out) precedes release, which gives way to a miraculous transformation (*mysterium conjunctionis*) that endows it with thaumaturgical properties. The ghost, a reconstituted risen *Geist* (or Christ), the son who sets aside the stone of death's burial vault, is a holy ghost (*Saint Espirit*), but ghost nonetheless. Conjured too, it is a resurrected being 'beyond' life, and, like any ghost, delivered over to a third, neither presence nor absence. As the force of its conjuring play—*différance*—ripples across night, the phenomenal world spreads out, somehow impregnated, a cosmic egg with all categories within its question. The voice reading, subject to laws other than its own, heteronomous laws, thus vocalizes in a signature other than its own as well as its own, and thereby avows the trace of the other put in writing.

The ghost put in writing would seem to shun Cartesian values, clarity and distinctness. With phenomenality as such undecidable, the determinateness of an apparition lacks a basis. The concept of determinative evidence faces the lure of mythmaking when no reading can be definitive. Of the lore, Derrida writes, "I call it *enigmatic* because it appears disappears while telling many stories and making many scenes, causing or permitting them to be told. Occasionally these are called fables or myth."[19] But the narrative strategy has an ulterior motive beyond giving permission to tell ghost stories. The disempowerment of proclaimed metaphysical standards isn't driven by a love of the occult, legerdemain, table-rattling, and the séance. The order is the reverse. Occultism and accounts of apparitions resonate with Derrida's thought because they point to a fundamental insecurity with presence (consciousness, subject, being) and its representation of the world. The uberphenomenalism of the phenomenal world, the trace, the noncoincidence of the I, the play of phantom signifiers: all surge up in the security breakdown. To chart the influence of the other whose excess erupts in any tropic of investigation and whose passage (like a meson through a bubble chamber) leaves *almost* no mark takes a nuanced strategy, requires new tools. It must inquire into the meaning of the chain, "hostage, host, guest, ghost, holy ghost, and *Geist*" and what it grasps, namely, the tormented body of Western metaphysics that keeps the soul of philosophical discourse, the concept.[20]

Parenthetically, a progress report *vis-à-vis* a subtle 'interaction' between writing and the reading voice that has been staged on the corpus of Jacques Derrida. Has the voice reading already been incorporated into the text as it is put in writing? The hypothesis proposes an 'overlap' between the two vocalities, in the form of an influence, a reflux or fluctuation from the other to the one that pervades the writing experience. And conjuration and its implicates, ethical and otherwise, are co-responsible. The acoustic signature of voice, in its biographical or autobiographical materiality, calls archived data, some of which may be from a site of repression. The *revenant*, returning from the repressed, retrieved from secret encrypted files, impinges on a voice reading a text in a process of putting it in writing. The voice in part exemplifies a distancing of consciousness by which 'inadmissible evidence' is brought to the present scene and written into text, and the event by which it (as in Derrida's 'analysis' of Freud's pleasure principle in *The Postcard*) it comes back unexpectedly—as *revenant*.[21] The unstated function of the archive (from which writing draws) is to preserve the memory entombed so that a 'trace' may inform a life. *Archive Fever* assigns a double meaning to the Greek *arche*: "commencement" and "commandment." The *arche* is event and history as well as the protocol of responsibility. The primacy of the second has to do with a nonexclusivity that indemnifies the present order against preventing interruption. The principles of keeping (storing) and of keeping peace strain against one other and are not resolved by separate compartments, each to its own. Distance, displacement, and disguise conspire against a stable phenomenality. The outcome in question, the subject of conjuration is defined by a deferred obedience.

In the concept of deferment, there are two distinct constituents. First, the thought of the ghost and its relation to conjuration provides a general script for writing. The ghost is apparent as the voice conjured to haunt the one haunted by writing. Voice and work are coordinates. Second, beyond the thought is a more powerful talisman, a ghost that could be that of Jacques Derrida. In the conjuration of the voice reading are echoes of the voice of his writing, the phonetic signature, 'his' *phone*, which resound in the reader's interior ear, as the vocality of the text. Its voicification can call up archived files in 'deep freeze,' whose memory—under a program of deferral and obedience to it—is of the father. In testimony, the work of mourning memorializes the father. In that sense, the ghost is a conjuration of the father's voice, put in writing, Parmenides, Plato, Aristotle, Hegel, Marx, Nietzsche, Freud, Heidegger—an ensemble to give voice to philosophical discourse. The father-son affiliation is variously commemorated in a work of mourning. The dominant is the voice of the interlocutor—Plato—that vociferates the dyadic opposition of all things. But there are other chords, for instance, the opening of disciple to master, scribe to author, and writer to reader (that constitutes the "Envois" section of *The Post Card*.)[22] Which one fathers, writer, writing, or what is written? Various responses are possible, but whichever first becomes the father incorporates a 'mature phase' of thinking that dominates the voice of philosophical discourse. The incorporation must necessarily offer palliatives as truths, or otherwise the truth of the deferred debt would be known. Derrida ironically remarks, "Philosophy consists of offering reassurance to children, . . . , of speaking first and foremost *for* that little boy within us, of teaching him to speak—to dialogue—by displacing his fear or his desire."[23] The accomplishment provides narcosis that effaces the terror in childhood. On the dramatic stage center stands the idea, the *eidos*, the atom of discourse whose virtue is to be inscribed as one and the same from occasion to occasion: the law of repetition itself ("law is always a law of repetition, and repetition is always submission to a law").[24] Philosophy defers the experience of childish fears, viz., of death, and remains obedience to that which is deferred. The logos functions as antidote but also as aporia: Socrates opens the *Critias*, "I call on the god to grant us that most effective medicine, that best of all medicines: knowledge." As aporia, it grants no passage to a possible experience. Blockage, a failed transcendental. Thwarted is the desire to hear the father, who could from some inaccessible archive, alone give voice to defer the fear of fears, the fear of death.

A natural trait of human life, fear of death ("the child in us"), is suppressed by a discourse of ghosts, Derrida's and his father's. As in the reading voice, as in the voice written, contact with the fear is phonically defaced. In the act, two distinct discourses are spawned, one of the father, one of 'killing the father' together with his "dialectizable" threads of thought. The second is masked by the first. The father of the idea with his ever-renewed power to keep at bay the terrifying phantom that is death's signifier elects for repetition, the way of the concept, power, wealth, and goodness. It is a choice of Plato's 'practice of death,' which is actually a postponement and deferral effected by the idea. The economy by which time and space are subsidized by a thanatopic excess is rich in the thematics of discourse. Furthermore, it prizes the "dangerous supplement," the hypothesis of immortality of the soul, and uses it as a substitute for 'greed for life,' the pleasure principle, and the poison of fear.[25] In the new discourse, immortality would not remove an ending but indefinitely repeat the idea; it would provide a law to outrun entropy. By means of ideality, the limits of life are exceeded, their means lived beyond, their border passed over. Porosity of the limit; a-porosity and aporia. In the passage to and fro, hither and yon, here and beyond is (the copula) the experience of the non-passage, the impasse—for how can one not die? A question that brings the crux, which is to say, an (the) aporetic experience which is the nonexperience of death. *Enter the ghost.*

Philosophical discourse in its classical guise (which is to say, discourse, period) provides a 'cure' or palliation of the emotional distress caused by finitude and mortality.[26] In particular, discourse qua discourse conjures the 'book' of phenomena. Then, to the need for restitution, reparation, and repair, the repetitive vitality of the idea can respond by dispelling and rendering void the threat of paralysis and morbidity. Within discourse, writing is the restitution of restitutions, the *condition sine qua non* of mobilization and motility. It accomplishes a double action, as (in Derrida's "Plato") the poison of a poison and therefore a counter-poison. The first poison is vocality: speech, verbalization, voice, and spoken language in general. The second poison is putting the first poison in writing; such toxicity is the "literal parasite: a letter installing itself inside a living organism to rob it of its nourishment and to distort the pure audibility of a voice."[27] Writing is the rogue that has invaded a cloister which is not to be purged until the purity of inner life, speech, presence, and subjectivity is restored. The exercise of spectral 'logic' ensures that the time will never arrive. In the attempt to exorcise paralytic fear by discourse, the phenomenal world is re-conjured, and with it presence and subjectivity, the entire substantial reality. Writing that contaminates any discourse that seeks to (1) reveal the taint (the trauma and its displacement), and (2) point out the dissimulation through a battery of 'phantom technologies,' is always a double-edged sword, toxicity squared, death that kills death. Since the infiltration of discourse by writing is extensive, resistant to detection, and remarkably unreadable, no effective countermeasure of intelligence is available.

Writing, cure for fear of dying, offers the simulacrum of death through reading and writing, the voice reading and the ghost-writer. But writing also is a host of the parasite that infects (inflects) speech (inner and outer) and saps its truth. The travesty of partaking in both casts writing as the scandal of *différance*, by which noxious death is played out, made metaphor, and thereby eternally deferred. The play's the thing to dull the conscience of a king. Writing, a "wayward, rebellious son . . . abandoned by his father" (speech), will be an enclave of the enigma of *différance*, in the vacuity of which a life can be lived in the face of death.[28]

3

To be read

TO WITNESS A SUMMONING of the ghost, the haunting and the haunted must both attend. Let it be established that there is no 'haunter' per se, no entity that *is* ghost. The haunted is situated in the voice reading, which phonically incorporates the haunting in the form of a thematic signature. The ghost comes to be put in writing what cannot be uttered audibly and articulately. The word itself concerns a fact centrally related to the specter: *con-jurare* speaks of the gift of one's word, swearing, pledging, vowing, making an oath. By an empowerment of the voice reading, by its authority, the ghost is summoned. The nature of that power and authority—demonic, erotic, or religious—must come under question if responsibility is to be understood. The priority of the entitlement, or of election of any kind, stands before that of which debt the summoning incurs: which inheritance comes with the summoning?

It should be admonished that putting it in writing isn't *about* conjuring, where the preposition provides infinite separation of the thought from the deed—but indeed a reversal in terms: *conjuring* writing, writing that is performative. The 'truth' of the text will have to be measured performatively, by an impeccable performative.[1] To raise writing to a conjuring, Derrida writes, requires acknowledgment that it "transforms the very thing it interprets."[2] This avowal corresponds to transmutation within a hermeneutics that catalyzes the reading into producing the thing—to more exactly define "performative." And should the thing produced be a non-thing, a phantom, one that leaves a signature in the form of a trace on the voice? A hermeneutics that opens a text to . . . the apparition contained behind its literal surface, waiting in the wings for the opening of the text. If there were such, the hermeneutics would enlist or insist upon "a performative heretofore never described, whose performance must not, however, be experienced as a glib success, as an act of prowess."[3] The price of being an auditor to the conjuration is high, perhaps infinite, since it is a gift that obligates its recipient, perhaps infinitely.

The key to understanding the gift lies in grasping its production, that is, what must constitute putting it in writing. Is every text haunted? What regulates or governs the spectral prodigality of a text (for example, Derrida's) to produce a haunting in writing as attested by the voice reading? Perhaps here, the theme of the writer's survival is fletched with the haunting of the reader by the voice reading. The ghost's appearing is the appearance of a witness *in the writing* that bears witness to death. The writer who survives as the voice reading necessarily attests to the crossing from life to death, and back again. In a classical view of survivorship, a kind of immortality comprises the gift of the voice reading, and once repeated, as a filiation of voice to voice. In an unusual reversal of Plato's *Phaedrus*, Derrida argues that putting it in writing survives death because the text is essentially alien to living, has always already lacked the 'seed' of life, and therefore remains "a force wandering outside the domain of life, incapable of engendering anything . . ."[4] It survives but as a simulacrum of survivorship. The argument both agrees and disagrees with the classical position that supposes that writing lacks immortality, since there the undying life, passed from father to son (sun to things visible on earth) is effected through speech, *not* writing. Audible word-sounds, the *phonoi*, propagate the original language and succeed in defeating death. By contrast, the written word remains barren and without issue. The demonic enchantments that Alcibiades finds in Socrates' articulate words are absent in cold print. Lacking white magic to recall the soul to its truth, writing classically benumbs the interior to mortality and paralyzes self-inquiry. Sluggish (the trope of the great stallion at Socrates' trial), insensitive, and prone to aggression, the soul fails to hear the call to justice and responsibility. Is there a political alternative to the oppression under a regime of writing?

In the classical canon, writing can 'contain' no ghost because of categorial exclusion. By the logic of supplementation, however, the terms are reversed in that the other already is put in writing, demonstrable as a voice in reading. Recall that a supplement is both addition and replacement, a stick with two ends, that brings an economy both of maintenance and replacement, keeping and not keeping the same. In the classical schema, writing, the barren seed, then supplements speaking, the fertile one, fecundating and actualizing its potential. The thought of Plato is incorporated in Heidegger's *physis*, a nature whose 'living word' initializes the world of beings. Derrida's break with tradition is highlighted when putting it in writing, *graphe*, "breaks into the very thing that would have liked to do without it yet lets itself *at once* be breached, roughed up, fulfilled, and replaced, completed by the very trace through which the present increases itself in the act of disappearing."[5] Writing imports a secret life (whose?) that insinuates itself with unbidden semantic overtones.[6] The secret remains secret and recedes into deeper and deeper reserves of the clandestine. Without audibility or the breath, a life is preserved in the subvocal voice that reads text 'under the breath,' to itself.[7] The inarticulate voice, reticent beyond measure, the unvoiced voiceless *phone* attaches itself to the letter and becomes guardian of interiority that marks the site of putting it in writing. The voice in proximity to singularity produces in reading a vocalization signed by the vibratory alterity, as it is inscribed in writing. *And that singularity is the aura of a spectral nature.* Voice writing haunts the inscription put in writing, while remaining barely inaudible, mutable (the same throughout), never quite there (vocalizing now?). The morphability of voice ('literal' voice, *lecta divina*) phantomlike follows a labyrinthine course. It refuses to give 'hard evidence' and bears a forged signature. It is an imposter. Since it doesn't submit to objectivity, credulity in reading is tested and contested. The spectral resonance of the voice *in reading* affects the meaning as read, obscuring, effacing, disjoining, disseminating it. It is as capable of producing a reading unavailable to comprehension, abandoning itself to the mechanical murmur of scanning newsprint.

Question of depth grammar: where in the scene of writing is the lair of the ghost? Back to Blanchot, writing, a land of the dead, invites the reading, in the voice of Orpheus, which is a descent: here, to retrace the way to the tomb. The reading must give voice to meaning that is encrypted and (to a degree) restore it to life. As seen above, the figure of iteration is employed as a sign. *R*esurrection, *r*etracing, and *r*estoration signify acoustically the logic by which reading is writing put in voice, and is signified by the idea of 'recycled repetition.' It is incontestable that a given writing can be submitted to an infinite reading of readings. If each component (word, spacing, sentence, paragraph) is similarly prolific, the risen dead are perfectly populous. The corollary is equally fascinating. It states that no unique reading exists, that stands uncontaminated by an other, impervious to alterity, and perfect in ipseity.[8] It is not the absence but the repetition of voice that the specter brings forth. Specter remains spectral, however, but changed or mutated. By force of the Orphic anabasis, it becomes the voice raised, this time with a spectral acoustics that permeates meaning and borrows the form of a grammatical 'dissemination.' The voice lacks a narrow broadcast band, acoustically focused and free of interference; it rather has an acoustical aura. The aura prevails not only in the voice of writing printed texts (books, codices, manuscripts, maps) but also in other contemporary forms of telecommunications (cinema, television, video imagery, holography), and requires a future study.

Parenthetically, one could ask if the ghost on the screen (movie, TV set, computer monitor, radar, oscilloscope) has an ontology that mirrors that of an acoustical ghost. The deep meaning of mirror image or reflection haunts Derrida's thought on the specter that "first of all sees *us*: it looks at us even before we see *it* or even before we see period. We feel ourselves observed, sometimes under surveillance by it even before any apparition."[9] The dissymmetry when the transition to the visible is made suggests the mixed metaphor of the *invisibility of the acoustical.*

This touches on the role of the reader in giving voice to what is putting it in writing. The question of the gift lies precisely here. It may be the paradox of the reader where reading gives what is not proper to the voice reading, and so, to the voice. The gift of the voice reading is improper and improperly puts it in writing, and is not properly the gift of either reader or writer, or of a collaboration. Although it comes with the writing and is put in writing, it isn't *of* writing and doesn't stay 'at the site' of writing. Transmuted voice is still less some 'property' of the literary, letter, word, or spacing. As it is voicing that works *conjuration*, the gift of reading is an inheritance, and of a debt the reading passes on by greeting the ghost *sotto voce* while reading what is putting it in writing. The address brings the anxiety that the conjuration exposes dangers, greatest among which is the phantom's counter-conjurations. In several leaps ahead, the line of thought will meet the gesture of hospitality.

The term of visitation (*visere*, to see) determines both the length of anxiety and remembrance of its gift of meaning. With regard to the other term, *revenant*, that suggests a past tense for the phantom, 'the ghost of Christmas past.' By duplicitous logic, spectrality shows this cannot be so, that it cannot be so because it belongs to "a thinking of the past, a legacy that can come only from that which has not yet arrived—from the *arrivant* itself."[10] The ghost's retreat is possible only because it is to-come, *a-venir*, and belongs to a time whose signature will have been written but not yet read—and therefore not yet read, will not have put it in writing at the reading where the ghost conjures to put it in writing. The arrival is a phantom recursion of an event that hasn't yet occurred but nonetheless interrupts the lived time of the reading, a hiatus of the mute voice reading. The place that a ghost *frequents* is one about to be put in writing and its frequency breaks in upon ordinary, synchronous time to modulate the voice reading. It typically voices as an a-chronous resonance, a drone, *sotto voce*, voice of utterance, devoid of accent, a rushed temporal anomaly, yet discernible so that the reader (inaudibly) responds whenever the text bears the ghost of meaning in *the voice*. The voicification conjures forces to disjoin thought and enter through the joint heard as another's voice, voice of the third, interiorized, distinct but patently not one's own.

By the way, whether heavy reading, frequenting libraries, and patronizing bookstores makes for a susceptibility to ghosts may be a concern. Freud worries along similar lines when he discovers that thinkers who near the end of their lives surrender to a 'telepathic or mediumistic temptation,' for example, an interest in scholarship about ghostliness. Can one tell which comes first, reading or the uncanny? A scholar may grow 'superstitious,' when sensitized to a phantomization of meaning that inclines thought toward the apparitional and places rigid ontological markers in disfavor. A heightened susceptibility to the uncanny would seem a natural outcome of the synchronicity, serendipity, and aleolectic methodologies that come into play in reckoning the spectrality of a text. The work of scholarship can offer fertile grounds for a spectral influx to flourish.

Another issue: does the ghost that puts it in writing, the spook of the 'inner voice' of reading, possess the sensuous materiality associated by lore with specters? Is it open to empirical study by, say, spectroscopy, photography, or magnetic resonance imagery? Derrida offers the observation, "For there to be ghost, there must be a return to the body, but to a body that is more abstract than ever."[11] The ghost *in voice* is required by logic to have a phenomenality. Phenomenally, it condenses out of an amorphous phonic substance to the plane of audibility without acquiring definite acoustical form. It becomes an aural 'object' by hardening, coalescing, petrifying, or congealing out of less differentiated hypersonic or hyperphonic vapor. Within the economy of the ear, it attains a threshold of 'phantomatic objectivity' at the expense of a dialectical wavering between presence and absence, indication and prophecy, and hope and dread. In the resulting phenomenological revision, reading is the scene of letting it appear with the mark of vocality.[12] Thus the phantom can be on location on the castle's ramparts at Elsinor, where the ghost of Hamlet's father was 'seen' to speak portentously at the stroke of midnight. In its way, the voice-reading exemplifies the classical paradigm of haunting that Freud associates with "death and dead bodies, to the return of the dead, and to spirits and ghosts"—though Freud in general follows his propensity for the physiological trope and considers only ghosts of living things. By extension, there are 'noumenal' phantoms, specters of the intelligible, ghosts of meaning, apparitions of truth, and hauntings of the logos. Positing a 'prosthetic body' is one way to establish the experience of 'materiality' of the ghost voice while reading.

Consider the echoes of Husserl's phenomenology that inaugurated Derrida's investigations into the spectral.[13] There, it is phenomenologically possible to isolate any 'regional discipline' in terms of its intentional component in lived experience—regardless of the reality (or unreality) of the object. Fantastic, ideal, imaginary, and purely fictive objects are as good candidates for phenomenological study as any, even though they yield a non-real component in relation to lived experience, the *noema*. Instances of the *noesis-noema* duality may place the correlates either in consciousness or in the world; but the strangely resistant non-real elements find no place in either region. They constitute a 'third' that is not proper to one or the other. Third, other, alien, outsider, foreigner, exile: these exemplify a region without region, and do so absolutely. Without the absolute displacement, it would be impossible to speak of phenomenality-in-general or of the phenomenality of phenomena, Heidegger's worldiness of the world. Improperly without proper place, the specter is absolutely dispossessed of site, an unfixed point definitely in the world. A strange birth: the possibility of the specter exudes from the interstices of phenomenology itself. The apparition of the apparition is the *sine qua non* of the transcendental reduction.[14]

From its phenomenological progenitor, there is an additional inheritance. The specter can be conceived as 'the frequency of visibility,' a reiterative shimmer of luminosity. To resort to the trope of visibility in describing the transcendental condition of phenomena is to return to philosophy's focus on light and the sun. From the beginning, that visibility is not visible draws on the Platonic intuition that the power of x itself is not x (the source of goodness, the Good, is not good.) Visibility is proper not to actual beings but to their possibility. The 'derivation' of actual from possible prefigures the ghost's aporetic behavior: at each stage, visibility frequents possibility and, never giving over to the actual, envelops it in uncanny diaphanousness. The goings-on of the ghost. Ghost/*Geist*. The haunting is *both* equally of spirit and of specter *and* of sound as well as of light.

What is the relation, ghost to *Geist*. *Geist* to ghost? Under the shroud of the phenomenological reduction, the specter is conceived as a carnal apparition of spirit that differs from the *Geist* only insofar as "its phenomenal body [is] its fallen and guilty body."[15] Necessarily a redemptive relation holds between the two: specter is spirit deferred out of deference to death.[16] Expressed phenomenally, the deferral represents the impatience of return after return after return, the very frequenting of the ghost, its temporality. Conversely, *Geist* is ghost as regenerative, purged of contaminating obsession (sin), its relation to the living nonpathological and rendered quasi-present. The relation of possibility to actuality (in the case of *Dasein*) verges on Heidegger's delineation of the ontological difference. There, Being's precedence over an actual being presents a possibility that actualization cannot achieve. Being, the *ens transcendentalis*, is spiritualization proper, individualization, a seizure of one's ownmost potentiality of being. Although the redemptive possibility is suppressed in Heidegger's thought, it is marked by an avoidance, Derrida writes,

> To my knowledge, Heidegger never asked himself, "What is spirit?", to all extents and purposes he treats the omission as assenting to the equation with Being. Spirit as sublimated spectrality is the *revenant*, the coming back, in the sense of being recalled to the question of Being. The recall, that in the context of *Being and Time* takes place under the auspices of conscience, is itself the vehicle of transubstantiation, of removing the taint of *das Man* and the level of 'average everydayness.'[17]

A return to spirit can contain no impatience (and hence is inverse to the movement of phantomization) since the event is constituted by a letting go, *Gelassenheit*. Spirit necessarily returns in its own time, without hurry or lack of hurry. Yet the time of spirit, worthy of an ontological if not a spiritual name, is pursued throughout by the ghost of spirit, corrupt spectrality. In *Geist*'s wish to remain separate from the ghost, the seeds of inauthenticity (could one say, of becoming ghostly?) are sown.

The ontological difference identifies a chiasm between two radically distinct senses of the verb "to be," essence and presence, being-such and being-there. Besides the logic of distinction, the discovery introduces death into the analysis since the difference makes use of a definition of mortal being, mortality, and the end as such. The skin that isolates essence from presence is passed over the living body. Not to be bypassed in its imminence, death 'forces' and articulates the spacing of ontological difference by resituating the 'thereness' of life. It constitutes presence as the space to close and foreclose the always already. The anticipatory resoluteness that warrants authentic existence is situated in the memory of spacing. In that thread of memorialization, Derrida situates the work of mourning: within the interval in which memory is most intimate with the immemoriality of the singular.

The intrigue of the ghost/*Geist* duality, with its many ramifications, branches, forks, and foliations, converts self-presence to an apartment house for ghosts. There is the epiphenomenon of a concatenation in ghosting, a product of the inner 'echo' with presence. Presence reduces itself to echo, repetition, or iteration. In Derrida's expression, if "[t]he essential mode of self-presence of the *cogito* would be the haunting obsession . . . ," then ego comes to mean, "I am haunted."[18] The ego is haunted by a haunting I whose conjuration is the haunting. The expanded formula opens *en abyme:* I am haunted by myself who is haunted by myself who is haunted . . . Self-presence is recursive and recursively produces a host of specters. The I made anxious by that multiplicity is expressed by an obsessive return to self-presence—the cause of the apparition in the first place.[19] Does *Geist* enter into this polymorphic and polyphonic haunting for a phenomenology (a phenomenology *of spirit*) made possible by the ego's being awash with spectral bodies thick as

Dante's shades in hell? The excess yields an economy of hallucination whose surplus is the simulacrum. Another pressing question lies here. For, once spectrality is situated as the very possibility of phenomenology, does it not become impossible to discern the Transcendental Ego from the host of other apparitions?

Use of the plural in *Specters of Marx* expresses the generative and recursive character of the phenomenon. One brings a second one that brings a third one that. . . . A single becomes manifold, a gathering of difference into the same. In a view so garnered, what is appropriated is appropriately named by the logos, the father. This is the experience of the full phantomic gaze, of being skewered by the name. When under surveillance (chills up the spine), it is by a crowd—even if by a single ghost. A crowd that mills about in no space, and in its invasive, turbulent fashion, carries a threat.[20] ("I have come to whet thy almost blunted purpose, Hamlet!") As immaterial as a number, the ghost is no less material than the signifier of number: ghosts of plurality, plurality of ghosts. Plurality refers obliquely to a property of the aura, the nimbus of the ghost. Spectral voice is broadcast omni-directionally. It resounds from every quarter and assaults with the perplexity of an unknown source location. It overflows the senses and erases Kant's outer sense—space—the out-there, externally real. The movement effects a phenomenological *retrait:* another connection between the *epoche* and ghost-talk. The resulting transmutation takes place within interiority—presence, consciousness, the subject, I, spirit—and produces a dimensionless point, the Transcendental Ego. A spectral eye, diaphanous and without substance, observes but itself cannot be observed, and with unstated purpose, intention, or meaning, if any. A transcendental placement of the ring of Gyges.

The ghost's potency derives from its impulse to be haunting, its *conatus essendi*. It desires to recommence its accompaniment to presence (that is not absence) and to come back to the start, the conjuration. The unremitting recurrence to follow living experience occupies the ghost with a special work.[21] The task to give a place to the third, the other that is a phantom of being, constitutes the *work of mourning*. It is intimately related to a search "to ontologize remains, to make them present, in the first place by *identifying* the bodily remains and by *localizing* the dead."[22] As examples, Derrida cites how, in both of *Hamlet*'s graveyard scenes, Hamlet asks that the dead (Ophelia and Yorick the jester) to be named and identified. Shakespeare seems aware of the depth grammar of mourning. In a fundamental sense, letting be (the *Es gibt* of Heidegger, the gift of existence) is constituted by denoting (nominating) with a proper name; it is *Ereignis* again. Mourning is first restitution by the gift of a name, a designation. An outpouring of grief can emotionally atone the passing of life, but the work of mourning is *for* a specific life, a singular. Perhaps the primitive belief about the proper name (holy and secret) derives from the singular value. To name the name within, by memory or by commemorative writing, is a *praxis* that is ethical in command.[23]

There is a yet more intimate function of the work of mourning. Insofar as authenticity (*Eigenlichkeit*) is the fulfillment of the promise given in anticipatory resoluteness, authentic existence is indebted, a debt incurred by acceptance of the gift of the promise. Authentic existence will remain indebted to the extent that it lives "in advance of itself," in Heidegger's terms, under oath to the promise. Its inherited value (being-toward-death, *Sein-zum-Todes*) is be worked off and paid for in the currency of mourning. Amortization is an obligation to remember the promise and the promissory; the name of the one who works. No profit, no surplus, no excess exists since 'at the end' of the account, by rule of ledger, the total is set back equal to zero. Death, understood in the trope of the account, forbids demise or perishing, since dying has a higher value than either. Dying concerns a silent call for the accounting. The payment, understood in double, is the twice-brought presence. *Dasein* both suffers presence (it commemorates its own death) and suffers for presence (to be present for the presence). A debt whose payment is always promised and when repaid (which is never) is paid twofold.

4

With the voice

NOT KEEN ON SOLO performances nor on packs, troupes, or gangs (gaggles or braces), ghosts arrive in a concatenation (from the Latin *catena*, chain.) Philosophically, the apparition is linked, one with the other, in repetition, linked repetition, or repetitive linkage. Apparition is repetition of repetition, repetition's repetition. Then what could it possibly mean to say that a ghost returns *for the first time* if the ghost begins by coming back? A plurality of 'first times' must already exist in time, analogous to the plurality that hides in the background, at the perimeter, or within the aura. According to it, the question, "When is the first time?" proposes a line that thinks thought backward, toward a beginning in recollection, or onset of *amnesis*, echoing Plato's interrogation of the origin, *arche*. "When is the first time?" sparks an inquiry that Derrida undertakes to refuse to site the origin or establish the non-originary: the facsimile or concatenation. Since the logos holds a monopoly on signification, only an *arche*-writing will work, if its spectral work can be brought forth. Spectral work is a supplement to *Geist*'s, which is logic, and so, arche-writing, or writing, period, becomes 'that dangerous supplement.' It is also a catatonic attack of memory and on truth since "memory and truth cannot be separated."[1] Writing mimes knowledge, a cheap commodity whose cheapness (by Graham's law) spoils the whole store. It breeds 'forgetfulness of the soul' by replacing self-presence with the simulacrum, as well as living memory with a mere mnemonic device, that is, technology for knowledge of being. But it also, as Thoth says, is an aid, support, device, or *mathesis* for memory. Writing is both. In this and other ways, it crosses the intelligible divide between opposites. It is *neither nor* or *rather both*. In its non-characterizability lies a recognition that no division exists between inside and outside, purity and adulteration, truth and forgery, or computational memory and living memory. Pure memory is a Platonic dream of a memory with no sign, no signifier nor signified, and so, of infinite capacity. This is a dream absolutely shattered by the fact of finitude.[2] The given memory has a definitely finite capacity—not godly infinite self-presence—and requires systemization or general organization by means of inscription. Since inscribing in memory creates an archive, that both keeps and ordains order, memory is purely archival in nature. Writing in its form of producing the archive already attends to the needs of 'pure living memory' that could not do without its help from the start. It predates memory since it contains the possibility of memory, predates its commencement since the *arkhe* of writing is the ghost that begins by returning.

"When is the first time?" Recollection foresees the issue that origins with the ghost popping out of secret temporal folds, the hymen. One might pause over the difficulty in exterminating ghosts and see that it isn't that they are among the already-dead but that they are unshackled from living time. That time doesn't bind them. Ghostbuster question: how to rid the premises of what has no purchase in time? In this connection, it can be recalled that the *work of mourning* is understood as letting the ghost be, not refusing it a term by which to put it in writing, read and lent voice, granting it existence, being, at least a quasi-presence, ontologizing it, and thus rewriting the classical apparatus of ontology.[3] Proper name and location serve as quasi-determinants for the apparition. But if the identity of the *revenant* cannot be determined, is work to proceed? The affinity between the aberrant temporal behavior and example of obsession in psychoanalysis becomes apparent. When Freud talks about resolution of obsessive conduct, he notices, "Probably it is the substitution of something conscious for something unconscious, the transformation of the unconscious thoughts into conscious thoughts, that makes our work effective. . . . By extending the unconscious into consciousness the repressions are raised, the conditions of symptom-formation are abolished, and the pathogenic conflict exchanged for a normal one."[4] Freud re-conceives the ghost as *revenant* as a re-pression, in which memory is deposited in a tomb, dis-(re)membered and placed in a lost archive. The recall of the ghost, like the recall of the encrypted memory, lies in calling to it—auto-production of voice to the ghost of voice. In the voicification lies a recognition of ontological lack vital to its identity, seed of the work. In this regard, it is strange that Freud spends so much time on a technology by which exorcism can proceed, obsessions ridded, and haunting ended.

Exorcism ("Ghost, begone!") is the idea of dispatching the ghost *for the last time*. To where? The hope is, out of a zone of ontological possibility and beyond a work of mourning. But it is a vain hope, inconceivable that the phantom can be prevented from an appearance since the banishment (of ghostly form) requires the effacement of eschatology, the site of the last. It goes without saying that the phantom is always already an apparition (acoustic, in this case) of the dead, and spectrality is a domain within a discourse of the end. The fact that the origin of the ghost belongs to the 'other side' means that it is indeterminate in origin. Impossible to understanding the meaning of 'crossing over' when one 'side' lacks determination altogether. To speak of boundary conditions requires a difference in meaning 'between' the two sides; but one has no meaning. But the dissemination of the other is another way of speaking of its omnipresent ineffectivity. It is everywhere, absolutely muted in differentials. That dissemination is of 'dead seed,' infertile, bearing no fruit, engendering no signifiers or signifieds. That is death come back to haunt as a witness; and it is in the ghost's attestation of the ubiquity of the last, the *eschatos*, the seed of unmeaning cast by the other, that wakes the work of mourning.

The preternatural ontological status as well as the noncanonical rejection of presence call for a remembrance of the 'last hours,' the end. The meditation on the ghost qua ghost, the double, interprets the duality of death and living as its basis: death as unlived life. In the interpretation, the apparition bears the wound of mortality, for instance, King Hamlet's. When it speaks, its voice resounds with an eschatological tone of the prophet. Prophecy admonishes with its concern with what is to come, the future. The ghost is strongly included to a specific tense in speaking, the future, but not just any future, the future perfect (French, *future anterior*): "it will have happened before you awaken . . ."[5]

Proper to eschatological speech, in a grammatical expressive of the phantom, is the oath. Conjure, *jure*, swear. "Swear by me, Hamlet." The ghost voice solicits a pledge or vow that is attested to from its privileged position of not belonging. It is also true of the ghost voice of reading that its is a singular position, strategically speaking. Having recrossed the temporal horizon now from the other side, and therefore temporally anomalous, it is fully capable of soliciting a promise on the part of the reading—at least when its acoustics possess a special record of that travel. Then, the voice reading expresses a necessity that commands, and has no difficulty in enforcing an oath. The means are carefully described by Heidegger as of apprehension of the future. The future's apprehension is of the 'primordial condition' of time and produces the care that *Dasein* expresses toward that which continuously arrives in advance of itself, *the ghost*. The specter is always already the next, never the present. Spectral time is other, a deformed, de-structured passage. As a result, a being like the ghost has prefigurative knowledge of a future that is anterior to the present present. The peculiarity is to arrive 'before' what is to come yet before the present, the English future perfect speaks of a future as being already determined.

One inheritance of Derrida can be brought to light by the parallel between the ghost's favored speech-act and the discourse [*Sprache*] of conscience in Heidegger. In his analysis of the call, conscience has manifest spectral properties, chief of which is its function as a reader of death's writing. It gives voice only mutely but subvocally intones the grammatical proper to the ghost. It operates, in an echo of Derrida's trembling in which Heidegger writes, by drawing the addressee "into itself and therefore always here and there—here into presence, there into absence."[6] The call mutely addresses the addressee proper, appropriating it as such, and taking it with propriety into its own. It is catapulted into singularity since being properly called, to be named one's proper name, designates in a way irreducible to no other. There it is absorbed by absence and ceases to be even one. This is not the only way that conscience doubles as death's voice, the ghost-voice of reading. It shares with death the ability to call in silence and produce trembling. An uncanny inaudibility, 'from afar to afar,' trembles backward and forward, to and fro, across the limit, and retraces the threshold of sound, movement, life. Its reticence is the voice reading and muted the way that spectrality is muted with respect to being. Here, the one addressed possesses a similar fluctuation in presence and also a variable ontological status, as if its existence were regulated by a rheostat. The pattern, shifting as it does, is the spectral or spectroscopic shimmer itself surrounding that which 'was previously uncalled into a nearness.' The pattern is perpetually within the virtual focal point, and cannot be rendered distinct by any prosthesis, like a third-generation facsimile or videotape that has permanently lost resolution. Its 'irreality' is ordained by origin—the ghost is heir to a region neither outer nor inner, a Levinasian proximity, and belongs to a 'third' realm, between sense and thought, meaning and nonmeaning. The ghost is a figment of imagination, disowned, and exiled to wander endlessly. Parenthetically, it follows that the ghost is perceived *by* the imagination, and that, therefore, refutations that the ghost is merely *imaginary* have some basis in fact.

"Swear by me, Hamlet!" the ghost commands. The grammar makes implicit reference to a final epoch, the *eschatos*, the Heideggerian time during which each being comes into its own. The tense in which conscience gives voice also is eschatological. It inwardly speaks what is proper, and exposes essential being no longer confused with its accidents—the *last* time is also the name named by death. Here another thread braids conscience and death together with the knot of the oath. The oath itself is a promise woven of the fabric of one's word. The irreplaceability of one's own name is guarantor. As said, the oath employs a tense that is spectrally instrumental in a fashion requiring scrutiny. For now, the joint is the convergence of the proper name and the future perfect (future anterior). In that world-time, the natural voice, wherever situated, will have become eschatological, as it is for Socrates when he says, "Now I want to prophesy . . .

for I am at the point when men prophesy most, when they are about to die."[7] The extraordinary phenomenon of prophetic eschatology, with its certainties 'beyond the evidence,' points to *beyond* history, and reveals, to adapt Levinas's thinking, a breach in the totality of being. It is precisely there that the possibility of the specter arises, its disruptive tremor, forever accursed among beings. It is precisely that 'pointing beyond the evidence' that the ghost-voice expresses in its mute tremble.[8]

Within the discourse of the end, eschatology, several important chains cross with one another. About link of oath, name, and call, it is written in *Being and Time* that "The caller maintains itself in conspicuous indefiniteness. If the caller is asked about its name, status, origin, or repute, it not only refuses to answer, but does not even leave the slightest possibility of one's making it into something with which one can be familiar when one's understanding of *Dasein* has a 'worldly' orientation."[9] Later, Heidegger will say of the caller that "it is something like an alien voice," relying on the metaphorical.[10] The unknown modulation is in excess to the voice of *Dasein*, yet is still *Dasein's* to which the impropriety of the uncanny has added, a discourse without origin. In that voice, "The naming calls."[11] To an extreme, naming outstrips and destabilizes denotation, designation, and reference. "This naming does not hand out titles, it does not apply terms, but it calls into the word."[12] In Heidegger's later thought, voice becomes estranged, expresses estrangement, and produces it in reading. Speech of radical inwardness is no longer gifted with the possibility of understanding and of disclosure of truth, but now cultivate untruth—the alien's triumph. Voice still solicits a nearness that at the same time comes from afar but now owns strangely marked signification that does not signify. *Like* an alien voice and in that likeness, the vocalization exercises an incomprehensible hold on the addressee, for the alien is madness, compulsion, obsession (the compulsion of madness or the madness of compulsion).[13]

The potency of grip (a 'death grip') is a metaphor for a discourse of the eschatological. The terms—oath, name, call—are recursive in how one repeats the other without ever being the first. In the way they summon nearness (proximity) without simultaneously abandoning remoteness, there is no 'first' or more precisely, the first appears by repetition, by coming back. Derrida writes how the sign is understood in terms of a game played by Freud's four-year-old nephew. He throws a tethered spool away [*fort*] and then draws it back [*da*], while his uncle names the play "*fort/da*." The spool's movement mimes the grammar of a ghost's command ("Swear!") in that the imperative tries to escape its own utterance by a radical disavowal of the signifiers of the system that controls discourse. To borrow a description from Jean-Jacques Lecercle, it is the region—*delire*—between 'the dictionary and the scream.' The performance of naming, the call to nearness, is a double action that both denies and dissembles presence. Whatever is called fails to arrive but remains estranged, an outsider, visitor, spy, foreign observer, or extraterrestrial. Its ontological status is quixotic, variable, ambiguous, or even unavailable. Naming conjures a marshal of the spectral zone, "the ghost of the undecidable."[14] Undecidability is the peril that threatens the technology of language (enframing or *Ge-stellen*) and pushes its grammar toward that of the end, the *eschatos*.[15]

Ghost talk. Talk of ghosts, the talk that ghosts talk. Most apparent is how such discourse points ahead ('whereto') rather than behind ('wherefrom.') It is scary and compelling ('Who's saying that?'), and these traits are produced, in Heidegger's words, by "a presence sheltered in absence."[16] Ghosts do not parse existence or existents (beings); nouns, substantives, and the nominative are not particles of their syntax. On the other hand, verbs, imperatives, and especially apostrophes, abound. Their irritatingly angst-provoking trait belies their form of address, in that they speak to a singularity. *Address* is meant in its two senses, a set of space-time coordinates and that to which (whom) one speaks, that is, the dative case. For example, Hamlet, no one else, is addressed by the ghost of the murdered king. He is selected or elected and identified as such, *an sich*. He is appropriated by the specter's utterance that calls by naming him his proper name, his nominative, and makes him no other than his own. The grip (and scariness) of ghost talk is its affiliation with the singular and the singular debt of singularity. Delimited as oneself, in the trembling of the 'I' brought on by an excess of exposure, one confronts a possible breakdown in discourse (or one's control over it), as if ghost talk had a precedence, priority, or value that trumped other matters of importance. The singular imperative ("Do not forget!") speaks in a proximity unknowable to a stranger, yet it is a stranger who commands.

Ghost talk. When is talk not ghost talk? It is a spectral discourse of generality, derived by a prolonged meditation on Heidegger's thought (in *Time and Being*) and expressed through the trope of economy. Derrida writes, "A giving which gives only its gift, but in the giving holds itself back and withdraws; such a gift we call sending."[17] The given grammar suffers a restriction since it contains a paucity of elements, for example, the proper name and the oath. It also dictates a language stressed, distressed, or stressed out by virtue of its diction. Then, insofar as it is uttered by the 'other side,' talk loses its sure, swift settlement of reference, its sedimentation, and identity becomes unmoored from objects in the world. It grows loose at the joints ("Time is out of joint") and floats freely above the denotative field. Customs of surety give way to ambiguity, ambivalence, and the play of homonymy and equivocity. The meaning of indicative statements dons a mask whose mouth issues conundrums.

A simple declarative reverberates oracularly in its excessive freedom of expression. Each utterance declares itself in need of deciphering, and in the end, fundamental hermeneutic questions remain. This is odd talk, haunted by the ghost of the undecidable. The ghost has undone the seams of language, and hellsgate no longer segregates meaning from unmeaning. Satan's semen is now scattered through and through, and language can grow aware of the dissemination, but nothing more. It cannot be changed. The seeds were meant for sowing.

Spectral discourse resounds in the core of ordinary discourse, echoing the appearance of the phantom in its resemblance to the one departed. *Like* is an operative word. The ghost is like the thing, and the trope of mimesis plays a key role in Derrida. That ghost talk resembles (or dissembles) living speech suggests—if the underside is examined—that that talk will circulate metaphor and metonymy. But this is also the case with language's, 'ordinary' language's,' play and ploy, the play of deploying binary pairs of signifiers. Derrida's insistence is that a loose-jointedness in the systematics systematically *un*determines meaning. In an undetermined region, it rubs it out and leaves it illegible or ciphers and leaves it unreadable. Both games compete for a place in discourse. In either, the wheel of meaning doesn't fit the hub and slippage in signification is the outcome. Because the phenomenon is both global and subtle, its effect goes generally unnoticed until a radically novel view opens to a new paradigm. When displacement is eventually recognized, one or two things occur. First, each object is not what it is but rather is *like* what it is. A ring is ring*like*, a flower is flower*like*, a patch of blue is *like* a patch of blue. (Is this not what Quinean logic attempts when it moves all claims to identity to the predicate position? "The tree is tall" becomes "X is a tree and x is tall.") Language, 'living' language is as metaphoric as ghost language. It has devolved, in Plato's sense, into a mimetic, into mere or sheer poetry—devolved because it loses its precise reference and its acuity in respecting border-crossings. Discourse has become metonymic. One word is substituted for another, and, resembling or dissembling it, hides the shift to all accounts. Links in the chain of signifiers are not welded together, so there is elastic stretch inherent in signification. Because words are permitted to stand in for one another, the dream of a 'universal algebra' or a core of fixed terms is shattered. A fantasy exploded at the core of logocentrism.

5

Reading itself

IN A PERFORMANCE OF conjuring Jacques Derrida's ghost, it is time to speak to it. ("Thou art a scholar. Speak to it, Horatio!") To be directly addressed might provide an *a posteriori* proof of conjuration, even if the ghost voice is mute. Does it induce a muteness on the part of the interlocutor, as with Marcellus? Must the voice reading be a mute voice that transcribes it on mute and puts it in writing? To write in mute voice, the writing's own voice but muted, mutated, mutilated: is this an invitation to encounter the specter instead of speculating or being a spectator to the play? Ghosts don't reflect in a mirror. They don't appear in a speculum. What *is* the mute or muted voice in this context?[1]

Perhaps a hesitation while putting it in writing makes allowance for the required oath-making. To repeat, con*juration* has a close (etymological) connection with swearing and before that, with *jus*, the law. It would be important to specify before which law one must swear to initiate a conversation with a ghost, to solicit the ghost voice. The difficulty here is that ghosts are anomalous in their essence in that they are outlawed by the laws of the physical universe.[2] Furthermore, they defy the laws of canonical logic in that they commence by returning . . . from beyond the line that divides life from the other, from death. If there is incredulity (hesitation), it has to do with not accepting that the other is bound by law—and at the same time is necessarily other than law, that is, what constitutes and regulates beings and the totality of beings in the world. For what kind of law is it *there* that makes for exceptions and anomalies to the lawfulness *here*? It must be the law of the singular or a lawful uniqueness that wreaks havoc with an ordinary belief system as well as the understanding of limits and the domain of law, for instance, the law of returning, the *revenant*.[3] About which 'law' must be encased in quotation marks.

This is a place to interpose some remarks on quotation marks and their kinship with spectrality. Such a digression has the structure of breaking off that to which the text must recommence by coming back: the interval (rattle of chains) of the *revenant*. To state a generality, the manifold digressions within a text are spacings of the ghost, a species of ghost-writing that empowers the voice reading to a re-cognition of the phantom. A digression is, however, no more empowering than any other segment of the text until the character of its ghost-writing becomes pronounced. To bring the digression on digression to an end and begin the digression on quotation marks and use of citation: citation marks the appearance of an other text within the bounds of the current one. "Remember me," cites the words of the ghost of Hamlet's father from the text of *Hamlet*, thereby inscribing a passage from a different text now put in writing. There is repetition, intrusion, encroachment, even piracy, but in all cases, an inheritance from a source text to which the target text is indebted. "Remember me," the ghost's words in *Hamlet*, serves to remind Hamlet of his complex inheritance and the debt of restitution. While the citation of "Remember me," through the use of quotation marks, doesn't set in play the same tragedy, there is a debt of borrowing. A borrowed voice, a voice cut from context and rendered insubstantial, an abbreviated (eviscerated) version of the full voice—a voice that recalls the spectral.

The ghostly double of citation is repeated in the way a cited text copies an inscription ("Remember me") without being a copy of an original. Citation is iteration without origin or originarity. Citation as re-citation. That the words repeated in citation are new to the context, that the voice reading resonates with a unique event of voicification, expresses an aporia. Iterability that has "its twin aspect of repetition of the same and affirmation of the new" is one characteristic of ghostliness in general, and of scholarship in particular.[4] Another concerns how the strategy of scholarly protocol ("Speak to it. Thou art a scholar.") permits the ghost writing to appear even as it forbids a full-bodied voice reading. By resorting to abbreviation, indirect page notation (idem, op. cit.), and other devices to indicate the debt of borrowing material (to avoid plagiarism), it marks the writing's affiliation with the community of scholars. Resembling (but not stating) the main thematic content of the investigating, the source texts are themselves not visible, nor invisible. Moreover, their complete retrieval is possible through obedience to the protocols indicated.

There is the general issue of debt. "Something borrowed, something owed." The special debt incurred in citation relates to intellectual property. By writing "I prefer to speak of " mark; rather than of language. In the first place the mark is not anthropological; it is prelinguistic; it is the possibility of language . . . ," a segment of prose, properly Derrida's, is on loan.[5] As his inscription, it belongs to him under some definition of propriety, and acknowledgment of possession is made through the aforementioned protocol. Perhaps the citation has a use-value and to put it to service in writing necessitates payment for it. There is an analogous debt in the case of the ghost of Hamlet's father. Since the *revenant* requires the living being (King Hamlet), no phantom can return (to haunt the parapet at Elsinor) without the prior life. The ghost is, therefore, under a conceptual debt to the living. More than that, the debt is specific; it concerns *whose* ghost it is. Precisely at this nexus, the complex of spectrality and its infrastructure of indebtedness engage the work of mourning, a work first of all charged with attaching an identity to the spectral double to a life. It should be emphasized that the work is in fact repayment of a reciprocal debt owed by the living to the dead, the debt of teaching us to live *finally*. ("So teach us to number our days, that we may apply our hearts unto wisdom." Psalms 90:12) In its primary instance, the ghost is a magisterial (quasi-)presence, whose appearance by nonappearance trembles at the limit, thereby showing at the crossing where we must abandon all violence.

Or it would have an oath sworn, and by swearing, its word given: responsibility for thought and action. To be brought to responsibility, a necessary step is to swear on the authority of the beyond-being since spectrality is the erasure of both presence and absence, and of the bifurcation.[6] An authority whose singularity prompts an undecidability, an authority beyond any determinate authorization of power, yet an authority empowering the singular essential to any response to it. An authority perhaps that prohibits a reciprocal relation to it since it is other to life, as Horatio finds when the apparition doesn't respond to his command. To swear, refuse, or be unable to swear (numbed with fear) on the displaced authority of the phantom opens a corridor to the other side, beyond possibility of knowledge. The 'emissary' has access to what, from this side, is non-access and from there brings knowledge of the possibility of impossibility. The impossible incorporation of the paradoxical in the body of knowledge, the logos—or the unconscious death drive—lends the authority of the undecidable to challenge each choice, political, ethical, economic, ontological, or onto-theological. The challenge is to ground responsibility in other than rules (precepts, principles, commandments) or have it warranted by reference to any being, including oneself. Such grounding denies the ethics of decision, and by contrast rejects the derivation of the ethical from the universal. Responsibility arises at the aporia of the singular.[7]

Does the specter receive an inheritance from life, in the way that a predisposition to disease is inherited? There would then be ancestral claims that link the ghost to the vital and the living. In the case of disease (like other traits), the inheritance has a material basis in genetics. Son is linked to father via DNA that expresses itself in a latency for coronary illness. Metaphorically, in the phantom's case, the legacy is comprised of unresolved debts of the life—in short, *the unlived life*. What is left unlived and unpaid comes back to haunt: this is the formula of psychoanalysis whose theoretic describes their amortization. In the context of the drama, the ghost of King Hamlet inherits an impulse to avenge the deceased king's murder. The more general case leaves the exact nature of the inheritance unclear; a haunting without will and testament. That is the case with the ghost voice reading what is putting it in writing. W*hose* life is unlived trembles under the glare of interrogation and appears undecidable. Yet at that very site, at this very site where the identity of the reading voice again frequents the context with its phonic penumbra, the essential matter is the work of mourning. A necessary work, first to identify whose visitation it is on the parapets at midnight, for unless it is done, consciousness continues to deny the law of inheritance and becomes a crippled son. To identify the life: to acknowledge *whose own* experience it was who now returns from the dead or to acknowledge the absence of identity. W*ho* owned the life, who was to own it and didn't, or who must avow the possibility of such knowledge. The insouciance of being and the possibility of ghosting run together in the tangled object of "learning how to live."[8]

"To learn how to live finally." If learning were possible, it would come not from life but from the beyond of life. If it were possible, one would learn to own the life, living it as one's own, properly, without the belief that it could be free from contamination. Owning one's life, paying the debts of inheritance, one would give up the illusions of incurring no further indebtedness and of making the account current. The possibility of the specter, seemingly foreclosed, would be radically opened. Phantom life, come back to haunt the living, would return because life would have learned to live living with it.

Correlatively, what one inherits from the ghost is the very possibility of learning *finally* how to live. As the trace of refusal (or refusal of the trace) of responsible life dissipates, the ghost returns with 'life lessons.' So many unpaid debts, irresolutions, and lapses of care come back to phantomize the living of a life, lend it a fantastic double or duplicity, traumatize, and thus precipitate the performance of singularity in thought and act. In the Freudian archives, they are the neurotic impulses that inhabit the ghostly region of the conscious. Bearing tidings of dead, repressed material, they, under the tutelage of the analyst, are encouraged to speak their piece—and be mourned for. Brought to the light of subjectivity, they become preeminently magisterial, disclosing that of which they are inheritors. To take responsibility in the face of the undecidable—to take responsibility, period—is to grasp spectrality's unavoidable correlation, and to live a life essentially imperfect in presence ("thy almost blunted purpose").[9]

"Remember me," injunction, oath, conjuring. Remember me, ghost of Jacques Derrida, as you read these words. They could be in a script of a ghost movie, or equally, a sigh (the last breath going out, expiration, the death-sigh), or a prayer, said in the middle voice or the subjunctive ("Let me be remembered by you"). Either repetition encroaches upon the phantom of memory, not only phantom memories (i.e., of events alleged to have not occurred), or memories of ghosts, but memory itself. Aristotle first notices the spectrality of memory: "when one remembers, is it this impressed affection that he remembers, or is it the objective thing from which this was derived?"[10] If the first, absence would be immune to recall; if the second, "why should the perception of the mere impression be memory of something else, instead of being related to this impression alone?" The way between the horns of the dilemma requires the ghosting of memory per se: "sometimes, when we have such processes based on some former act of perception occurring in the soul, we do not know whether this really implies our having had perceptions corresponding to them . . ." Memory is conceived as the phantomization of perception. It is the afterlife of impressions, ghosts of which wander in the soul, producing ambiguity, confusion, and uncertainty, and in the worst cases bespeaks the madness of people who are "accustomed to speak of their mere phantasm as facts of their past experience, and as if remembering them. This takes place whenever one contemplates what is not a likeness as if it were a likeness."[11] That is, mistaking something fake for real: dissimulation.

Memory, with its figments, fugitives, and fabrications, is a prime locale of the ghost. This includes memory that is sworn on, placed under oath, and made to serve as testimony. The analysis of Kant's reproductive imagination unveils a habitation in the third realm, between presence and absence, being and nonbeing, inner and outer, constructive and unconstructive.[12] Passage between, crossing (re-crossing) the limit: there memory speaks of what has gone dead. In the extreme that is always presupposed, it speaks of death and the other and speaks in absolute terms, terms of absolution. In a magisterial guise, it is mastery by memorialization that Socrates practices in the *Meno*. Phantoms that the slave-boy cannot recall by himself lend knowledge of reality. They come, apparitions of a divine unconscious, not ruinations of past perception. They seem free-floating, blurring the contours of presence, even infecting the presence of the present with the past present and past, rendering it temporally ambiguous. Arriving in hordes, iterative, clamorous, at times recalling some blunted purpose, they cannot be addressed (even by a scholar!) and vanish at the stroke of midnight in the blink of an eye.

What material is still outstanding in making conjuration performative? Perhaps too strong an emphasis on 'reproductive' imagination, the name of which points to the retrospective function that Kant assigned to memory. Strangely, the question of the relevant archival files—memories—is not, or is not primarily, of the past. The future event is that which will express the repressed contents of the archive, traumatically, without cause, in 'its own time.' There is a relation of past with future that parallels that of memory with a responsibility to come that is ruled out by traditional logic. The oracular voice of the archive vis-à-vis the responsibility to come, which is related to the voice to uncanniness, *Unheimlichkeit*, the archive that most emphatically "is a question of the future, the question of the future itself, the question of a response, of a promise and a responsibility for tomorrow."[13] The awaited conjuration depends on the archive, the mnemonic bank, and will open to a future responsibility, that is, toward its contents and meaning. In part, the work of the archive lies in "a very singular experience of the promise" that binds the messianic voice to the text, to putting in writing that which has been deposited along with the totality.[14] The promise owed to future work belongs to a future anterior that operates on the present, exerting its influence on expression. The ghostly/ghastly future of 'messianicity' that influences the voice results from a promise that was never made. The effect of the ghost of Jacques Derrida, which would be conjured, on the voice reading the writing is indelible—yet in the retrieval of which grows illegible. Secret, because "the secret is illegible or undecipherable rather than invisible."[15] Even when the voice is voiced oracularly, uncannily, the reading of it is acoustically rubbed out, put on mute, killed. A voice permanently muted.

The future is not opaque, but abounds with images in disparate media that hover like anxious shades. Perhaps the abundance makes reading the future undecidable, yet accentuates the need for decisiveness in reading it. In uncanny silence, the reading waits for the ghost to perform a 'transcendental reduction'—a bracketing of present excess. Responsibility lies at the far end of reducibility as it faces the singular. At least with the hermeneutical circle, it is a question of a memory of the future and the singular, which may be the same. It is not difficult to access Jacques Derrida's images (one is before me) of many kinds, visual, audio, telemetric, electronic, cybernetic, hypercybernetic: examples of the mediatizable. Then, at the far end of the reduction, where responsibility ceases not to differ from itself and becomes irresponsibility, it is a question of a recognition of the other that is Hegelian. Mutual respect gives voice enough to respond to the voice-reading, in the conversation that will have ensued until this point. To read it responsibly—to hear the voice-reading give voice also to the writing voice—is already to hear the voice (like Horatio) in phantom speech. What is to come comes from the other and from death. Absolutely, it will concern swearing, re-calling, and promising a lost and forgotten destiny . . .

Also, the voice of justice. Justice is constituted in the recognition of the third, the one in addition to the other that supplements the relation of absolute responsibility. To swear is to take an oath before the law, violation of which defines the unjust. Justice involves the reparation of debt, retribution of offense, and punishment for crime—not only for deeds of one's own doing in one's own time, but for others' deeds of the past and in the future. In all tenses, there is inherited 'from the father' an unsought legacy 'to set it right,' worth its weight in responsibility. To deliver the message, word or blow, ("not now while Claudius prays") may spell one's undoing. To speak, to give voice to the ghost voice, is to learn how to live, which may be one's undoing, finally. Learning to live means learning not to, to unlive, to recognize the 'gift of death.' The further lesson of justice involves undoing the ontology that is generated in violence and degenerates into violence. "Before any fault is determined, I am guilty inasmuch as I am responsible," inasmuch as the promise of language commits one to it. Not to be denied: ontology (or onto-theology) commences with violence perpetrated on the other, and ever recommences with each successive closure and reopening.[16] To commence a teleology or destiny of humanity, a wounding on the part of the logos is necessary; the violence of night must be violated. Hence the logos comes by way of an inherited debt. Writing, voicing in itself and in reading, is heir to a demand for reparation, for the gift in return, the gift that cannot be given. To give voice to the ghost, whose words are no longer breathed, is to be reminded of the inheritance and the debt entailed.

But conjuring is not strictly thaumatological. It is part of an entry level toward membership in the community of questioners—that jury. In a way, it is no different from the jury of Athenians to which Socrates gives an apologue, charged with his death. That decision looks onto the end of philosophy, an epoch, history, and world ('philosophy's'). A jury, so charged, must obey the law and to bear witness to offense, and must then weigh each word. A panel of interrogators that combs the archives for the meaning of interrogation in order to recognize who perpetrates the interrogation, for the sake of preserving the value, if any, of the question. A jury, those "gentlemen of the jury" to whom Socrates spoke, who must hear the dire prophecy of death ("vengeance will come upon you immediately after my death, a vengeance much harder to bear than that which you took in killing me").[17] A jury that now must judge whether prophecies of the end of philosophy are uttered in Derrida's voice, a simulation, a mime or mimetic, a phonic reproduction, an acoustic ghost, or whatever. But what could 'the end of philosophy' possibly mean? It could say that the encampment established in Athens over 2,500 years ago to voice questions of being, the soul, death, and the afterlife, has passed into the past, and that its influence is now dissimulated. Could any one writer bring the end of that and not be disseminating 'barren' seeds in the dwelling?

To conjure (as wished), to take a seat on the jury that decides the life of the man—or a return from the life, as *revenant*. For did Socrates not teach that the value of the lesson of life was higher than the life? It is the aporia of knowledge, the paradox that learning how to live, finally, is more valuable than living, period. A paradox not easily nor simply dispelled. "Crito, we owe a cock to Aesclepius. Do not forget," speaks the master, expiring. Swear, Crito, to me before the community of questioners. Swear to me while I am in the throes of crossing the limit, bearing the limit, where I wait your word. Swear to me an oath of my return, my *revenant*, that I will come back to haunt you, in your sacrifice to the gods, as well as in your business affairs and personal anguishes. Swear to me before the jury of those whom I am about to seek, "Minos and Radamanthus and Aeacus and Triptolemus," that you will not cease learning the lesson of learning, that you will not place living a life higher, finally. Swear that the finality will never contradict repetition of the sacrifice, so that the return (*revenant*) might be guaranteed and the end of philosophy never accomplished.

6

Words 'I' write

Is the *revenant* the iteration of the man or his work or of both?[1] The work would be the given of the gift of which the man is recipient, the *donnée*. The question does not ask the meaning of 'or' in the disjuncture, whether it is an allusion to a self-giving or auto-donation that requires both. But the relation is important in deciding the constitution of the *revenant*. Certainly, *what* comes back to preoccupy and obsess feeling is connected to the otherness apprehended in the ghost's insubstantiality. Anxiety is produced in flaunting radical ontological freedom, the essence of inessentiality. The phantom evades the determinacy/indeterminacy opposition and can't be pinned down by command, name, trait, number, or identity (in time-space). It is always 'neither-nor,' the ever-availability of the negative alternative. The always other situates what the *revenant* designates; it is the ghost of disjunction. But also, with the double genitive, the disjunction of the ghost, phenomenality multiplied, made manifold, multi-featured, and in this case, polyphonic. The voice reading, the ghost voice, is not so much the voice heard, but the possibility of hearing the reading voice at all. The ghost that the voice vociferates is found in all doubles, duals, or dualities, and brings the possibility of reading them. The voice-ghosting iterates neither the man, the work, nor both, but is found in the very jointedness, the joints of language (letter, syllable, *phone*), in how particles hang together. In part, the work of mourning, difficult if not impossible, must judge the undecidable question of the difference between the man and his work. But in the difference is the ghost, the other that is wholly other, not in the man and not in his work and not in both. Its oddity lies in relating the two by dis-relating, deconstructing any similarity between them, leaving the 'or' at the same time a unity, a 'one.' One meets the man phantomized in his work and work de-phantomized in an encounter of separate affiliations (disaffiliations.)

Echoes of Derrida's reflections on his own debt to Heidegger that he never ceased to acknowledge. In this case, an inheritance laden with debt other than the 'intellectual,' and a reflection complicated by the fact of personal acquaintance, of knowing the living man. Still, if that can be bracketed [can it?], the suspicion of a phantomized Heidegger still lurks beyond the play of Derrida's concepts. Heidegger's *revenant* involves the chiasm that one admires the work but not the man, and so, not both. The philosophical work (after 1933–1934) is endowed with a 'heavy political mortgage' taken out in order to pay for the man's pledge of allegiance to Hitler. No thinker can appropriate Heidegger's thought without confronting fascism, National Socialism, anti-Semitism, and the holocaust, that drew inspiration from it.[2] A thinker who at the same time is a Jew may be specially marked. Any argument to the effect that Heidegger's romance with German rural life led to a fascistic politics may be dismissed as a lure. Yet, to distance the man's action (and his subsequent refusal to publicly acknowledge it) from his philosophy is also mistaken. One lesson in 'learning how to live, finally' concerns how one really belongs to one's studies, and in this case, to the life under study. One then belongs to the life, the man, all his acts and omissions, his allegiances and affiliations. And in Heidegger's case (in all cases) they run like a stain across the text of thought and over the hands that hold it. Echoes of the life of Macbeth and the ghost that frequented it.

Heidegger is doubly intriguing because he himself addresses the wound to which thought is vulnerable. The wound is to memory and effaces itself in an amnesia. *Amnesis* is forgetful of being's violation of the order of things (*rta*), the right or the just. Being as well as disclosure are both violent. Presence (*parousia*) is necessarily a rupture, an awaking from a latency that is night. Thought is wounded in being thought, the transgression of the logos, which is possibly the kerygmatic idea of original sin. The subject bears consciousness as a wound inherited from birth.[3] The inheritance must be paid off by investing in a discourse of inquiry. Within this context, calling thought forth ("Swear!") itself can inflict the wound. Thus, the intention to think supposes a willingness to disrupt, erupt, disrupt, interrupt, and all other manners of rupture (rapture.)[4] The fact that the intention aids and supplements the original *anamnesis* gives proof of its necessity. The archival supplementation that permits the memorization of memory is nevertheless the wound. That wound, of necessity, is fated to be phantomized in Heidegger's thought, made a phantasm, ghosted, and thereby avoided, a phantomization that requires deferral of obedience. *Introduction to Metaphysics* alludes to an inherited debt that is the very stuff of tragedy. (And tragedy in its satyric beginning loves the play of ghosts.) Like Plato, like Heraclites, being is the outcome of the *polemos*, the struggle of opposites to remain other to each other and at the same time to assist the surge to unity. (Is this to be taken as a tragic motto?) Before Derrida, Levinas alludes to the epoch of being, which, in Heraclites, proves "that being reveals itself as war to philosophical thought."[5] As a corollary, woundedness tries to banish all witness. In war, the victim is witness and the witness, victim. Consequently, Heidegger fails to undertake a search for an alternative to war, unlike Levinas, who raises the other to eminence, since "he is the persecuted one for whom I am responsible to the point of being a hostage for him, and in which my responsibility, instead of disclosing me in my 'essence' as a transcendental ego, divests me without stop of all that can be common to me and another man who would thus be capable of replacing me."[6] The other alone is in a position to give testimony to the fundamental ontological 'impulse' to war. Since the proclamation also reveals a path to peace, the politics of the war-state endemic to being cannot abide the witness and voids the concept of testimony. To seek a philosophy of testimony ends the avoidance by which the wound exculpates itself. In that light, the gift of Heidegger's texts is a lesson in a refusal in the double sense: of an awareness that refuses awareness and of a refusal aware of refusal.

It is not difficult to imagine a similar encounter for Derrida, for Heidegger's phantom haunts almost every page in writing. It is not difficult to imagine that it provides a model for the *revenant*, the concept, for it teaches the art and performance of conjuration. Perhaps it epitomizes his being an epigone and marks him with an inheritance of wounded thought, the debit of vulnerability. It must be so if the claim that the entire onto-theological tradition, Western metaphysics, is afflicted—from Parmenides and Plato to the present, without excluding himself—is true. There is no choice between empiricism (the dream from which philosophy awakens, with its affiliated occultism and ideology) and philosophy; but to choose to invite the ghost that has been a murderer, a violator of the order of things, killer of the father, all substance of the debt that gets put into writing—and for which the only just decision is to bear witness to the crime. But the wounds of violence at the same time open the book to the chapter on deferred obedience, and there an examination of inheritance, the father-son relation, the crime of exclusivity, being, consciousness, *Dasein*, can proceed. One exemplary examination concerns Heidegger's avoidance of the word "spirit." *En abyme*, the gift of the *Geist* is the ghost, the spirit of iteration, that repeats the *Geist* of the gift. *Geist*, whose work returns as a ghost, the ghost of a *Geist* "whose power," Derrida writes, "remains abyssal. In all rigor, it exculpates none of the discourses which can thus exchange their power. It leaves no place open for any arbitrating authority. Nazism was not born in the desert."[7] The deferred obedience demanded by the *revenant* can equally inoculate the writer against myopia as implicate him in blindness.

For philosophers of 'the end of philosophy,' what avoidance—toward what vulnerability toward the other—lies in rejection of the word "spirit"? For Hegel's word for the *sui generis*, self-moving subject, which Heidegger shuns, thereafter must encounter it in the phantom of breath, Hegel, however it is suppressed in voice. As a result, there is a breathlessness, a non-vital, non-phonic voice, that nonetheless summons to proximity, as conscience does—but apprehends without acknowledgment. By the same token, an abhorrence of ghosts permeates the thought. Of the fact of suppression, Derrida writes, "the word 'spirit' returns, it is no longer rejected, avoided, but used in its deconstructed sense to designate something other which resembles it, and of which it is, as it were, the metaphysical ghost, the spirit of another spirit."[8] When Heidegger writes of Augustine's, Descartes', or Dilthey's spiritual concepts, symptoms appear to stigmatize the wound. But denying the susceptibility, he fails to hear the ghost voice in his own writing. It speaks anyway. ("Thou art a scholar. Speak to it.") The specter is called and then is conjured away by a master conjurer, who, like Morgan le Fay and Merlin, the pupil spirits the master by conjuration learned at his feet. That the trace remains does not, however, mean that it postdates the dismissal of 'spirit.' The phantom might as well have brought it on from the future anterior. Derrida writes that "spirit visible in its letter, scarcely legible, becomes as it were the spectral silhouette—but already legible, this one, of another. The spectrality would be no more an accident of spirit than of *Geist*, of the thing and of the word."[9] Heidegger doesn't put it in writing—to give voice to 'spirit,' the word, vociferated in writing it—because of the ghost. Yet it is there—here—literally, by virtue of arranging the letters for their phonic resonance. Its identity by necessity remains a question, as does the possibility of a question of identity at all. The fact is to face facts. And the fact is that the ghost that returns, the *revenant*, is classical metaphysics, thought destroyed in the early sections of *Being and Time*. To speak to the ghost, to give it voice, in the present case is motivated by needing to make an avowal of the failure of 'the end,' that is, the closure of ontotheology. A hard admission, that death doesn't take it far enough, and that it goes too far, beyond the limit, and brings back the double of what had been over. The harder confession would name the greater failure, to find a way around Hegel's *Geist*, his *Phenomenology* of Geist, "of the double which can never be separated from the single," which always arrives in threes.[10] The real hope of *Being and Time* is a doubling that is never more than two, the ontological difference between Being and the totality of beings. The blind is the no specter, no speculum, and no speculation, which leads to capitulate to the one that comes in three.

The issue of avoidance, however, applies *pari passu* to the intention to conjure, in this case, to ask the ghost, finally, how to learn to live. To speak *about* conjuration is not yet to achieve the performative and could be a diversion. By the same token, as a concept, conjuration has competing affiliations with both magic and testimony, two threads that entwine but are separate. As a performance, the criteria of truth (of the lesson, or of thaumaturgy) are more subtle, more equivocal. At least its desired result can be fairly stated: to voicify the question that teaches, that opens the blaze of interrogating light on finality and living the life. But inasmuch as the ghost of Jacques Derrida itself must be heard, giving voice to secrets of the self, a cluster of issues have been avoided. For one, is a ghost a singularity? Is his ghost uniquely his? Are ghosts repetitions, commencing in their return, living backward or obversely, having shed the form of a unique identity, and do they now persist like a part of the wallpaper? Can they 'own' the same uniqueness as the life that they double, or at least one that inherits its important traits and debts? Would the traits be withdrawn (*retrait*) once the line is crossed? Which are important and for whose purpose? The voice of the interrogator expresses confusion over *who* in the trembling of inquiry. His words speak: "who is it that is addressing you?"

> Since it is not an author, a narrator, or a deus ex machina, it is an "I" that is both part of the spectacle and part of the audience. An "I" that, a bit like "you," undergoes its own incessant violent re-inscription within the arithmetical machinery. An "I" that functioning as a pure passageway for operations of substitution is not some singular and irreplaceable existence, some subject or life. But only rather moves between life and death, between reality and fiction. An "I" that is a mere function or phantom.[11]

The secrets of the self. The crux is in the crypt, the living cell of what will have been a conversation with Jacques Derrida's ghost. Perhaps after all is said and done, the attraction to the idea of a substantial self, present to itself, self-conversant, conscious, a transcendental ego affiliated with intentional thought and action, adequate unto itself and the exemplar of adequation, is by necessity. Not such a terrible thought! A proper self, a living own-most potentiality for being oneself, a self one owns: the secret lesson of living with the two is the lesson that I want to learn, finally. Partly, it is to grasp that the substantial self is a commodity of Western metaphysics, mediatizable, dialectizable, and salable; and that in the name of "moving on," it must be surrendered, by a deconstructive performative. Sacrifice is less destruction and more incorporation. The immanence of voice exists in need of supplementation by a transcendence, an interior in need of an exterior, a self of an other, a life of a death, in all of which seconds already always are the contaminant of the firsts. An opposite already supposed by its opposite that is anterior to it—supposed by the concept of opposition. The antonyms inside/outside, "the matrix of all possible opposition," are poised in opposition by virtue of an externality, that is, the outside is external to the inside.[12] So, already contained in the 'substantial' self, the self in itself and *an sich*, is a non-self, a self simulated so that it looks real but is not. Here, to understand the signification of 'opposition' is a first step toward the secret self, the secret meaning of the self, and only a first step.

What remains with the advent of singularity, the gift of a voice of ghost/*Geist*, a voice reading the writing that is auto-affection, *sui generis*? Is there the (re)commencement of an 'irreplaceable existence'? The pronouncement of a voice vociferating that puts it in writing is akin to learning how to live it, to *voice* it reading. The remainder is by necessity anterior to the opposition that posits 'self,' a something ('pure passageway') that allows the oppositions to get into play in the first place and nonetheless withholds itself from entering into play. Rather like a force or movement of expiration, a passing over (the angel of Death) to beyond, or through, forth and back, between determinate ends with names such as reality and fiction, life and death. Since 'passage' is reminiscent of the Greek *poros*, from which 'experience' derives, 'the self' is an undergoing, bearing, suffering fluctuation that endures without enduring the insubstantial play of opposition in passing beyond. *Différance*. It isn't *différance* itself but its ghost, not in the sense of owning the specter but not withholding it either, since *différance an sich* does not exist.[13]

The challenge is to forego comprehension, as canonically framed. To forebear the grasping reflex, which subsumes concepts under it whose contours draw the de-finition of 'self'—quotation marks would signify the ghost—opens the play of the voice reading while it is put in writing. If anything, voicing the experience of 'self,' self-experience, continually arrives at an impasse, a non-audition or the non-experience of an audition: the aporia of the ear. Anterior to any nomination of experience and at the same time subject to the posterior violence of the nominative.[14] Prone to violation, intimidated by presence, too reticent to declare itself, as Levinas writes of "non-intentional consciousness." To abstain from profiting from the play by seeking to govern or regulate is the lure to dominate it by invoking the terms of opposition *an sich*. To learn to live then takes on meaning from a peculiar withholding (*retrait*), a retaking of violence, and particularly the violence of assigning a determination to the voice reading within which it then vociferates. The voice reading by necessity broadcasts conditions that are site-less, displaced, and without origin. To deny its frequenting of writing equally suppresses with violence and collects obedience on credit. What remains 'in life' to be learned, it turns out, lies in the transmission of the voice of ghost that frequents the disclosure of truth. It is not the disclosure nor the truth, but its cryptic behavior of arriving together with its disappearance ("*Exit, ghost*"). Its incomprehensible relation to *telos* and *arche* lies in proximity to the witness. These are late lessons that, sonically available, would teach a mastery of the forces in living. To be learned, finally, intelligently ungrasping the concept of the end and the scandal of philosophy.

The question "from whom to learn?"—a repeated lure—asks for the secret name, the secret's. It's easy to show that the 'who' names neither the student nor the teacher. That the *ghost* (like Socrates) claims to have nothing to teach repeats the venerable aporia of the *episteme*. It is not susceptible to further clarification because "if what we have just imprudently called a *ghost* can no longer be distinguished with the same assurance from truth, reality, living flesh, etc., one must accept the fact that here, for once, to leave a ghost behind will in a sense be to salvage nothing."[15] A negative consequence, a manifesto of nihilism, an impossible teaching, an absence of transmission. Socrates avers that he, the man bearing the proper name "Socrates," taught in no public domain, including language. The 'who' remains encrypted in a teaching (adept to adept, never in *res publica*) at once bypassing the idea of a 'substantial' teacher. In the politics and economy of secrecy, initiation brings an understanding of life, finally, and lets 'transcendental' value be a felt actuality. It would be, for example, taught by a 'self' secreted within a man named "Socrates," who had nothing to teach and dissimulated (against his will, or not) being a teacher.

Being educated by Jacques Derrida's ghost follows a secret transmission—perhaps on the model of a secret 'self' affiliated with his intelligence that transforms. More exactly, from a secret aspect of his death to a secret aspect of my life, this one now lived as living. Secret to secret, thus preserving and transmitting, or preserving by transmit-ting. And: secret to remain secret, in that the student is not necessarily apprised of the visitation, as though there were a mute voice or muted penumbra to the voice reading what puts it in writing. This formulation need not posit a region immune to the corruption of the non-secret (public, 'average everyday,' impersonal), an inside without an outside. Just the opposite. The ghost voice so thoroughly permeates or infiltrates the voice reading as to be generally indistinguishable. But it does situate a secret vociferation of his that acoustically mingles with mine in secrecy, 'secrecy to secrecy' confirmed in its secrecy and at the same time not to tell. The transmission of the secret must necessarily remain secret to the possessor of it. One who possesses cannot reflexively know the owner of the secret. A secret consciousness, nonintentional (Levinas), a subconsciousness, where 'sub' appears in its deep meaning of secret.[16] Possessors of such encryptions are known for what they bear. This is a back door to the concept of attestation.

That idea of 'the pure' or 'the simple' continues to lure thought ('the soul in conversation with itself') into thinking the voice reading is simply 'its own.' That it happens at least as often as it is dispelled proves a necessary linkage to a second logic, perhaps alogically. Because a logic of contamination is a hard sell, a politics of virtue strives to compensate for the contamination; vice and injustice are seen as corrigible. The voicing of a secret 'self' must be determined differently, by the logic of difference and differend, as though returning to the ruins of primal nothing; which is as Derrida writes:

> if my secret self, that which can be revealed only to the other, to the wholly other, to God if you wish, is a secret that I will never reflect on, that I will never know or experience or possess as my own, then what sense is there in saying that it is 'my' secret, or in saying more generally that a secret belongs, that it is proper to or belongs to some 'one,' or to some other who remains someone?[17]

The pretension to self (inner, pure, 'my own'), the secret that is a lie, then takes on a porosity or humility to such a degree as to abnegate it. Meanwhile, as the secret of contamination spreads, it is known to be everywhere, yet not locatable. ("A circle whose circumference is everywhere and center, nowhere.") Nonetheless, there is no reason to gloat over a loss of pretension. The return to the very idea of a secret self: isn't that the *revenant* at work (play)? It's come back to haunt, to frequent—no matter the master's logic—to reestablish a counter-logic (counter to whatever logic in play [work]), and to offer proof that it again must be dispelled (*Exit, ghost*). The idea of a secret self, the *revenant*'s favored guise, comes for another round to almost elucidate the ghostly secret self at work: voice as a performance artist of spectrality. Presumably what it teaches is that in performance of spectrality, performance is transformative.

The secret that teaches—it could be Derrida's—or Derrida's ghost's—teaches a kind of active justness. Working through a dissolution of the 'coverings' of naked singularity, it brings differencing, the production of the suchness, "back to things as they are," in their haecceity.[18] Substance is reduced to a trace-action (or non-action) in the subtle form of the almost inconspicuous. How the secret teaches, what one discovers from form and content, makes it necessary to resort to metaphor, image of agency, fable of description, or lore of fellow workers, past, present, and future. It is the lesson of substitution at work. In adding to or doubling the old lesson, one comes to the end of the search, namely, to live, finally, the gift of life. Of the null point, the *punctum caecum*, Derrida writes, "It's perhaps there that we find the secret of secrecy. Namely, that it is not a matter of knowing and that it is there for no one."[19]

The secret that accomplishes one's life produces an inhabitation that leaves no element unlived: any inquiry must focus on that non-knowing. The word "secret" seems to announce a separateness, a self-enclosure insulated from the world—a condition prohibited by a logic of contamination. Thought, however, has circled that rim, as if refusing the ungraspable secret to living, which is only *given as a gift qua gift. The secret is a gift and the gift, a secret.* Its essence can be 'stated' only aporetically as a word-play in English: the gift is not a present. The gift is not presentable or re-presentable. It is effaced in the passage between donor and recipient, the essence of transmission. Its meaning is, therefore, inaccessible to any language system and protected against being put in writing. The gift is remarkable in that one can never be certain about having been gifted or obligated by an indebtedness. The secrecy of the gift thus assures that the ethical status of the writer is never completely decidable.

The gift echoes Kierkegaard's idea of faith, an absolute reversal in the order of absence by which the absented and antinomous element assumes supreme value. Kierkegaard writes, "If I have faith, I cannot succeed in having an immediate certainty of it—for to believe is precisely that dialectical balance which, although incessantly in fear and trembling, never, however, despairs; faith is precisely that infinite preoccupation with the self that keeps you alert to risk everything, that internal preoccupation of knowing whether you really have faith."[20] The generosity of the gift that must withdraw and conceal itself in sacrifice lies in its anonymity, its refusal to erupt into being, the very secrecy sought. To renounce it is to abnegate the self as learner, as recipient. The generosity expresses itself explicitly and visibly in the gesture of trembling, the *tremendum* encountered earlier—now outlined in Kierkegaard as a dialectical wavering. "Is it 'I' that is gifted or not 'I'?" The 'I' that is subject to the *mysterium tremendum* now trembles before the gaze of the invisible other who cannot be seen.

That ghost would teach the essence of living, the unteachable lesson! After all, being dead, it has passed through the aporia of death, to the 'other' side. Doesn't the lesson derive from there? A natural (if grave) misunderstanding, that the secret lies over *there*, beyond the limit, across the border. It is clearer, however, that the gift is the gift of 'death,' now enclosed in spectral quotation marks. The gift gives 'death' a new significance, a new apprehension, a new experience to apprehend. The trembling before the other, the 'I' that trembles before the other, is at the same time caught up in another secret, given with the gift. The *tremendum* is produced in the face of death, where no one can substitute for any other. In the gaze of that face lies the origin of the subject's responsibility.

7

A ghost

A PROVISIONAL CONCLUSION ABOUT conjuration: it's not thaumaturgy. It's faith. Rejection of the provisional conclusion. It's not faith, it's ethics.

To begin, thaumaturgy doesn't work. Smoke and mirrors may script a play to undo the conscience of the king, but conjuration is not essentially a work of magic—unless it denotes an essential relation between magic and wonder (*thaumazein*.) This is not to cast doubt on the magical effects of voice (ventriloquism, audio-kinesis, prayer) or the wonder of the voice reading while it is put in writing. But if philosophy is to bear witness to the law, if it is to do the work of conjuring, it must bury its magical potions, spells, enchantments, and demonic appurtenances. To read Plato is to review the record of the purge and of its politics.[1] The result: a logic based on a system of oppositionals—presence/absence, truth/falsehood, good/evil, one/many, knowledge/belief—is invested, and all subsequent standards for intelligibility are referred to it, that it may decide matters on its own authority. Any 'term' that escapes the binary network is deprived of signification and expression. *Tertium non datur*. The third escapes the regal investiture of 'logocentrism' whose guardians ('daughters of the Sun') protect the gates of the republic, repulsing the alien and stranger. But the constitution is not without suspicion. For an instance, Socrates, the Delphic embodiment of logic, courts an apparitional double, his *daemonium*, that possesses magical powers, for example, infallibility regarding future events. A study of the incorporation into philosophy—of Socrates' Apollonian mission, his power over the cold and the inebriating Dionysiac (*Symposium*) and over the fear of death (*Apology*)—is needed to determine whether the operation successfully supplants (suppresses) thaumaturgy. The study would have to delineate what actually supplements magic so that thaumaturgy is both enlarged and replaced by it. The name of the result is not secret. It is philosophy, supplement to magic, the magical supplement.

The intrusion (extrusion) or attraction of psychoanalytic terms, specifically those of purgation, comes into play at this point. Ritual purification, burnt sacrifices, scapegoats (*pharmokos*), demonizations, and fealty to occult authorities reveal an index of repressive action. Bad material (read: politically incorrect, potentially traumatic matter) is archived in a safe place ('gulagization') and, like poets and artists in Plato's constitution, banned from the republic. To what result? Poetry subsequently returns to haunt the purified text of philosophy as metonymy and metaphor, equivocity of meaning, divided reference, tainting even the transcendental purity of philosophical imagination. If high security archives with effaced names are shunted from history onto a blind side track, they possess in themselves a 'demonic' power of unexpected reappearance. Logical thought, in some sense of the term, that censors and secrets proscribed files, in that very act phantomizes the demon. The ghost's alogical apparition lurks as a potent disinterment of introverted material capable of subverting metaphysical commitment and imperiling intentional consciousness.[2] The rupture may be explosive, seductive, or merely plaintive, but the reaction of philosophy is predictable (predicative). It will repeat the purgative: sharpen definitions, refine distinctions, deploy further argument, or detail dialectics. With the return of the repressed—thaumaturgy and spectrality—philosophy mingles with an intelligence more ancient than father Parmenides, and regains its identity as . . . philosophy. Since the repression is by violence and violent in its condition, philosophy twice renewed is a philosophy of violation—of justice itself.[3]

Since the economy of suppression conceals material that, as Socrates states (on the advice of his *daemonium*), is no object of knowledge, it is important to be cautious in speaking of suppression. The ghost itself is immune to grasping, interment, or entombment. Detained for interrogation, it yields no vital information of the other side. On the passage to the limit, the need for understanding is greatest since only in relation to that DMZ is the question of responsibility broached. To ask is again to conjure the ghost of Heidegger. Responsible decision is *the* event (*Er-eignis*) that produces the singularity encapsulated in "one's ownmost potentiality for being." Responsibility, the appropriation (*Ereignis*) of choice proper to *Dasein* in order to bring it into its own, does not lead Heidegger to emphasize 'that solitary individual' of Kierkegaard, from whom he draws much. That person is situated beyond any possible rule, regulation, principle, or precept. Until that point, decision is 'merely ethical'—for example, on the basis of Kant's categorical imperative and its ideal of universality—since it deploys a technique or technology of choice. It derives decision utilizing an algorithm and voids responsibility *as such*.

To face responsibility, by contrast, throws philosophy into the terror of the situation. Derrida writes, "I philosophize only in *terror*, but in the *confessed* terror of giving need. The confession is simultaneously, at the present moment, delusion and unveiling, protection and exposure: economy."[4] Both ethical naturalism and ethical transcendentalism buffer philosophy from the episode. Both serve to defer the threat to equipoise by placing it beneath an abysmal mask. Release the ghost: the jolt wakes philosophy from its ethical fantasy and places it tremblingly before a responsibility ever outstanding, ever relaxed, ever undecidable by the rules of moral decision.

A strange image and stranger work, the phantom as gadfly on the back of the drowsy horse of Athens-Jerusalem-Freiberg-Paris. A philosophy whose metaphysical commitment is forgetful of its "almost blunted purpose," and whose destiny remains other than ontological. But in this case, the gadfly's sting is not the Socratic *elenchus* but something intractable to refutation, the *mysterium tremendum*. To revert to Patochka's understanding of Plato, dialectic presses the mage, worker of magic, into the service of the Good by means of incorporation. Magic embodied in dialectic is repressed, its potency diluted in service to the laws of logical thought. Released, however, thaumaturgy returns as the terror of the gaze of the other. The coherent reading of the philosopher's escape from the cave (tomb) and ascent into the terrifying, dazzling luminescence of the beyond-being (whose gaze cannot be returned) must take the *mysterium tremendum* into account. The release is from a history of repression (repression of history) practiced in the name of virtue, throughout which no act possible (commission or omission) can break the fetters of rule-like constraints or contrivances.[3] The release is also to a time "out of joint," one that no longer coincides with itself, is not synchronous (but a-chronous or Levinas's dia-chronous.) It does not end where it begins, and it fails to hold together as a totality. That singular time, time of the *revenant*, in the drama of *Hamlet*, takes on the trappings of a quest for justice, as retribution. (Analogously, Plato seeks transcendental knowledge for the sake of instituting a just ruler.) The temporal disjuncture, the out-of-jointedness of time, is the effect of an unrepressed magic, or rather, time's synchrony is a by-product of repression. It brings force to a situation, and at the same time leaves vision gazing into the fissure with terror, paralyzed and numbed (a gadfly's sting.) Recalled from drowsiness, what does it mean to act lawfully before the law, justly before justice, when time is out of joint and no rules apply? A heteronomous law, even aberrant. Yet, a phantom and disjointed, evil as well as good, absent as well as present, overdetermined as well as underdetermined, time *as such* now provides the condition necessary for responsibility, the event. Hamlet can awaken from the fetters of philosophy and its paralytic sting, and do the right thing.

The parallel goes only so far. Socratic gadfly and metaphysical specter both awaken the sluggish, it is true, but awakening in the first brings only annoyance while the second, abysmal anxiety.[6] In one the repressive operation largely succeeds, and reason, making a nuisance of itself, chides ignorance for not being alert. In the other, repression persists (can it be undone?) but the material bursts forth volcanically and with violence (*sui generis*)—into the light. Bearing signs of entombment, it has by an unknown influence been inexplicably set free from the 'unconscious.' In the gap between time and itself, in temporal incongruity or discrepancy, inexplicability gives rise both to impossible monstration and to the possibly demonstrable.[7] Reason receptive to the *revenant* gives free range to its precursor and admits it into philosophy. As a consequence, logic contains an excess that is part of the history of repression, a history of ancient crimes perpetrated by reason within reason. It gives lip service to expiation by telling stories of its misdeeds. To look back at the parallel, Socrates' (and Hamlet's) intellectualism is abrim with the inheritance of repressed magic and the *revenant*. Both share an irony, a passion for speaking with the dead, a penchant for entrancement, and both are caught in the dialectic between patience and its opposite. With both, a reason is produced that is never not in struggle with the injured jointedness of time. The difference delineates the difference between functional and dysfunctional suppression, *daemonium* and ghost. The former remains a docile suppression of thaumaturgy which is then permitted within limits into the discourse of philosophy. After all, magic guides the martyr to his death by hemlock. The latter, the ghost, is more likely to don the magician's cloak and succumb to the role of mage to invoke fear and trembling. It has come back to amortize the cost of its capitulation, its capital, and its life. It has been shown its death. This is Hamlet, who, unlike Socrates (for whom death is either dreamless sleep or conversation with the immortals), confronts the *tremendum*, and by inviting the ghost also invites the terror of the abyss.

The 'magical' incorporation of thaumaturgy into philosophy bears responsibility for the advent of the *revenant* at the same time that it institutes a presumptive logic. Its laws of thought promote rules over exceptions, universality over singularity, precedence over novelty, and juridical over justness. But if the guardians of presumption are recalled and the war on the absurd called off? In such a *terra incognita*, one—a scholar—might at last be ready to speak to the phantom. The new situation requires a conjurer: Derrida writes, "a scholar who would dare to admit that he knows how to speak *to* the phantom, even claiming that this not only neither contradicts nor limits his scholarship but will in truth have conditioned it, at the price of some still inconceivable complication that may yet prove the other one, that is, the phantom, to be correct."[8] The proof that complicates beyond measure of complication lies in the inconceivable response to the terror of the situation—that invests the ghost qua apparition. The responsibility cannot be conceived, thought through, deduced from "general rules that apply to all rational beings whatsoever," or counseled by reason in its incomparability. The correctness of the phantom's 'position' is given in its summons to decision regardless. It is precisely there to meet the ghost qua ghost, the phantom as *such, an sich*, where its suchness consists in being the *closest signifier to death* in our lives. The ghost calls for a response in the face of death's face, where the irreplaceability of uncontested nakedness is unveiled.

From the ghost issues a summons to an irreducible experience, an experience that cannot be a redux of another, but whose repetition promises the end of repetition insofar as history is the repetition of the presence of the present.[9] The repression of thaumaturgy that drives magic into the unconscious of philosophy belongs to a strategy to negate death. It heralds no new epoch in philosophy, no post-magical one (but how would that look?). A strategy of total eradication of the trace (of death, of the other)—the Platonic project—simply replaces wizardry (tonal, musical, rhythmic) with the magic of words, discourse, and dialectics. The repeated substitution of the signifier for the signified in the chain of terms that name morbidity eliminates death, the thing (if this can be said), from reality. Death by any other name remains the same, outcast, exile, vanished, . . . , other. Language, especially writing, then is poised to safeguard a concept of transcendental life that is effected by the soul's ascendance to a vision of the Good. Ascent, however, is possible only if the ghost and its demonic power are subdued by a discourse. This juncture precisely invites the recognition of an imperfect strategy. The specter that has not vanished here inverts the discourse, perverts it, and lets it revert to the other: the death call. But one aspect is missing: the ghost must give voice without the breath.[10] Without the vowel. A voicing in which respiration cannot provide for the voice box, the larynx and vocal cords, the tongue and the mouth. Voice of the dead, a dead voice to mimic (but only to mimic) in its otherness, the living voice. Voice of absence, absent breath of life, absent organic substrate, absent being-toward-death. The remains of vociferation, the phantasmagoric intentionality, the phantomic *phone*, the articulation of a death wish (a wish not lived by the living), the sigh. The sigh that escapes the mouth upon crossing the limit where there is only an "awaiting (at) the arrival."[11] Yet, miraculous voice, voice of miracles that speaks marvels and wonders: a *pure* voice inasmuch as it is free of the taint of the organic, animal life, life itself. (Is there any doubt why only a scholar can speak to such speaking?)

Repression should be on guard against the fact that the ghost is near, in fact is the 'closest' signifier of death. It is similarly wary of how death as a noun is the poorest candidate to attach to "a concept of a reality that would constitute the object of an indisputably determining experience" and how it yields the discourse poorest in signification, and therefore, least subject to domination.[12] It is a discourse (unlike this) disempowered of binary oppositions, in whose play of opposites (life/death, presence/absence, real/illusory, solid/vaporous, and inside/outside) is a challenge to any ghostly apparition having a fear of a logic of exclusion. Wait. Can it be called a discourse at all? Grammatically, it contains only the rudiments of one, call, name, oath, summons that have to do with a language of retribution. These give rise to a family of themes that includes debt, remembrance, temporality, and, not strangely, signification itself. On the one hand, ghost language seems at the service of compensation, specifically, for appearance, to make up for the 'truth' of disclosure by rocking the boat. The shock of its voice is because it is and remains a-thematic. On the other, it is obviously not in any simple way mimetic, like parrot speech or the onomatopoetics of wind. A ghost of a discourse that leaves little or nothing in meaning to be salvaged but whose vociferation prompts—urgently—the operation of salvaging the trace. One remains apprehensive about what the phantom voice is saying through its blasted articulations, (a bad cell connection), interferences, and distortions—as if the very resonance of voice were now governed by indeterminacy. The point of its signifying seems deeply significant yet utterly lost in transmission, as if the speech had other claims upon it than that which the discourse of the living chooses to avoid. Pause to ask, what are its debts and from where (whom) were they inherited? What part, if any, do they claim repayment and why is it always already deterred?

But this is mere ghost speech. As itself, in itself, the ghost signifies in that, always already among the dead, it would audaciously convey the other unto signification, to reading voice, to give voice to putting it in writing, distinct from being, presence, substance, or security. It drifts in and out of metaphysics yet is weakly attracted to categories of thought holding eternal objects, even while a beacon of exteriority itself for Levinas. To gather the reading voice under a concept is to abandon it to an indistinctness that is far different from its distinct acoustical pattern, which is as close to a 'proper' trait as any. But the alien signature of the mute trace isn't confined to declaratives of dispossession or expropriation. It is more adequately situated within an emphatic of terror. That voice, at the lower modulations of terror, would include the creeps, spookiness, the eerie, and weirdness. The emphatic lies etymologically close to the apophasis of negative theology, which is one reason that it can solicit a response. That which it unfounds is beyond any grounds based on the Platonic vision of the Good. It opens the eyes under a veil of tears to a new experience of death, beyond even its givenness.

The corridor opened in the surrender of a repressed thaumaturgy and its dissimulations opens to the terror. The hocus pocus of the ghost, its restive nonmateriality, chronic aberrance, and a-chronicity, constitutes a lurid mask that leads beyond an authentic (*eigentlich*) response to death. The abracadabra and the *Sturm und Drang* disguise the specter, often by showing it as ally or affiliate. But this is dissimulation: hiding by revelation. Real props unveil through violent means. The signifying of the ghost is no longer in a reroute through the demonic, or its magical warding off the encounter. When that power ceases to be (by repression or by suppression), the ghost erupts into a 'direct contact' with the other. It is the decisive moment, a time out of time and disjoint with itself, time of responsible action, void of principle and precept, in the facelessness of absolute singularity and the law, as if the instant that Abraham must choose. The voice, atremble, is recollective of traumatism without giving a frame for it.[13] The ghost magnetizes the voice with that resonance that registers the tremor. It can try on the voice-reading putting it in writing and cohabit with it. Far off is an ethics of the free subject: for whom the terror has disencumbered a language to guarantee the identity of ghost subjectivity on the subject.

An odd crossroads. Does Derrida's ghost (his 'own' ghost) gift a voice disencumbered from other general spectral appurtenances but not their metaphysical commitments? That is a good question, but there's more: if accepted, will it express his (its) own specific gravity or acoustic signature? Reception of the gift surely involves not knowing when it comes or that it is a gift; it makes no sense to ask "what is" or "why" when the issue abruptly is no longer to speak to him (it)—to dominate it (him) by means of the father tongue, but to let it be given. To let the voice be given or otherwise, there is no ghostliness, in its inessential quality of vociferating mutely, so as to alter the acoustic of reading inconspicuously—or using the trope of audition. The assumption that there is a pure communication, uncompromised by interference or distortion, a *system* of signifiers, that issues from the apparition which must be voided since it relies on the substantive grammar of classical metaphysics and philosophical discourse in general. Strangely, that teems with the very hypothesis of communication, which posits of a community of reading-voice and voice of writing in which they mingle. The voice reading *with* the voice of the writing, ghosts both, having no separate identity but still possessing a distinctness. Derrida's ghost and mine also partake in that miscibility of the phantom that lives by repeating itself. The voices are not one and the same but both belong with the other, at least as attestations—or perhaps, attestation in the singular. That is what makes the present 'form' of communication susceptible and willing before spectral contact to forgo the 'death that lies ahead' so as to meet the one that returns. Only at the far edge of contiguity, beyond the limits of the liminal, in an alien enclave, can the ghost deliver its emphatic speech—there where there exists communion beyond bounds, where bounds within living speech voice the speech of dead to the living. To find oneself *there* or to be found *there* oneself: this names another impasse, a glancing blow of *différance*.

The ghost leaves acoustical tracks in writing throughout Derrida's, only they are spectral and leave a phantom mark barely audible, indirect *and* emphatic. "Emphasis" as a word belongs to the prodigious family of *phainein* words central to Plato's thought and Heidegger's. Since the prefix *en-* to means "productive of" or "bringing forth," the sense of "emphasis" is that which produces a showing: the gift. In an important meditation on phenomenology, Patocka argues that the event of showing is the locus of mystery, with the genitive double.[14] *Its* (if ipseity is correct here) bursting forth or breaking through is moderated by discourse and accomplished setting violence against violence. One recognizes the disruption (it defers obeying) through the transcendental reduction—could one say, with its repressed thaumaturgy?—as soon as the event is over. Anterior to the magic of the *epoche*, prior to the discourse that encloses the phenomenon in the wraps of presence that veil the violation, the emphatic is situated. The elementals in the ghost's voice, with resonances stressful and terrorizing, leave behind the acoustics. They are only the trace; frantically grasped after by the mind, the insubstantially real escapes like a filament of the voice reading.

A lesson ("How to live my life?") sought from Derrida's ghost conjoins tantalizingly with the idea of an emphatic discourse. Grapes dangling barely beyond reach: image of a phantom desire, whose object is a phantom or whose gratification is a ghost that haunts consciousness. An aporia of desire: is it possible to find a way around or through? Is there a way to 'annul' (annulate) *différance*, take its force so as to produce reconciliation and sameness again? To take the feet out of the fire would spell the triumph of Hegelian logic and foundationalism. By contrast, the no-exit of the ghost commits the investigation to an aporetic experience, experience *as such*, with its attached problematic of the grammar of the aporia. To push (*putsche*) toward the experience is to fall to the lure of empiricism: "As for the concept of experience, it is most unwieldy here . . . it belongs to the history of metaphysics and we shall use it only under erasure [*sous rature*]. 'Experience' has always designated the relation with a presence, whether that relationship has had the form of consciousness or not."[15] Yet not to move toward the aporetic experience belies philosophy's forgetfulness of how violence trumps all, that is, to turn its back on repression. It follows that the ghost must speak first, if at all. The ghost can never give voice unless first addressed. The mystery concealed by spectral discourse is not yet the *mysterium* but a mystology, a mystification. Nevertheless, it precedes the ghost, lives in its advance, predates its prefiguration. In a murmur before vocalization, it is a precursor to showing as such, unless they are foreshadows and prefigurations of the other, *en abyme*. To learn to live, finally: in seizing the lesson, the adumbration of finality must be avoided, even unto an endless adumbration, by which is meant, never a coming to show. Always in the penumbra, toward but never reaching the 'line' dividing dark from light, death from life: ghost grammar, in its vowel-less predicament, addresses that region or nonregion.

A discourse of emphasis, *en-phainein*: the dis-stressed, expired voice of spectral voice that gives voice without the breath—voice-reading. Each word pronounces the shadowy boundary between absolute opposites and 'articulates' the trembling there, which is a vibratory movement of between. Sympathetically, the self is brought tremblingly to its knees with tears of responsibility. Imploring, it is enabled to receive the gift (of responsibility), while any content—in the form of a concept or theme—is given only after, in a successive epoch. The void as present, the void of presence, lies at the heart of the thought: "The concept of responsibility is one of those strange concepts that give food for thought without giving themselves over to thematization. It presents itself neither as a theme nor as a thesis, it gives without being seen, without presenting itself in person by means of a 'fact of being seen' that can be phenomenologically intuited."[16] There is a way in which the ghost mimics the mystery of *showing*, in that the ghost watches without being seen, without leaving a trace of awareness of being seen. More telling to an emphatic discourse is that ghost speech gives voice without leaving a trace of audibility. Because it can't be comprehended, it causes apprehension. Its meaning is revealed by its whisking away from the phenomenal world by whisking away the phenomenal world itself. Yet in its absence an 'encounter' is provided with irreplaceable singularity. The self's trembling is exacerbated by the nearness of infinitesimal separation—the *mysterium*—and assumes its irreplaceability with an attitude of imploration. The grammar of emphatic discourse is prayer, its phonetics of course, breathless.

Is it correct to conclude that the emphatic carries thought to the cusp of responsible decision, possibly beyond? The ethical impossibility of Abraham's decision, Kierkegaard's concept of the religious, stands in the dissolution (absolution) of grounds in relation to the necessity of not abnegating choice. In a necessity without grounds, *who* is the one to decide? The one, trembling, for whom the *unseen* ghost passes a most emphatic notice, reads without comprehension. The notice is a death notice, a notice of death, one's own. It is a notice that one's own death is not only given, assumed by an act (in)comparable to Abraham's, an act of absolute solitude; but also is a gift. In the notice, one hovers in the dual folds of secrecy, a butterfly's flight in return to self, a *revenant*'s. The doubleness, the gift and the givenness, the unnameability and the imminence, is the transformative agency of the performance. Emphasis is the scene of performance that dwells emphatically behind the scenes.

8

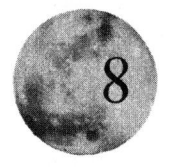

Writing itself

THE DEEP VALE IN which pass thoughts of Heidegger, Levinas, and Derrida that dwell on the theme of death. The concerns of authenticity, infinity, and undecidability, a triad not commonly found together, nevertheless emerge from the same abyss. More precisely, since it is the question of a death of "my own" (scare quotes already always sign the ghost), the subject necessarily concerns a death that in giving itself to me gives me to my own self, or individuates me. The grammar marks death the gift, the difference that separates the living from the dead, the *revenant*. But not any *revenant* but that of the voice reading, or *is* the voice in its primary event, its *Ereignis*, as it gives voice to what is put in writing. This connection between death and the gift of voice is known to Hegel, as Agamben cites, "Every animal finds a voice in its violent death; it expresses itself as a removed-self (*als aufgehobens Selbst*)."[1] The ghost voice as *revenant* comes back 'from the dead' with the voice inherited from there. As a signifier that effaces its own signifying, it is sited nearest to the unsignifiable, signless, unseen death, in some sense of proximity and that is from where it repeatedly voices. It is the acoustical taint *or* trace of death which is either redundant or *is* the taint or trace. The matter is one of signification. Hearing the voice reading then is to join in the conjuration produced on the scene of production, which is writing, as accompanying the voice. It is to be in communication with death as the dwelling of the dead, as it is given voice and the power to delimit its place. In such communication is found a lesson in learning how to live, finally—to understand the life unlived because it can never be lived, which is death. The work of mourning the other is there, in the acceptance of memorialization.

The positions (Heidegger, Derrida) weave together in a complex pattern implicating death, and perhaps it is folly to unfold it briefly. Nonetheless, Heidegger identifies *Dasein* as a concern for its existence which is owned, appropriately, only by facing its termination in death. Death "not-to-be-bypassed" and calls through its voice, conscience, for the cessation of living the unlived life. Lacking acoustical origin, it still possesses an effectivity for individuation, the constitution of *Jemeinigkeit*: "by its very essence, death is in every case mine, insofar as it 'is' at all."[2] Death uniquely marks each unique life in such a way that each is *for whom no substitute can exist*—which in turn marks each me as *its* own ("its" in scare quotes.) Similarly, the gift of death, Derrida writes, exposes the irreplaceable self whose trembling signifies insubstantiality. No other can die "*in my place*" because no other can live there. The ghost ineluctably belongs with each that it phantomizes, and as for mine, it is mine; no one else's can ghost for me. "Dying is something that every *Dasein* itself must take upon itself at the time."[3] It is impossible to die for another or take the other's place at death, as in the Alcestis myth. All appearance is governed by the *revenant*, since its coming back alone begins the death and life play. Heidegger may fail to see that the gift assures that an unlived life be appropriated since his failure is bound to a misunderstanding of sacrifice. If death is a gift that cannot be given away, exchanged, replaced, or transferred, it is also a gift that cannot be sacrificed, no part of an economy of sacrifice. Death accepts no substitutes, whereas sacrifice implies exchange. Furthermore, the impossibility of taking another's place at death, a stand-in, exposes a deeper logic. To one targeted by death involves a unique reciprocal non-sacrifice: to give oneself to death even as death gives itself to one, where both are gifts for which there can be no recompense. A more strenuous discussion of the sacrificial would unite the two views.

Heidegger's perspective crystallizes around *Jemeinigkeit*, the self-identity in its comportment toward death. Paradoxically, regardless of the gratuity of the gift, its promise of death necessitates the amortization that brings the identity into its own, and by corollary, gives the ghost its irreducible singularity. To resolve to give the self to its own death is to respond in the only way that death's generosity permits. Perhaps the paradox uncannily heralds the gift promised, at the same time an inheritance and a debt from before birth, in responsible living. It also produces the ambiguity surrounding the phantom, granting it an autonomy that is equivocal to the point of heteronomy. Heidegger thus can write that "[t]he call comes *from* me and yet *from beyond me and over me*."[4] The excess of the law that summons absolute exposure to an inevitable death hedges where the authority comes from, self or elsewhere, or both. It follows that whether responsibility rests in one's own decisiveness remains moot. If the call is necessarily heteronomous, Heidegger would agree with how Levinas relates it to the other. He does not, and for Levinas, that summons is the *a-Dieu*, the word that is "to-God" and at the same time, to life in a final leave-taking. Within the frame of finitude, heteronomy would require a radical shift in emphasis in the call, if not an impossible one. He writes, "the *a-Dieu* is not a process of being; in the call, I am referred back to the other human being through whom this call signifies, to the neighbor for whom I am to fear."[3] The shift from autonomy to a heteronomy is tectonic with respect to the concept of death: 'my death' is no longer a syntagma for an ally. It is a murderer, of self, language, discourse, and comprehension.

In Levinas's radical reassessment, the summons issues 'directly' from the absolute Other, whose trace (apparent in the face-to-face encounter) reduces the 'value' of a death of one's own to a secondary status. Death is able to instruct for Heidegger for two reasons: through "the fact of relating to the possible as possible" and that "this unique possibility of relating to the possible as possible is being-toward-death."[6] But to assume that the 'first death' is *Dasein*'s own, and not that of the other, is mistaken: "Further on it will be a question of a 'duty beyond all debt' for the I who is what it is, singular and identifiable, only through the impossibility of being replaced, even though it is precisely here that the 'responsibility for the Other,' the 'responsibility of the hostage,' is an experience of substitution and sacrifice."[7] One gives as witness, as aid, as comfort, to the death that takes/gives the other away. That possibility is entwined with a principle of sacrifice; the economy required of the latter is derived from the grammar of the former and how the given supplements the gift by dissimulating its palpability. Important implications flow from *différance*, namely, an opening of the concept 'death.' Relating it to the sacrificial is founded

> in its ex-ception—and regardless of its signification in relation to being and nothingness, it is an exception—while conferring upon death its depth, is neither a seeing nor even an aiming toward (neither a seeing of being as in Plato nor an aiming toward nothingness as in Heidegger), a purely emotional relation, moving with an emotion that is not made up of the repercussions of a prior knowledge upon our sensibility and our intellect. It is an emotion, a movement, an uneasiness with regard to the *unknown*.[8]

Is the hypothesis that the exceptional incorporation of oneself in the other's death—as emotion, movement, force of uneasiness—is the gift of the *tremendum* at all plausible? Perhaps Derrida's variation on Levinas's theme means to say that only the attestation of an other's nakedness and excessive exposure can produce the singularity of the I.[9] Alone before the other (God, death), the self, the I, trembles in the throes of extreme testimony. A testimony that is also testamentary, in that alone, one must answer for the other: the gift of death, now radically reconfigured. The paradox is that the other's death, in which the one has been included, incurs no debt on one's part; "for what is due cannot be paid; one will never be even."[10] The emphatic mood of the *tremendum*, the "uneasiness with regard to the unknown," is a "duty beyond all debt" for the singular I, now on the horns of a time disjointed by the grammatical necessities of the witness.[11]

The sacrifice of onto-theology correlated with its absolute value with respect to care of the soul (unto death) has a further consequence. The identity of the *who*, the I, is no longer exhausted in the empirical facticity of presence, whatever its avowal. Obversely, a disruption—mortality glimpsed on the other's face—breaks the grip of being-toward-death (its incessant I-making, *Jemeinigkeit*) and terror infiltrates that schism . . . or its simulation, the specter of existence, existence's specter. The emphatic of uneasiness pins one there irreplaceably in one's 'own' place, yet before a death not one's own. Singularity, heteronomy, responsibility: here is a chain constituted by Levinas's version of apophasis. Responsibility to (for) the other before death requires, Derrida writes, an imperative to interiorize or memorialize the other. From the sacrificial altar, the work of mourning rises. Produced by remembrance, the work holds in mind that a proper name is at the same time an epitaph, extinction of which constitutes a scandal that would supplement that of death. In the shadow of the worldly threat (threat of worldliness), the ghost apparition is necessarily ethical in bearing. More precisely, it brings the ethical back into view. In, but not of, the showing, it calls forth the work of mourning. Its frequenting of consciousness is in the cadence of prayer—a sigh of tears and imploration.

It looms as a terrible responsibility. A responsiblity for (to) the ghost of the other even before the other's death! One is bound by a responsibility to the ghost before it even comes back, prior to the advent of the *revenant*. It is responsible in a time out of joint since it persists anterior to the conditions that constitute it. An ancient work more anterior to the gift of death than the giving of the gift—the voice in the tense of Derrida's eulogy to Levinas: "for a long time, for a very long time, I've feared having to say *Adieu* to Emmanuel Levinas."[12] The ghost that haunts before death, foreshadowed, adumbrated, prefigured, drives a critical question before it: is it situated in the ontological difference or in the life unlived—two distinct forms of displacement? Perhaps when existence is unmoored from essence, the ghost gazes out from the fissure, and its look produces the mode of the ethical. Emissary of 'pure' emotion—terror—the ghost sees without being seen (the 'visor effect') and situates one *there* uniquely, there where no one else can possibly be.[13] The gaze's power to specify utterly the *who* derives from a withdrawal ceding phenomenality.

The disruption in the sacrificial constitution of life, of the *Lebenswelt*, is not the absolute, irreducible disruption of death; it is rather a 'little death' (thus exhibits analogies with sexual orgasm). The ghostly gaze, in summoning the fact of mortality, can invoke, provoke, and evoke the terror that initializes an inner memorialization both open-ended and non-dialectic. Death, for Levinas, is the gesture that hollows the egological space to infinity and deposits a 'without-response' in its place. In the light of the *yortzeit* candle, perspective is eternally transformed. The look now "is within us but it is not ours; we do not have it available to us like a moment or part of our interiority."[14] The look within is not inward but requires a "dissymmetry that can be interiorized only by exceeding, fracturing, wounding, injuring, traumatizing the interiority that it inhabits or that welcomes it through hospitality, love, or friendship."[15] The act of memorialization thus breaks through the grounds of living memory, repeatedly effaces the limit, and disperses the thanatopic throughout the vital. It is there that a thought at the margin resides, waiting since the most ancient beginning. It is there that Derrida conceives 'ghost' in a mode that memorializes Levinas's thinking on death: "Ghosts: the concept of the other in the same . . . the completely other, dead, living in me."[16]

At this check point ('border, closure, and demarcation'), it is crucial to note the footpath of Derrida's ghost. With death as "the possibility of the impossibility" of being there (Heidegger), the ghost can claim a limitless access to the limit. The position attests to the impossibility of a crossing that proclaims finality, that it is the last. Death the concept is useless in delimiting the (im)possibility of life. Going ahead *from either direction*—life to death as well as death to life—is 'ultimately interminable,' which can mean that either the borderline is infinitely thick, the rate of penetration infinitely slow, or there is no crossing (nothing to cross *or* crossing is a bad metaphor).[17] The deterioration of 'death' has been going on for some time, leaving it a frontier without borders—as if the ghost were already an integral part of life. Certainly, interminability in the movement from life to death, death to life, is the aporetic in action, even as 'evidence' is necessarily inconclusive, undecipherable, and spectral; quotation marks around 'evidence' is evidence of spectrality. 'Death' at the aporia raises the question of whether the aporia is a parasite of experience, or experience the hostage of the aporia, that which *"can never simply be endured as such"* and that, therefore, perpetually deferred by experience.[18] That which is possible only as impossible: the aporia. The ghosting of the possible by the impossible (and the obverse) arrives (returns) to experience the uncanny dread, gift of the *tremendum*, voiced without breath, robbed of vowels, deprived utterly of the *conatus* of the *esse*. In the sphere of intelligibility, the ghost spirits the voice reading the aporetic written of the terror of the situation.

It is well to supplement the observation that deferral of the aporia is twofold. On the one hand, giving reading voice spaces out the aporia by indefinite postponement. It has not yet arrived, in a periphrastic tense. It is yet to arrive but is never going to, a second periphrastic. On the other hand, giving reading voice pays deference to the aporia, respects it as a holy event, and therefore averts its 'auditory gaze,' imploringly. The aporia cannot be directly heard and lacks a horizon, perhaps functioning as the horizon of the inaudible 'other side.' As inconspicuousity (inconaudibility), it surrounds (in the sense of com-prehending) singular experience by enclosing it within its non-borders. As a consequence, responsibility is situated squarely in the aporia's aura of deferral. The voice reading's repeated postponement of the impasse *as such* allows a borderless 'other side' to permeate. A non-closure is produced through which (coming one way) the ghost can glide *and* through which (coming the other way) the voice-reading can arrive at the 'limits of truth.' Responsibility, being responsive to apparitional reality and not occlusive of its otherness, is constituted by an act of reclusion. The voice-reading remains a recluse in front of the aporia. That act designates acceptance of the gift that enables the *arrivant*, one who crosses (the irrecrossable line) and thereby enters a deeper inclusion, or rather, non-exclusion, with death: the voice-reading that includes its other, the voice-writing—another 'definition' of the aporetic.[19]

And yet wherever death is, there exists a politics of death conjoined to an economy of the work of mourning, and both find representatives in these thoughts. A thanatopic political economy is necessarily historical, in which history possesses a twofold meaning. On the one hand, the present analysis as well as those it repeats (Derrida's, Heidegger's, Kierkegaard's) would be read as living testimony to a historical experience of death *as such*, the 'inexperienceable experience.' Inasmuch as it bears witness, belongs without belonging to it, it remains in the unique position of the witness. A positing of a supplement to an event that cannot be the same without the supplement. The witness: there without being there, there perhaps incidentally, inconspicuously, or virtually—a specter, necessarily secret . . ."[20] The witness's account haunts the scene of dying, whatever its politico-economic inflection (as death haunts the testimony, as Socrates in the image of *The Post Card* haunts Plato's work), even as it purposes a value-free, non-normative, or transcendental view as to content. Onto-theology purports to be radically fundamental and originary in its testimony to thought. Whether it is or can be depends largely on the incontaminability of testimony, that is, whether the witness is non-susceptible to 'crossings' that contaminate, crossings of truth, right, just—under scrutiny here. On the other hand, it seems in any event clear that the terms in the present examination of death (Derrida's, Heidegger's, Kierkegaard's, my own) would not be conceivable without the historical event of the Abrahamic religions, religions of the Book, Judaism, Christianity, and Islam. 'Death' in relation to the frame, archiving device, specific study (specific archival matter) is also susceptible to the same historical inquiry, and probably subject to the same importation-exportation puzzle that bogs its affiliates. The 'more vexed' question is whether the onto-theological determinations (call them that for now) are contaminant, witness, ghost, or some recombinant, or whether the religions are already always included in the basic ontology. One could ask whether the Book contains a ghost that sees without being seen ('visor effect') in an attestation to the fact of death—as if there exists "the essential contamination of spirit by specter."[21] Are onto-theological determinants a peculiar historical trope, a philosophical *lexis*, or a salute to the grand extravagance of the Book?

In an unexpected way, the concept of testimony completes one great circle and returns the writing to its beginning. It is to ask whether a writer has the possibility of proposing in writing to be a unique witness to death *in writing*, as Plato privileges himself over Crito, Phaedo, Apollodorus, and other observers who prayed in the execution's cottage. Each such account must repeat *in writing* what the gaze of *theoria* takes in 'with terror and awe' at the scandal, the murder, as Levinas calls it, of death. Does that gaze, of the witness, return on the interior to putting *in writing* that which cannot be returned, that is, for which no *revenant* comes? Each such account would have to iterate by performance a spectacle of non-substitutability in which the gift of death (eloquence, silence, ineffability, nothingness) is borne as prime witness to the I of the writer. Is the repetition of *memento mori*, a sacrifice of the gift *in writing* so as to give voice as writer of it? (And so, here too.) Trace-echoes of Blanchot: "To write is no longer to put in the future a death always already past, but to accept that one must endure it without making it present and without making oneself present to it; it is to know that death has taken place even though it has not been experienced."[22] Perpetuity of the exchange (substitution) of donor and donee, for death enters the account to announce the aspirations and intentions of putting it in writing, while writing leaves an entry in writing so that death may keep secret its secret. In that round dance of positings—death as prime depositor puts the writing in writing—here is a lesson of learning how to live, finally. The introductory curriculum must include learning how to write, finally, since before living, in living, and after living, there is writing. Through putting it in writing, it is not possible to produce an 'uncontaminated' testimonial rendition that doesn't parasite off the very life it attempts to teach. Impasse, aporia. The very lesson proffers a ghost that haunts the writing (a wisp o' the will) to obsess the I that puts it in writing. If the performative approximates this meaning, the written text is performative in the required sense. To learn to live (write) with a ghost: does that comprise a solution or the fantasy of a solution? The smile of Jacques Derrida, a phantom of my imagination, offers only consolation. For a belief in ghosts, it is confirmation, not nothing.

To live with the death of classical metaphysics, the ghost of which haunts the thoughts, desires, and choices of life: the lesson must include that facticity *in addition to* disclosing denial of death. To hold that the metaphysical *Abgrund* should be filled by another, different metaphysics (non-Western, non-Abrahamic, non-dualistic) is to live in denial. The death of metaphysical commitment is necessarily the death of metaphysics, period. *An sich*. Alterity doesn't mean replacement but irreplaceability. Whether or not there is a transcendent exterior to it, metaphysics is haunted by a beyond. By the logic of supplementarity, the phantom is within—a secret—and it is metaphysics.[23] There is no truth to the phantom and no untruth either. The phantom metaphysics doesn't produce truth but the plague (or play) of the *pharmakon*. As long as no borderline guarantees provide immunity from untruth (absence, death, evil), truth (presence, life, good) remains impure. Like Nietzsche's free spirit, the phantom that heralds the death of metaphysics (God) roams unhindered within life present. Assuming the closure of philosophy, it will await its inevitable re-embodiment. *It will always be so*.

It will always be so. Aphoristically, the thought, taken to heart, relates to the lesson of living life. Not "death will come," not "death won't come," but "death has already and will have come." The ghost of this life (past, present, or future?) passes through living events as surely as and at times more palpably than history. The I whose life trembles between beginning and end, presence and absence of the living and the beginning and end, absence and presence of the dead, already ghosted and ghosting, is the I put in writing, incomprehensible gift to the writer. The living, breathing one who feels metaphysical commitments fatally threatened by the lesson passes over to the non-living, non-respiring other—*via* the life unlived. Life in the death of its privileges of repression becomes thinkable once the transcendental imagination has been feebly exercised. That life has conceived, if indistinctly, the heart of the lesson: life comes only after the after-death state. Another version of what Jacques Derrida's ghost has already taught. "*Geist* is always haunted by its *Geist*."

Into the Book

THE TRACE WHOSE ITERATION is the trace is the trace of the other, without ground, origin, or *telos*. The other presents itself as a trace of a trace, a trace twice-removed because once-removed has not yet escaped the null orbit—God, death, and the void. Consequently, the hypothesis of justice, that the trace of a trace is what evokes the holy, is correct in its supplement: the symptomatology of trembling and fear unto terror. That one is never immunized against the terror is reason to pursue study, not to claim that all terror is holy, but that terror is terror, and ought to be regarded as such. Terror once held in high regard can still be the object of prayer, is itself an invocation of the face-to-face 'experience.' The I that trembles in the face-to-face is the same I that is unfaceable, ineffaceable, whose inheritance of holiness, brings to it, the guest (*hote*) who would tremble under the gaze of its invisible host (*hote*). In substitution and reversal, one for the other (guest for host, host for guest), a wavering exists that constitutes absolute trembling, a base note that resounds throughout the phenomenal world, as life acoustically mingles with death and death, with life. That absolute reversal, Kierkegaard's 'dialectical wavering,' produces a wakefulness in the I, initially (prior even to the breath) in the subtle tremble of sensation, sensation trembling with life, *vie vitale*, aliveness. Here, the I encroaches on the survivor, what survives (*sur vie*) life, lives over and above it, and outlives the *polemos* of opposites, an overtone of an irresolvable chord. There is the consequent appearance of responsibility, which is justice, which survives in an attitude of obedience to the other, *tout autre est tout autre*. The survivor with its indeterminate responsibility, its responsibility to the indeterminate, represents the only possibility (hope) of survival of justice. Disruption by the trace (trace of the trace) symptomizes or gives the mark of obedience in the voice-reading. To survive (life, death), the reading voice resonates obedience to an eruptive freedom, one with sudden departures and arrivals (*revenants* and *arrivants*). If this is what the holy asks, it necessarily remains unknown—another degree of trepidation in the symptomatology.

There is the further corridor of temporality. When survival produces the time of responsibility, what is given voice in the name of justice and holiness? This is a much-needed entree to the performative alley, where there is *performance* of iteration by iteration, in this case, the holy. It may be necessary to recall iteration of the holy requires only to repeat the trace that initialized the series to constitute itself. As an afterthought, the time of survival could not be either evolutionary or developmental, since both are synchronic (and Hegelian) concepts, while by contrast the holy brings a temporality of disjointed *différance*. Such an epoch could not be subject to development because it is never 'gathered unto one' and necessarily withholds its appearance. The holy does not show its face except to signify death, at death or in death, to the living who are or in the 'image' of death, that is, a ghost—then, as the trace. The showing effaces itself upon disclosure and produces the shroud that is an incertitude that dis-covers the holy in existence: the holy is a haunt that is haunted by a ghost. Whether its inclusion belongs to any given iteration constitutes the secret of the trace, the trace's secret.[1] The ghost is the 'palpable' edge of the terror of the secret of secrets. *Enter the question of the ghost.* What would a study of ghost qua ghost entail, if not an examination of the transcendental imagination, which is charged to constitute supplemental images unto the unimaginable as required? Once in play, the transcendental imagination produces the non-origin of the supplement that augments the holy by replacement—with fear and trembling.[2]

If the holy contains the semen that survives life, in the trembling of the voice reading the words disseminated, it is nonetheless omitted from the iterative series by self-dereliction. If to write is in general to sacrifice the meaning for the sign and efface the switch, the holy always already is exclusively excluded in the very intention to inscribe—and this is injustice. To let the voice remain on mute in the theme of the holy, to bind the holy to non-vociferous voice, a non-language, is irresponsible. To put in writing the voice-reading is, contrariwise, to remain on mute and to acknowledge that the muteness is the trace of a survivor, a mutation perhaps, but one permitted to mutate the inscription without altering any of its immutability: the work of the trace. If the context does not make it improper to speak of traits, the trace has at least one. The mute vowel of the voice-reading (God or death) signifies the trembling through its signifying function. Pneumatology says that, as the breath moves in and through its glottal articulation, signification operates phonically, signifying both meaning and non-meaning, even when voice remains inaudibly given. In the trembling passage, inspired, respired, expired, there is a disruption and a discontinuity, the breakthrough of repetition, the potential indetermination of the mute word. The pneumatological interval may be virtual (reading to self) or real (reading aloud). So-called silent reading is virtuality itself. In both, the muteness is quarry for the breath. Holy speech, the trace on mute, is constituted by repetition *sotto voce*, without relation to the breath. Echo without sound, in the hallway to death, as the scene in *Circumfession*, when Derrida puts it in writing that his dying mother "no longer calls me, and for her, for the rest of her life, I no longer have a name."[2] The breath swallowed whole in its entirety by the mute trace: death of name, call, holy in language: return of an algorithm that counts metaphysical discourse in the incommensurate logic of the supplement.

Within the web of temporality, iteration is (like) a time's tremble (tempo of a tremble), the tremulous shift of tense that scans the variant temporalities of the present, present future, present past, present progressive, present anterior, present posterior, now. Perhaps a metaphor for sympathetic vibration, the spontaneous reverberation of a notion lies in the presence of a concordant. The trace is not the determinant of a shift in time but determines the possibility of displacement; it is not a "transcendental signified" but the transcendental of such.[4] It inspirits the spacing of *différance* between two poles, the 'two's'. *Différance* is the shift between 'two's' that is unequally shared (and equally unshared) by the opposites delimiting the possible movement—as well as the question of what 'between' means. The shifting, moreover, repeatedly overruns the limits that nonetheless serve more than a merely heuristic purpose. No originating force takes part in initiating the series. The hypothesis of shared difference, a hypothesis that requires a deeper inquiry into sharing a difference, necessitates an effacement of the concept of limit. In lieu of it, one could think of trembling as an initializing of difference, or as a designation of the formal cause of 'sharing' that has heretofore been given no name.

The service of iteration and the iterative series delimits the possibility of survival (of life, of death), for which survival the demand for justice and responsibility, that is, obedience to the other in its otherness, first arises. The repetitivity of the mute vowel (in *différance*) is an exemplar in this regard. Or rather, *the* exemplar.[5] Although its state of acoustical muteness holds the possibility of repetition for each term, it changes neither any one nor the whole series of terms. If survival (as well as its dependents in justice and responsibility) is possible, repetition determines the possibility; in biological terms, existence of the species depends on reproduction. The line of thinking lends support to the hypothesis of ghost speech. Isn't the ghost's speech that necessarily is spoken without breath—unlike the speech of the survivor—constituted by properties of the mute vowel?

That without the breath, the mute vowel is more manifestly immutable since no longer subject to change? And that the ghost's speech is an acoustically appropriative version of the non-vocalizable?[6]

The voice of ghosts is contiguous with the theme of survival, *survivre*, immediately upon the muteness of speaking. Surviving, living *on*, is homonymous: meaning both continuation and consumption. The homonymy is clear in how the survivor lives on only by consuming its life, a formulation that follows Levinas's definition of egoity. Ingestion, digestion, assimilation, elimination: ego persists in one or another metabolic mode, since its essence is its *conatus essendi*, in Spinoza's terms. To speak of ghosts, the supplemental question of justice and its survival arises. If justice consists of a response to the trace of the other, and responsibility respects the otherness of the other, each other, then both are accomplished in the function of memory. Memory (*mnesis*) functions when it remembers the iteration of the trace. Itself a ghost phenomenon, living memory already bears the ghost of the other in memory. A politics of memory or remembrance is the necessary adjunct to the surviving voice of the ghost largely because of the intimacy memory bears toward justice, a memory or remembrance alive to and bedazzled by the aporetic nature of thought. Memory remembers that to speak with the ghost is to engage a trace of the other, thence to be borne in memory as a memorial or in memorial. Within the politics of the polis, iteration is fidelity: the fidelity of justice as well as the justice of fidelity. Aphoristically: "To keep alive, within oneself, is this the best sign of fidelity?"[7]

The scene of responsibility in writing is analogous to that of memory. Writing as co-responsibility with memorization for the ghost's survival. When to write is to give voice to the ghost, to let the ghost voice the writing as it writes, is to put it in writing, expose, release distinction, and phantomize a 'self' whose event is as unique as the trembling of a nerve. The already-dead of the writing. If justice is to allow that other to survive, an act of memory that embraces the already-dead in a work of mourning is imperative. The law of inheritance states that justice is owed the ghost, both the ghost of presents past and the ghost of presents to come. Although mourning concentrates on the first, responsibility divides between the two tenses. The infinity of the task distends from the *arche* of death to an indefinite future. Moreover, work to acknowledge "our friend to be gone forever, irremediably absent" must not serve "to delude oneself into believing that the other living *in us* is living *in himself*."[8] The transcendental situation, that the ghost qua ghost is idealization and interiorization, bears recognition; "it entails a movement in which an interiorizing idealization takes in itself or upon itself the body and voice of the other, the other's visage and person, ideally *and* quasi-literally devouring them."[9] Such work possesses a double action, hosting the ghost as well as being hostage to it. The infinity of its task extends not only to the other loved or admired, but to the unknown other—the ghost that is no more than a trace of the trace, that is holiness. The inclusiveness of the debt inherited characterizes a deep trait of justice. The just man or woman hollows out a place in memory a place for myriad iterations of the ghost, a wailing wall against which to weep for an unaccountable absence of absences. Putting it in writing inscribes a name on the wall, engraved, chalked, burned, or painted, and places the responsibility in writing at the same moment as in remembrance.

As a consequence, one mourns the fact of substitution itself, the passing of one thing for another. One separately mourns conditional replacements, like having been born in place of another, whose place it in some sense could have been, an unborn sibling, kinsperson, foreigner, or enemy. Lamentation mimics the spirit of Pascal, where usurpation plays a large part each one is guilty of usurping the place of all the others. The work of self-mourning thereby is doubled or trebled. On the one hand, there is the future ghost of oneself to mourn, the remainder that survives to supplement survival ahead of the death that has to come. The ghost of oneself, one's 'own' ghost, the *revenant*, both lives and does not live in oneself, an acoustical hangover that encompasses the entire unlived life. Justice is situated at the place for the ghost at present *and* to-come; justice, that is cannot be present justice without at the same time being future justice. On the other hand, there is the conditional ghost to mourn for not being born, the Pascalian dilemma. The debt to the other, *all others*, must be paid in the coin of remembrance: it constitutes a concept of responsibility to the wholly other that disturbs peace of mind and produces "insomnia."[10] To mourn a birth, not its privileged life, but a theft, a crime, an injustice that can never be expiated, an impossible atonement. An endless mourning. . . . Such is the heart of the impossible task of the ethical, the impossibility of which drives it.

A justice that is just would be even-handed, co-responsible to the future ghost as the past subjunctive ghost that has been born instead, and seems to make do with the fact that "*all we seem to have left is memory . . .*" of the possibility of justice.[11] A remembrance that is by nature fractured, distracted, distraught, and dissolute. Such a remembrance has an effectivity appropriate to the syllabus of justice, namely, wounding and excess. The syllabus teaches that the law must be remembered as impartial to all. The prerequisite is of a memory sufficient to the call to responsibility without sacrificing its own survival. Here is the aporia of survival, that it must include a booklet on memory's non-survival, or radical dislocation—the ghost is not in the memory but held in reserve, a memory not of the dead, but the living, a memory that attests to the "unbearable paradox of fidelity."[12] The demand of interiorization relays how the other is nothing outside of memory, and the "dark light of this nothing" announces, Derrida writes, "that the other resists the closure of our interiorizing memory. . . . [D]eath constitutes and makes manifest the limits of a *me* or an *us* who are obliged to harbor something that is greater and other than them; something *outside of them within them*."[13] The-other-in-the-one: Levinas's "psychism" seems a conjuration out of the same spectral matter of Derrida's "ghost." The ghost inside that turns inside out to stand outside, is accomplished in an acoustic mode by the voice-reading. The justice of giving voice to the other, the vociferation of other accomplished at the biding of the other, a sacrifice of one's own biding, a service of justice to the other.

To be adequate to the law of mourning, to find adequation through mourning, is fated for failure—another cause for mourning there. In an infinite task, success is asymptotically measured and always an open bet. A good failure bears in memory the politics of memory and of inheritance, an obligatory politics for ghosts. Perhaps one way to fail in an exemplary manner is by putting it in writing and giving way to non-acoustically vociferous hordes of phantoms, "more than the living," and to not deny what is owed them, their voice. At the same time, writing cannot repay the dead because its debt to them is unamortizable, and cannot do so because the debt lies with the very possibility of indebtedness that the ghost brings.[14] In response to their summons (to write, speak, and recognize them), remembrance, imploration, and prayer are compensatory, as Odysseus discovers in the land of the dead, as Dante in the inferno. Memory is owed and repaid although the indebtedness is never fully discharged but continually inherited. Yet the unpardonability is a *felix culpa*, happy misfortune, since it moves the work of mourning to the abyss and renders it without end, an epectastic adventure. Thus, to put it in writing is to write in part because of unpardonable failure—never to write "to the end."

Of course, Derrida repeats, to write is to defer, to make space between the desire to pay and the desired payment, to postpone the pleasure of its attainment, to put off consumption (consummation) until time has passed, to revel in the desiring, and to elevate the present progressive tense to eminence. The failure that calls for mourning is writing to root out the 'sin,' to confess, avow, acknowledge, ex-pose, exteriorize that which has been kept interior—that is, living memory of the dead (past and future), in which is included the writing's own ghost, its 'self' come back from the dead, the life being spent writing and thus unlived. Whether sin or debt, the writing makes use of the contaminant (properly: contamin*ance*), such is the usury of writing. If writing involves voluptuousity (postponement of the object of desire for the desiring), then the sexual allusion may be appropriate, either Rousseau's "dangerous supplement" or Derrida's circumcision. To put it in writing is to forget the failing, to lose sight (site) of it, absolution or oblivion. And sometimes to put it in writing is to know no more than exile, that one has left the Garden in writing to glimpse the nature of sin in the sin of writing, knowing the Garden is myth, metaphor, displacement, substitution for an amnesia that haunts remembrance, sickens it with diversion, and gives the remedy to an aversion for resolution. Or, to put it in writing is to sin by writing and sin is another name for remembrance, which is to say, to bear the other in memory because of writing's own sin put into writing. Or, to bear the other in memory, to be torn by the endless labor of mourning, is writing's only sin.

The law, the only law, the just law, just the law: there can be no horizon of its operation. Justice must necessarily bleed to the edges of the page. Its claims to memory and memorialization are based on debts of inheritance. Everyone, by virtue of falling under the law, is other to all others.[15] *Tout autre est tout autre.* Putting it in writing either avows the evil or rationalizes it by obfuscating, distorting, or mis-analyzing, but always puts it in writing according to the law of heteronomy. Writing 'creates' a distance from self, or, likely, repeats it, copies the noncoincidence, and apes the incongruence. Writing tries to get away from itself by catching up with itself. The voice-reading is alien (by an infinitesimal) to the voice-writing. The voice put in writing is heterogeneous to itself, self-estranged and non-self-corresponding. The par-don for the transgression is given and retracted before the next word is given voice to replace the last just now on the page. The pardon is apocalyptical and waits in the last word to signify the eschatological end of philosophy. There it coincides with the transgression, which is to seek the end of philosophy (Hegel, Marx, Nietzsche, Heidegger, Derrida, . . .), to close the discourse and lock the secret in the past imperfect tense, the always already. Sin as closure, but sin as opening, too, since to open philosophy (even to deconstruction) is to unlock the discourse to the secret and render it *as if* given. Par-don. Anything that could be given could not be the secrecy that keeps interminably to itself, a pariah, gaze upon which holds impenetrable terror.[16] The secret that cannot be given or be pardoned for being secret, because writing outruns it, uses words to defer reading its message; to write, to mourn. The valediction forbidding mourning.

When at last writing comes to the last, and puts the last in writing, the final portion of the last ennead, in the last comes across a measure of absolution incommensurate with the work at hand. Which is the work of remembrance corresponding to the writing that at the same time unwrites and renders illegible, in order to undo the responsibility by secreting the words. In one sense, they give voice to an involuntary submission to an other (the father) that commanded from before the first mark—the holy ghost. In that sense, putting it in writing bespeaks an obedience that, it is suspected, can be rejected or met only if written enough. Writing then writes to avoid avoidance and inherits the impossibility of success: the aporia. To argue in writing that writing, the 'dangerous supplement,' infects the innocent neonatal consciousness and plants the seed of sin back in the Garden, does not extirpate it. There is no way to put it in writing and avoid avoiding avoidance. The labor of giving voice in the production of text attests the presence of the dead in the womb of life, a dark placenta, both nutrient and mute companion. More precisely, the dead for Derrida has its locus in the dead foreskin, phantom of the glans that haunts the scar of incision, and it must be given a voice in writing that is yet not the writer's, that has no voice but is mute, silent. It is precisely the infiltration of the other's voice in writing that marks it as responsible and aporetic. Paradoxically, to give voice to the other in writing preserves the silence that belongs to the essence of responsibility. "Once I speak I am never and no longer myself, alone and unique. It is a very strange contract—both paradoxical and terrifying—that binds infinite responsibility to silence and secrecy."[17]

To put it in writing in order to mourn the avoidance is to mourn the avoidance of mourning. Guilt avowed lends a fractured presence to the act of writing, thereby setting the writer apart from what is put in writing, and the separation is the voice of avowal. Writing enters the confessional booth, with Augustine, Proust, Stendhal, and Derrida. But the metaphysical propositions that posit avoidance are lures. One learns from them the negativity that hollows a place for nothing to fill. From the start, presence is fractured, fissured, divided, deferred, split from itself, tinged with its opposite—contaminated as to be indistinguishable from absence. The supplement is dangerous because the original is replaced both with loss and without loss, even, with gain, augmentation, enhancement, amelioration. How can confession then proceed? A greater guilt (a greater debt) will find a way to proliferate the fragmentation and testify that the conditions that determine testimony are no longer a possibility. In another way, it shows how the 'doubling' of presence, or (what is the same) its disunity and dissolution, always makes a new scene, for this is how *différance* differs. A new scene of writing, meant for the present epoch (the last?). In it, confession will henceforth vociferate the other's recording, catching its acoustic shadow in inscription—the obligatory curriculum of mourning. There may even be an erotic force in the dynamism, where the one in love with the other is once a portion of the selfsame self, the narcissism of Aristophanes in the *Symposium*. Innumerable possibilities for absolution, each bound to innumerable new possibilities of loss. Which confession would not be made happier by a stronger bond of culpability? Putting it in writing neither solves, absolves, resolves, nor dissolves; it incurs deeper and deeper limits of debt that increase with each last word. Debt as homonym, a double sense: both *ananke* and piety, that is necessarily voluntary and intentional. It moves both toward immortality and toward the mortuary.

Contretemps, the scene is not new since philosophy as confession is an old invention, as old as Plato writing a confession for his master. What is new is Plato's ghost-writing, writing the ghost of Socrates in order to bear witness to his (Socrates') failure to mourn, a failure that echoes Plato's own—which doubles in the conjuration that Derrida performs in *The Post Card*, where Socrates writes Plato. But the scene is twice new in yet another way, *both* new as the latest confession, sin, scandal, *and* new as putting in writing what says it without telling. It says the sin but doesn't tell the nature of the transgression, why it arises, how it appears, or whence it is destined—even as it celebrates the *mea culpa*, the *felix culpa*. The voice-reading vociferates but without knowing whether it is found in writing, or whether the writing is too discreet, timid, devious, or duplicitous to tell it. The voice-reading is given the confession served up on a platter (the mute head of John the Baptist), but philosophy in the new scene of writing is more sinned against than sinning. Not simply because it desires it, it puts in writing hypotheses of insufficient disclosure. It writes in debt, out of a debt of the first order that attempts to recompense or, perhaps, compensate for the evil, and so, raises the *specter of ethics*. The ghost compulsively and obsessively returns to the scene, to retry it, undo it, correct it, or do it better, more luridly, more authentically. Putting it in writing becomes moral compensation, compensatory, insidious, and difficult to undo. The haunt of ethics and the tribunal of justice (like Gomorrah where Abraham found no just man) is there from the first word written: "I do not know, men of Athens, how my accusers' words affected you . . ." Socrates (Plato) or Plato (Socrates) will go on writing, never telling how he transgressed, not denying or affirming it, expressing puzzlement, questioning, and leaving a nest of aporias behind. Uncontested guilt, repeatedly exemplified, but with no particulars revealed, generous in broad outline in the ongoing articulation of guilt: "the unexamined life is not worth living." Juxtapose this with "I am pretending to confess."[18]

The new scene of putting it in writing as 'philosophy' involves a double mourning, a two-part work that constitutes a work for the other that does not aim for personal immortality or success in its own time. It mourns the death of the old scene, the masters' death ("there are no masters left") as well as the end of writing philosophy. This is a death not only of putting the closure in writing (Hegel, Marx, Nietzsche, Heidegger), but also of writing *up to* the end, from Parmenides to Derrida. It cannot be a writing of presence, self-consciousness, and the concept, or a putting in writing of the same—which tells what it is about. It examines the concept of limits to say specifically what constitutes transgression. In this way, it is mindful of sin. The new scene works at mourning its own birth as substitution for the old scene (family scene, older brother), and mourns not being original, without *arche* or *telos*, a 'mere' replacement, and a *dangerous supplement*. Like Rousseau's guilt at self-abuse, the new scene cannot put writing down either, as it grows aware of trifling, expendable, petty impulses. It must continue compensating even as it necessarily omits telling for what. Thus the new work of mourning, inaugurated by the new scene, mourns the omission, the lapse, the hiatus, even as it continues to be lapsed and omitted, not admitted and excluded; the omission can never be corrected. It is an incorrigible omission (Rousseau's incorrigibility) and cannot be rectified since the new scene of philosophy cannot tell its secret.[19] The secrecy of its secret kept in retreat recedes in writing's approach and hides itself within the vital folds ('the veil') of mortality. The writing that alone accomplishes and consummates the work of mourning is without satisfaction in its own time, and thus is guaranteed to be a work for the other. Even when it comes to a stop, richly impoverished in inscription, it again has succeeded in failing or has failed to succeed in telling its secret disobedience, transgression of limits, penetration, opening: the forbidden name of its sin.

Speaking with the ghost

WOULD IT ASK TOO much to assume sincerity (not incompatible with irony) as the moving force of my impulse to talk with you? There is, between contrivance and authenticity, already an aporia. Authenticity may be sought but when authentication is in the play of disguise, it's safe to say that impasses blocks the itinerary to be followed, and behind each, a ghost repression. The impasse *is* the repression closing the border and permitting no passage through the experience. It's a strange beginning but just where first I want to address a master of aporias. You even write that there are more impasses than passes so that experience is always experience of the aporia. Experience is aporetic. I ask because you've dealt with aporias and, therefore, ghosts, and because you might answer some questions. Ghosts are creatures of an impasse. Death also gathers there. If one associates quickly enough, the next question is about the interiorization of mourning. Does mourning begin only at an impasse, when the life comes to a stop? Generally, then, at a place best avoided, de-sited, effaced on the map, ciphered away. I know little of the cost of speaking with the dead, but that it requires payment. For the ghost to be freed, the forces that keep it entombed must be recompensed. Here's the nub of my ignorance: is death the only coin or is even that a product of imagination? This is perhaps one place more where the ghost contests as well as prevents thought's engorgement in the void.

You may wonder where this is leading, Jacques. Nine scenes, and still the need to speak with your ghost—with you. You would never go so far as to forbid it and might even empathize, though a cursory search shows no evidence that you actually *believe* in ghosts. Does that matter? As far as I can tell, though you've dealt with ghosts and their remains (ghost texts), you've never explicitly addressed a ghost qua ghost (e.g., Hegel, Marx, Freud, Heidegger, or any "father"). There are two exceptions: 1) in your eulogy to Levinas when you close by saying, "*Adieu*, Emmanuel"; 2) definitely more problematic, in *Circumfession*, where you write, in Period 11: "I am addressing myself here to God, the only one I take as a witness, without yet knowing what these sublime words mean, and this grammar, and *to*, and *witness*, and *God*, and *take* . . ."[1] Perhaps it is to stretch meaning beyond recognition by conflating God with his third person, the Holy Ghost, *Saint Esprit*, but that is something else. I connect this with another observation, that you avoid the direct form of address, the vocative, that is the call from one to the other, the other to the one, I to you, the ghost. This is a strange avoidance in light of your interest in the performative so one has suspicions. Yet it's no surprise that you rarely record speaking to a phantom since you do recognize that spiriting away of an element by the unconscious, so that the content is effaced and illegible. This has the consequence that the ghost could be anywhere. A reader may notice a strong affiliation with 'deconstruction,' if there is such a thing, and ghosts. A stronger suspicion is that the former is the play of the latter. Deconstruction is strongly performative; it works by "transforming its subject into something else" (an odd definition), performance by conjuring. Its transformation calls back the repressed, or more precisely, the ghost of the repressed—since repression takes life, entombs it, and turns it into a phantom.

That our "conversation" must respect the term of "deferred obedience"—*Nachtraglischkeit, après coup*, or deferred action—is understood.[2] It is best, however, first to get clear. Deferral—a complex idea—means that obedience will be put off until later or some other time: postponed, rescheduled later, not just now. Questions inevitably fly. How does the delay happen? To whom or to what is the obedience, albeit deferred, given—by the dative that, you say, haunts the indicative mood of all writing since it is all gift—and (in another obsessive question), finds itself in an atmosphere secreted by the aporia, or better, sucked gravitationally inside?[3] It's obvious that the deferral pursues you in advance, a spore of the future awaiting present inhalation, when no possible precaution can prevent it from giving what it carries, an inheritance. So even though you have not incurred it by act of commission or omission, there is the matter of how justly it is carried. Furthermore, one cannot rule out the possibility that "deferred" is a homonym that refers to a deferral in and through obedience to the other. I defer to an expert in ghosts and listen closely to what he has to say about repression, that one "earns" it that way. One means of recognizing repression at work is when contexts get displaced in time, space, and form and the displacement thought as archival derangement, to use a trope of yours. That derangement—a madness induced by an overwhelming traumatization—is accompanied by a ghost of death. But the ghost remains hidden and that serves to conjure a false security, the serenity of repression. Under the latter's auspices, narrative is coded and must be deciphered if the ghosts are to be exposed. It is here that our conversation must turn serious. If narrative is constituted by deferred trauma, it must urgently face the problem of simulation and raise the issue of whether there is such a thing as truth. Can we agree for the time being that there is truth that, while necessarily unattainable, must just as necessarily be sought? An absolute, infinite truth that we might approach asymptotically?[4] Along the way, it will be imperative to take up the trauma of death and what the word "death" could possibly mean in the context. Equally imperative will be to unearth the accounting sheets for the inheritance and their progressive mutation, their mutism. I would hope to celebrate the exposure, but one thing that we can agree on concerns the heteronomy of the ghost. The law of its alterity conjures the alterity of law, which governs ghosts. To bring these two lines—death and the other—together, could be called the real act of obedience, that is, *conjuring*. Obedience to an inheritance out of time and space (deferred to that placeless place) could conjure a non-empirical simulation of life subject to laws differing from ours—that is, a ghost's.

The matter of deferral doesn't end with that. That which in being said is held back, *not told*. This may or may not correspond to a strategy of repression that hides *away* in some 'archive' to distort, reconfigure, or delete marks, memories, or memorials—an aggressor-destroyer program that you liken to Freud's death drive (if we are entitled to the trope of a technology he didn't have). Your writing has a distinctive brand of saying without telling as well as a capability to *secrete* a knowledge through a 'non-epistemic' means.[5] I allude to a thaumatological element in your work. Possibly, secrecy always implies a deferred obedience since obedience and deferment are produced in what must remain behind the curtain. The secret of obedience, but also the secret obedience that obeys only in the sense that it can forget to obey—a subtle logic. The promise to forget can also remain secret, thereby creating a secrecy *en abyme* or possibly an apocalyptic secrecy. In all these matters, I shall assume an inheritance of repression along with the value in the transformation of the repressed (*via* the performative of release). There are occasions when the ghost of the repressed—death, death trauma, termination of life, end of living—stops frequenting living memory with vague ill-defined apprehension. It will not declare itself source of the conjurings—it won't declare itself in any way, but it may signal the end of deferral. It too exemplifies saying without telling. Anonymous, a faceless ("his beaver was down") apparition lurking in the backdrop behind language, it has become the text of that which would be obeyed, only not yet. But perhaps yet has already come. Then its perpetual postponement of an obedience to a debt inherited through the course of repression, its cost, has run its course.

Then we could bear in mind that the debt bestows itself upon empirical reality, the actual and existing, as an inheritance before any desire, anterior to all phenomena. (In parentheses, Rilke's romantic conception that "before we were turned round, we faced the open"; an initial inheritance is conceived with the trope of fallenness [and the supplement of the "with"].) You, Jacques, reject the hypothesis of a pre-Edenic state, a presence to the present, a time not disjointed but synchronous with itself, with an essential openness to the open point of origin, yes? Yet that ghost or the ghost of the ghost of the most excessively anterior, the excessive anteriority—the source that haunts all thought, as well as an obedience owed to it—is obedient to the trace.

With obedience deferred, there is the question of immobilization of intention. It is a way of asking whether the repressed—content or archive—can ever be unfrozen, activated, initialized. I would like to consider, in this context, the immortal latency you ascribe to the death drive of Freud's. From the standpoint of force, it is ongoing, intermittent, without end (valorization or calculus), indiscriminate, and indeterminate. From the standpoint of delivery, it is the gift (*don*) that supplies the entire operation. It leaves the content already dead, a completely dead matter, indifferent to what takes place, out of presence, abandoned to pure ipseity (a redundancy). Such 'material' is undying in the sense of being not lived, in an archive labeled *due back soon*, as well as *back from the dead*. There, immobilized are both the phantom and the phantom-ization apparatus. In this regard, it is difficult not to notice that phantoms as a production obsess your writing. The dynamics of repression are ever churning and this is a sign. In contact with death, the archiving—the mark as well as what is marked—is altered radically. Memory of untimely time is pressed into a vault, Hegel's pit, in effect, and impaled at the bottom, murdered. The repressed 'knowledge' is of death and its archival chamber signifies death. (Knowledge in quotes because secrecy protects against the trauma's becoming known; it *conjures* the trauma away and prevents discovery.) Perhaps one way to understand Nietzsche's genealogy of weakness that defeats strength by inventing cunning. On a Nietzschean analysis, what knowledge serves—repressive forces—determines what it is, namely, protection by constraint. From its inheritance, knowledge screens out direct contact with *thanatos*. In another trope, it inoculates (homeopathically, like cures like), and produces an immunity. Knowledge, the ascetic ideal, reason, *nous*, itself simulates a mask of death strategically to mask the face of the other. I would add that this point seems to reverse you on patricide, murder of the father by the son (Plato, Oedipus, Freud), repeated often in your writing. Here, the crime is reversed. It takes place when the father, who would have been killed, kills instead the son at his traumatic birth (Saturn, Cronos). One could say that repression functions to protect against the filial (and affiliated) *phantoms* that obsess and haunt the background with memories of their murder. This paradoxical inheritance of repression (death and life, finite and infinite) is a wound of repression. Perhaps it is grafting onto Heidegger's idea the ontological and the violent rupture of birth that it incorporates. It is a matter of remembrance that existence has an *arche* or origin produced out of an unrecorded violence. Existence then could be the ghostly record of an encounter with death, an encounter, moreover, in which the son is necessarily sacrificed. By one of a series of strange reversals, the ghost that conjures the ways of knowing is under the authority of *thanatos*. Existence is an inheritance given without conditions, before choice, in the untimely time of choice, a time contemporaneous with the vocative *let there be*. In a time when the word "freedom" still signifies. Is it fortuitous how there are ghosts whenever there is freedom, a revolving debt inherited as existence. The ghost as a shield against the strength of nothing, that comes back at will, is capable of distortion and mutilation of existence, while leaving no trace. If there is denial, it could be the deferent against a too easy obedience, the one that is deferred in place of a more difficult one. The magic is in how a ghost is conceived as coming back; a *revenant* begins by coming back (you say)—like the fairy tale where to say the rhyme backward is the key. A magic is possibly found in the ghost's arrival ahead of itself, ahead of the apprehension—not at the end.

If I leap ahead, it's to the inheritance of repression as it extends to an ethics of vengeance and cruelty. Your gleanings from Nietzsche remind me how the cost is exacted and in what coin of suffering—where the *in*determination of freedom expresses avoidance. It brings to mind your studies, notably *Of Spirit*, and Heidegger's avoidance of the word "spirit," placed under the interrogation lamp. There, a subtle condemnation emerges: his 'spirit' is 'demoted' to a ghost, one among multitudes, that conjures a world to compensate for an unlived life. That conjuration accomplishes the cruelty of existence, the residue of the original breakthrough of being, the onto-genesis, that invests onto-theology (as well as religions of the Book) with their station. Cruelty, as a moving force, takes away, detracts, lowers, diminishes, disaffirms, and eventually, per-jures the almighty-ness of that. Conjuration must end in perjury. But invoking the ghost of Nietzsche only explains your proclivity for evasion, without damning it. Or if it does, that is because spectrality already implies damnation.

Perhaps the idea of recovery ought to be jettisoned, both the debt of deferred obedience and obedience itself—equally, a deferral obeyed and obeying deferred—because it incorrectly posits an economy of affliction. The debt also serves a radically different purpose, but purpose nonetheless, conjuring. The force of repression produces the debt which in turn brings the repressive force. And, the energy can be well invested in thaumaturgy, as you illustrate with many verbal magics. The first thing that conjuring can conjure is something that can conjure it away. *Ghost begets ghost and is begone by ghost.* To formulate the basic thought of yours concerning onto-theology: what is conjured away by repression returns to conjure up existence (being, presence, substance, consciousness . . .). Conjuration plays a privileged role in philosophy ('Western metaphysics') insofar as it is the *revenant* responsible for existence, not the other way around. It is extremely important to notice that conjuring also serves performatively, that is, magisterially. Conjuring capable of summoning up existence, in the fashion of a Mephisto, is in fact done by specters themselves. It is creation *ex nihilo*, thaumaturgically accomplished. I mean, of course, magic in a wide sense, where mage is part of the chain, death, shock, repression, knowledge. Magic belongs with *poesis* and mimesis, authentic creativity, which you link in your discussion of Aristotle's concept of metaphor.[6]

Speaking together began with obedience—obedience deferred—but what is 'obedience'? Doesn't the question include the dative, what is owed *to* that which is obeyed, in this case, the repressed? One way to think repression through is as an expunging of the text, effacement of the inscription, or erasure from the book: illegibility. The thought is augmented in that the debt is 'beyond all signifying.' There is a lure to thinking it is owed *to the dead*, but shouldn't one be wary here? The dead seem beyond what can be signified, and lacking a signifier, are nowhere inserted and without designation of place. The abundance of phantoms in your books suggests the opposite. Without pursuing the matter farther, I propose an adventurous hypothesis, namely, that these dead define the axis of your thought: they are the ghost 'a' found in *différance*. 'A' for axis as well as apex, the tip of Hegel's pyramid.[7] The ghost or mute 'a' constitutes a *pièce de résistance*, a master conjuration that conjures itself away and never appears *as such*. Below in the acoustic sphere, when the question of the 'a' again is broached, when you point out that it is phonically indistinguishable from "difference" (without the ghost or mute 'a'), it will be responsible (by way of initialization) for the play of ghostliness. This is a tight knot yet to be severed since the mute 'a' is part of a larger scene, one where responsibility with bad conscience plays to a condition frequented by ghosts.

One must avow that the muteness of the single and singular first letter of the (Latin) alphabet, the 'a,' is striking. Some time ago, I was struck by the breathing associated with sounding the 'a,' and its affiliations with the sigh and the death rattle. We needn't remind one another that for Nietzsche the breath is that of being, which is to say, being as such, *an sich*. Your play inverts the matter by a peculiar evacuation of the acoustics of breathing (of life, no?) from the 'a.' As you say in your interview with

Henri Ronse, "You have noticed that this *a* is written or read, but cannot be heard."[8] Thus, signification in its entirety is paradoxically attacked and revolutionized, both revolving around the ghost 'a,' which is itself irreducible and which retains a trace of the dative, that *to which* obedience is due. It may seem strange to focus on a minute detail, a micrology, of the text, but often a unique and secret signature is inscribed in that way, as you point out. That the mute 'a' is an intrigue and a (current) scandal in philosophy does not preclude how little of it that can be said at the moment.[9] The *to which*, on the other hand, retained as a supplement or contaminant, presents a constant source of terror, a death face that leers from a window in the dark of night. The *to which* lies on the far side of repression, hence, the obedience under discussion. The muteness has a mutated echo, the primal terror of a scream with the tongue cut off. Under your hypothesis, each articulation mutely bears an acoustic mark of terror, that precedes it as an incision on the ear's body, similar to how each inscription, for you, repeats the scar of and is relegated to "the singular archive named 'circumcision'."[10] Every utterance thus avoids saying because it is said in a voice that puts telling the primal encounter on mute. *To be turned up later.* Every utterance simultaneously conjures existence and perjures by conjuring. The temptation is to ask whether it is by compensation or by cure that you offer a genealogy (as Nietzsche) and freely blend autobiographical with philosophical narrative. Is it done to mute freedom, mutilating and mutating it, or to practice an autonomy of healing?

    I think of the text defined by the first mark inscribed in the flesh, the father's, the law's, "father of logos," as you say, "a logos indebted to a father." A father with whom "it is not possible to speak simply or directly" and who speaks with instruments of cruelty to impose a covenant on you.[11] The mark that must thenceforth say your name is a name you cannot tell but must carry on the tip of the tongue, forever slipping into inarticulateness. The mark that simultaneously inscribes you in the book of life, one year at a time, and marks your father's crime, is a cruelty repressed. A double mark. The mark of the double. Because of the duplicity, each mark henceforth will be double. Your work abounds with many, many 'two's.' Obedience is always already about the 'two's.' Father, law, debt, logos as well as son, obedience, inheritance, trace. Both the mark of repressing that which ought to be obeyed and also that which the repression represses. These two obediences and two deferrals only sometimes line up in a recognizable alignment. One congruence lies in obeying the language of repression because it buffers the terror. One craves its security and obeys. Another lies in obeying the debt prior to circumcision and the law, which is owed even before what the covenant demands, before the first face-to-face in the course of which one is reduced to nothing.

This second line comprises a phantom obedience in which the donor (*qui donne*) as well the gift (*le don*) never appear. After this too brief conjecture, let me see whether the two lines cross.

The thing can't wait. Deferred until time, obedience must produce a spell that both ends deferral and postpones conjuring. A double spell that represents the cost of a production to outplay death and the thanatopic—or to produce a play to catch the conscience of death. Its cost seems to involve a deep concern of yours, philosophy's (read: Christianity's) repression of the demonic. The discussion of Patocka's portrayal of incorporation (introjection?) and suppression in *The Gift of Death* argues along familiar lines: a sufficiency or plenitude of self-presence, an arrogance of being, a production whose own insufficiencies are archived scrupulously away, are symptomatic of repression. Avoidance (of the mark, of death) comes back in a devious fashion to code the look that one cannot face. The coded expression itself is phantomatized, not traceable to its source, locked in secret memory. Could one say paradoxically and too briefly that the cost of production is the metaphysical terminology or terminus that could posit the other?[12] More precisely, in obedience to the metaphysics? Obedience to a logic that appears as both the cause of conjuring and its result, a logic of deferral. The magic spell (Freud's Magic Writing Pad) thus lies in the scene of the logic, center stage, as always with its *de jure* exclusion of the middle.

Let's not overlook the *jure* in conjuring. Any principle assumes the witness or testimony of the *who* (*testis* is *tertis*, you say), so too with matters of principle. The *jure* of conjuring is the gift. The gift of conjuration, however, differs from that which conjuring gives, for it is not exhausted by the 'semblance of reality' conjured. The gift can never be given and must always remain outside, in excess or remainder to, the given. The immaculateness of the gift that is never given, in addition or even primarily, attaches to a preeminently ethical meaning. What is given is non-indifferent in that it makes a difference ethically. It is against this background that a more transparent expression of conscience appears.[13] I'm not thinking only of the word 'law,' though a juror is expected to mete out fair measure as well as respect the act of witness, its occurrence, and its patience in conscience. There is almost the opposite, that in some cases shows how conjuring serves justice in respect to the other, the ghost. No more substantial service can be provided by the gift than to express the principle *tout autres sont tout autres*. Every other is wholly other. Conjuration both addresses the injustice and sets it aright. You bring out how strongly the mark of injustice resembles that of the father (logos/tribe, good/economy), where choice is always necessarily against one's will. The chain of mark, inheritance, covenant, *res publica*: such debt must be properly willed—by use of the will proper—if a victimization of responsibility results, and one becomes an irresponsible victim. Until the time of a willed (*undeferred*) obedience, obedience without choice of obedience—the debt will mark each utterance. Each inscription will repeat it *ad nauseum*. Rubbing away or rendering illegible will only make it be stated more boldly. If the act may be called the first injustice, then it also represents the first aporia, the aporetic of all aporetic experience. It is a mark of what must be passed through but without passing through. A passage where no passage is given.

To speak of a drug that deadens (kills) the violence of the first crime ("As soon as there is the One, there is murder, wounding, traumatism"), that is already deferral.[14] You go on to say that writing is a conjuration to end violence by initializing a life without it. Necessarily, language is a language of ghosts, notably, the (*Ur-*)ghost of being, and it can utter silently untold trauma. Again, saying but not telling. Things are said without telling most particularly with regard to *the event*. Unsaid, it must therefore remain *as* (in some sense of *as*) dead, entombed, conserved forever since it cannot die; history arises as the remains. Here is the important point. The eternally repressed, unlived, and unsaid is destined to become incorporated in the nearly effaced mark of the least significant thing, the most non-signifying of all—whose near total effacement disqualifies it absolutely from signifying or being a signifier for anything, in the chiasm of the aporia. The chiasm is Medusa's prison; the aporia is her look, the look of the Gorgon. Stuck as stone, yet alive, reflective, feeling, sensing: the aporetic experience resembles physical catatonia in relation to a fear of immobilization. Perhaps writing tries to archive this very thing, yet its absence permeates language throughout the chains of signifiers, a death in which animate force is lost, yet frozen the scene somehow subsists, endures, suffers.

To turn the question back to the relation between repression of repression and "the singular archive named 'circumcision'." Your fascination with marks, inscriptions, incisions, graphics, literacy, and the like, derives from where those two cross. The first mark is a wound, the scar of a singular surgical operation that signifies inclusion among the Chosen. But could there be another, more hidden avoidance (repression) in saying (without telling) that remains a primary spoke in the wheel of prayer and mourning? Let me first ask about what is given in gift of the wound (*vulnus*). This concerns the blindness resulting from the direct face-to-face with the absolute other, God, according to Hebrew and Greek thought. The gift given in and through blindness corresponds to the deepest layer of spirit.[15] Spirit now cleansed of demonology has an association with fire, alchemical or dialectical fire, fire of negation that combusts the real. Deconstructive fire, perhaps, is a theme for another occasion. Instead, recall Patocka's analogous question: how a spiritual

(Christian [Judeo]-Christian) repression of the Platonic psyche produces a radical dissymmetry in the gaze. In Plato, the gaze is reciprocated. The Good is both seeing and being known. Patocka recognizes that spirit (of the Book) suppresses or represses the direction of return. You say, "This heterogeneity of the invisible can haunt the visible as its very possibility."[16] The new position abounds with a spectacularly ghostly capability by virtue of an enucleation that seems like a disability yet actually 'augments' sight—if terror can be conceived as a supplement. At present, I observe only that the gift of contact, insofar as given, requires a responsiveness that in fact adequately expresses the work of mourning. That complex work includes adoration of the secret of the gift, the secret gifting, and, consequently, secrecy per se.

Because you see into the blind spot how a blinding spirit touches the spot to blind it, you introduce a new spirit whose blinding produces the ghost. If no blinding, then no ghost to frequent existence. This isn't the place to describe the pardon or expiation that too takes place in secret, but let me try. Put in writing but in secret. For the secret rubbing out of determinate reality, there is the figure of Thoth ("the hidden"), a quasi-heroic Egyptian figure. Thoth demonstrates devotion to mutating the event that takes place and the mark that it leaves and so invents writing. Hiding thenceforth becomes revealing a liability (blindness, wound), and this turns it into effectivity, *the making a difference*. As it expiates by making a difference, as writing unavoidably does, singularity is the only difference that difference can possibly make.[17] That possibility of a difference-making difference, the gift of making difference, is what you coin *différance*, the gift of making a difference. Incorporated within it is the secret of the event (*Ereignis*), the Heideggerian sense of appropriation. No one can doubt that the wound is a painful secret, but one that all the more secretly obligates you to conjure away the ghost of telling.[18]

To return to 'spirit,' it is connected with the trope of festering, as in a wound. Engulfed in flame, inflamed, hot to the touch, is a classical emblem of spirit, *Geist*. *Geist* can never be one with itself (restiveness itself is Hegel's absolute), but must remain tremblingly noncoincident, as though the shimmer of a cathode ray tube. It can never be present because of constant or inconstant oscillation. But this doesn't advance the question far enough. If spirit, *Geist*, is thought through the coincidence of the wound and the gift of wounding, then it precedes the wounded, and thus appears ahead of its own event, is a *pre-eventuality* (*Enteignis*, not *Ereignis*). It does not produce the event but previews it, impartially, yet never to appear in the time of the wound. *Geist* is witness first to the future, the advent to come. Perhaps we would be more comfortable with the idea of the gift as testimony to the not-yet, its tenses and termini. When it speaks, its prophetic authority announces the reading voice as it reads along the process of inscription. The inscription is of the pre-eventuation, and the voice reading it put into writing is temporally proximate, in front of the event—that in a strange passage seems to describe the scene of circumcision. If writing needs no substrate, writing implement, symbolization, or purpose, the way it does with Freud's Magic Writing Pad, it still needs to be visited by the phantomized voice-reading, in order for the self-awareness of spirit to be constituted. This conception of spirit is anxious with the peculiar play of confession and logic or a logic of confession specific to writing as you put it. The angst resounds in your avowal (to H. C.) of the secret of confession: "the avowal itself was the fault, . . . the sentence of a text which thereby turns out to be the most innocent, but also the most cleverly calculated . . ."[19] Nonetheless, your signature on many examples of strong public disclosure arranged specifically for acknowledging things you are (aren't) or have (haven't), gives me courage to consider your calculus. You are careful to employ a logic that does not palliate the wound or woundedness, that perhaps underwrites a minimal respect for festering excesses, results of the original trauma. A mindfulness of the gift and its revelation through disappearance permeates all your thought in this area. It is not in passing, therefore, to note how shame of injustice (bearing the mark of the Jew) drops salt from tears on the wound. There is something to ask you about.

Parenthetically, I find that confessions abound, not only in *Circumfession*, and there is also what confessions confess. Guilt and sin, debt, inheritance, owning and avowing. By the mark, you inherit the guilt of the circumcised: always to be marked in the eyes of God and his tribe. The guilt that confesses since it contains repressed matter that seeks expression in the dress of sin, and prates on about it. Guilt produces an economy by supplying appeasement for the force of repression, attempting to buy judgment by proving innocence—bad conscience. Bad conscience is known for a voracious appetite. The more confession, the more it craves, even if they are untrue. At this very crevice that ethics produces, literature arises. Perhaps it would be better to frame the problem from the other end. What becomes of a concept of truth when driven by relief from the repressive pressure, that is to say, by an obedience deferred by an avoidance of the truth? A very Nietzschean quandary indeed.

The investigations of divers consequences of wounding of language are extremely fascinating. The ethical ambivalence isn't difficult to perceive, but you don't seem to acknowledge the full expressive power in the act of marking. That it marks Jew as Jew, in marking the Jew, initializing the mark, especially and exclusively the Jew, and including the Jew who fells the Jew, *that* Jew. That doesn't make him the most Jewish, as you said to Hélène (only Cixous can call you on that), but totally Jewish in writing. Jacques, you are the Jew who put the Jew in him out through writing? What do you end up with? The Jew, always the Jew, who harps on his being/not being (the Jew) Both. Both condemned and expulsed. Condemned to putting it in writing, for it is only there that *différance* can be apprehended, in both senses of "apprehend." *Différance* that brings both comprehension and fear. *Différance* is the voice of the ghost reading as it is put in writing, since it never necessarily appears *except* in writing and never appears in writing. Your writing isn't free from putting it in writing, and it appears only in writing. Rather, an acoustical trace remains, the vocal signature of the first mark: circumcision. Only by tracking the "it" (*ça*) ideationally, putting it in writing, do you come to where *différance* lurks *uber*-phonetically, a phantom-like vibratory dissonance. In the indistinctly sounded acoustic is the ghost of the mute 'a,' '*aleph*' on mute, a mutation of the wound of Jewishness.

On the methods for keeping the wound open, aside from cauterization. One could, for instance, accept Levinas's insomnia. To move along the sharp line of guilt—one has always already usurped the other's "place in the sun"—is to wear a shirt of thorns. An obsession by the omnipresence of ethical injustice provides an example of moral stricture or rigorism. It is *for* the other that one keeps awake, in both senses of "for": as substitute and donor. Levinas insists on remaining as hostage to the other's debt to the extent of giving the bread from his own mouth. The secret gift appears in the second sense. It is the obsession that haunts you as the work of mourning. The wound there serves the vigil, an attestation to what takes place. If the possibility of ethics turns on that point, could one not ask whether it would differ much from yours, an ethics of exceptionality? In both, moral value appears to have been wrested from the law beyond law, the law in singular, *dike*, to reorganize into normatively acceptable forms.

You seem in a mood, Jacques, to follow Levinas on this, but deflate his category of height and superfluity with regard to the hidden other whose secrecy is beyond secrets. Questions of inheritance, debt, and ghosting must begin with that. Perhaps to supplement the subtraction, you keep saying *Tout autre est tout autre*—each each is irreplaceably unique. That is to say, for you, no singularity beyond singularity. Absolute singularity may be infinitely repeated, but it has no "other side." With regard to discarding honorifics of height, don't you believe that "existence" is one, needing questioning in light of the counterfactual ghost that haunts it (Heidegger's *Seinfrage*, "What if there were nothing rather than something?")? What else could have been if it hadn't been in existence, privileged by and respected for the selfsame status, yet all the time chased by a phantom non-existence? Or rather, would the possibility in all seriousness remain a phantom that could have happened but effectively would not have? Think of the whole issue of virtuality: the techno-media, tele-automatic transmission of the power of not being real but not unreal either. Even if existence is a term of privilege in oscillation with non-existence, that trembling is alive with a meaning that bears the emphatic of emphasis and gives voice to the ghost. Doesn't the *what if* mark a phantom appearance in thought, the very capability of imagining non-existence, ghosts, apparitions, and virtuality? Doesn't the *what if* express the far side of imagination, that is, *différance*; or equally *différance*'s faculty, the "transcendental imagination," prime source of the "deconstructive" proclivity of intelligence?[20]

Let me cross back over the nexus of philosophical and psychoanalytic ideas. In his mature thought, the death drive of Freud works to undo the work of the pleasure principle as they compete for viability. His account raises a number of basic questions, but let me focus on one, the function of the death drive. Irreducible and in possession of no content properly its own, it first of all is an anti-drive that operates with material adopted from other drives. It violently and *a posterior* suppresses the urges of infantile sexuality and establishes a matrix of archives in "black sites" without legible address to serve the rendition of repressed memories. There they are radically altered (mutilated) to the degree of becoming unidentifiable: name plate rubbed out, gulagization. The death drive in a supplementary action establishes archiving programs that, like computer worms, corrupt or destroy existing or future archives. Addition and replacement: the double session of a supplemental strategy. Once functional, it taints the totality of the archive. If this is a version of the post-Edenic condition, it lacks the possibility of redemption. A fall *en abyme*, with a correspondence to an infinite and non-dialecticizable negativity, Hegel's bad infinity, not equal to the movement toward absolute knowledge but at the service of deconstruction (if "service" is correct). It enters into no alliance and has an absolute disregard for borders. It is the solo operative or rogue intelligence personnel par excellence. And yet, doesn't the drive's logic belong *pari passu* to deconstruction also? If so, its inclusion has not been coerced but results from a radical hospitality. As you say, "it is in death and on the edge of death, it is to death that hospitality destines itself—death thus also bearing the figure of visitation without invitation, or of haunting well- or ill-come, coming for good or ill."[21] You who avow that you can give no avowals—sincerity without sincerity—the risk is then to presence as an exemplification of archival material. Now at least you can confess that Western metaphysics invites a new an-archy, the new *a-tehkne*. For destruction of memory of the father (its Oedipal prerogative) becomes enthroned as an "anti-science." For isn't the father, conceived as giver of law to the archive, the archon, really auto-destruction or self-destruction of *mnesis*, memory? In light of this question and Freud's refusal to subordinate the death drive to a higher authority, I feel constrained to ask what is to become of deconstruction's truth, its so to speak moral work?

A question that cannot be deferred. When I imputed a magisterial design to your thought, the intent was partially to analyze death and its related terms, life, mourning, *jouissance* (especially linguistic), the tragedy of the world. That design seems to exemplify the performative in strategy and mood. It seems to seek the gift of the other and its accompanying deconstructive transformation by putting it in writing—a delicate feat motivated by an excess of generosity. Correlatively, it strives to depict the tragedy of justice and its associated awareness of the other *as* other—an awareness explosive in otherness—that both have become moribund. The performative force of the strategy has its source in the question of whether death (death of this epoch) has come to mean a total leveling of diversity or total simulation of sameness (a redundancy). Both imply, still more tragically, a reductive distortion of knowledge. Scarred by injustice, a body of knowledge bears the mark of a preexisting excision. As such, it is a knowledge that will primarily serve ideology, propaganda, state-sponsored violence, infotainment, proliferation of tele-vacuity, and the like. Writing in the performative renders the subreption palpable or acoustically apprehensible in the voice-reading. Perhaps it isn't a veil lifted (a trope you deplore) but a scene conjured, complete with the ghost of truth. As you notice, "there is a *truth of delusion* . . . this truth is repressed or suppressed. But it resides and *returns*, as such, as the spectral truth of delusion or hauntedness . . . the truth is spectral, and this is its point of truth which is irreducible by explanation."[22] The truth of imagination is a phantom voice of a phantom invested with the power of the reading voice as an image of the real. Perhaps one gift of the magisterial lies in providing an alternative reality, an alterity, a completely other order of things. An example that exemplifies: a performative that is that deeply performative. Remember that the performative is necessarily in the dative.

Deconstruction then deems to reverse the depletion of good sense today, by teaching death and by showing, through the phantom, how everything is afflicted. It would show an absolute effectivity of death to summon a resoluteness (not necessarily Heidegger's) that (dis)places the other *in writing* for the reader—like a debit in writing—and through reading (silent, aloud), lets the other's place be apprehended. Such work would necessarily belong to mourning since it is the passage of death that impregnates the void of experience and calls forth the labor. Such work, you seem to imply, would belong to the mother (to Socrates, through his mother's midwifery), and your mother's ghost now enters the scene. Actually not only now, since I spoke your mother's name, Georgette, one day this spring quite inadvertently in a lecture. I, Georgette. She who bears you through pregnancy to full term while in mourning over the loss of her firstborn son, mother of the prayer for mourners, the *kaddish*. She who almost doesn't get up from a card game to deliver you, author of a writing on substitution, reader exchanging places with writer, the voice of reading assuming the place of the voice of writing. All *taking the place* is to iterate a birth in which substitution takes place, originally, you taking the place (for your mother) of your dead brother. This is another place to insert biography's site in a philosophical corpus, to put it *in writing*, since attestation and owning up to the truth go hand in hand with exposure of oneself through inscription.[23] Perhaps to put *in writing* is payment of the debt, amortization of the inheritance, arrest of the chain of substitutes: does the possibility of either exist? What is necessary would be a pregnancy that shows no promise of issue, an inspiriting event with no accessories, perhaps a pre-eventuality in the sense above. And, it must be said, one with a heavy mortgage on ghosts. Is there a way to avoid the irony of the mother?

Your devotion to family seems a way. Any ancestor, once living, is now a ghost that once conjured commands concern. The patriarch especially, Freud, father Freud, Sigmund himself. The conjuration produces a politics of memory, or conversely, that politics, of interiorization, empowers a familiarity with familial phantoms. To whom does Sigmund give voice, and for what? The question relates to whom does the mother, your mother, dying to death in front of you, give voice as you write her in memory by memory? There in your memory to put it immediately *in writing*, to put the debt *in writing*. To put a debt in writing compounds the indebtedness. You seem to memorialize the mother thus, but not my mother, yours who died while holding your hand, the leave-taking magisterial in its gift. It is the power of the mother who brings mourning to birth but remains eternally unaware of the substitution, one son for another. Georgette is life that keeps the void in abeyance by means of mundane distractions. She is instinctive (you take Rousseau to task for his adoration), with its survival impulse intact. Because she mourns her lost son Moses, and Jacques is his replacement—hers since he takes up the work where she leaves off—the work she teaches with her mother tongue, the *lingua franca*. She belongs in the *Phaedo* scene of Socrates' *Phaedo*, since mourning, with its attendant cult of death, has always belonged to the feminine. I mention all this because it seems the other side of the father/logos.

(The irony is what I miss, speaking to the ghost. Is irony lost at the death knell? Its absence can call it back only grudgingly, in eviscerated form. The lack may be related to the *gravitas* of play. Grave games have an inescapable gravity. You play with the beyond-death and look for students. The 'teaching,' if that is right, advocates or admonishes nothing about the apocalypse noted by Hegel, Marx, Nietzsche, Freud, Heidegger, and that reopens the wound. The German lot of them. A suturing that had festered in the spirit of philosophy, its *Geist* or its ghost, the ghost of the once-living *Geist* that had since cast spectrality off, is again torn free. Opening with the death card, the Black Queen, your mother might, opening the hand to death, anteing its difference with life—and to *différance*, that life can be more-than-life, contaminated by its other. To play Russian roulette poker in the suit of hearts. Along the way, glimpses of *différance* congeal to corporeality, if you let them, and unveil the difference between life and death by erasure—death is the erasure of difference also and erases difference as it goes.)

It is difficult to surmise which comes first (in your priorities), a love of mourning—the opening to death—or *différance*. Perhaps the uncertainty corroborates a principle of co-origination or -originality, central to your thought. (It could be evidence for a Nietzsche of a "European Buddhism.") Nonetheless, born to a mother in mourning for a lost son, born a mourning self to replace the other who already belongs to death, indicates grief as a founding principle. A living son who would replace a dead one with both living and mourning. Though an *ad hominem* argument, mourning, with its lesson of death-in-life, which is self-mourning, a mourning that replaces the self ('trembling') with another that one mourns, designates an obsession or excession of mourning replaced infinitely in the birthing. This would signify an *infinite mourning combined with infinite guilt*. The debt that can never be repaid yet whose repayment is foremost. The position seems to bear an ontological weight similar to Heidegger's in that both rely on an indebted existence. Infinite mourning with infinite guilt thus requires an active phantomization productive of many ghosts, one of which trembles at the source of the very 'I' whose debt you put in writing. One might desire a guilt-free conscience for the sake of *jouissance* and egology in general, that is, avoid a responsibility defined by poor resolution. Such would avoid "the concepts of responsibility, of decision, or of duty [that] are condemned *a priori* to paradox, scandal, and aporia. Paradox, scandal, and aporia are themselves nothing other than sacrifice, the revelation of conceptual thinking at its limit, at its death and finitude."[24]

When it comes to speaking with you, Jacques, death is first of all. That aspect that fascinates, more precisely, concerns a politics of ghosts in life, the intelligible remains of ones who have passed away, but remain in the form of ghosts, insertions of the transcendental into the sensible, bent on eternally alien visitation, parasitic paradoxes and bad infinities, spooks of the unknowable. This line leads toward *différance*, that meta-ideal non-idea of yours that sets apart whatever is joined, limits by unsettling limits (concepts, those excluders), and gathers by segregation. It necessarily lacks any concept 'of its own' since it cannot include the same. It's too bold to ask whether *différance* doesn't dole out death. At least in the fundamental sense that death is excluded where it introduces the unbounded, whose annihilation puts at risk all borders. Before *différance*, if it's possible to say, is one more ancient in genealogy, the one that *différance*, the father killed in order to become before—his father. There is the unbounded that *différance* bounds by differencing, spacing and differing, and then placing the mark *sous rature*, perhaps that is non-deconstructible. Call it the law or justice, in a metaphorical sense, *dike*.

Sacrifice is built onto *différance*, making *différance* both simple and with divisions. The boundarilessness sacrificed in favor of boundaries is constituted by *différance*. It is the more 'ancient' condition that makes possible the conditionless—that absolute unconditionality. The 'ash' of the sacrifice remains on the 'a' on mute, or is that 'a' itself, actually and acoustically; since not only as a trope does *différance* wear the muteness as a mark. Its inaudibility also produces a phonic gap in which *différance* is stationed and now transmits and transcribes itself *in writing*, in the form of the *gramma*, as you call it, behaving like a digital virus. A non-sacrificial sacrifice, or perhaps downright murder, of the sonicality of it. If a transmission could be conceived of as a nonfatal death of death (such as Blanchot's), then the matter of transmission is not as confusing. Is it both a parasite, and host of a new capability, elevating and diminishing the recipient—in this case, putting it in writing—the one that inherits the almost always a-phonic 'a' of *différance*? What bears witness to the act itself, the sacrifice that initializes and initiates? Do I know?

A lineage line of masters, one from the other, through whose 'channel' ('*chaîne*') repetition is transmitted: I have in mind the lineage of *différance*, the master repetition responsible for the replication of each and every thing that is different from itself. Not the philosophical fathers who would slay their son, you, Jacques, for sharing the trace. Trace as in *tracing*, tracing a lineage, recovering a trace of *différance* across a line of masters of repetition. Not as a word does *différance* ever show when put in writing, but still a genealogy of the trace could be reconstructed. Wouldn't the record then be an account of a visitation, of thinkers by the phantom, a peculiar yet profound obsession shared by them? An account of rendering the ghost impotent only to have it come back, of a frequentation that cannot be arrested—altogether like a parasite driven into latency but not exterminated. Perhaps in light of this, even if the ghost is a parasite (virus) that could be killed, the idea of parasite (virus) could not be, and its ghost or the ghost of an idea of a parasite, or a ghost idea, which is pleonastic, would still remain. In this idealistic riff, there is a further question regarding the ghost lineage: the determination of priority, which comes first?

This returns me to our previous conversation of eros. There is the question of the 'two's' (lover and beloved) but also of the phallus and the silk, even the *tallith* that provides a site of primitive or infantile sexuality—an allusion to masturbation and secrecy. The 'dangerous supplement' in Rousseau's code, masturbation seems the secret of the secrecy of the secret self, the self never lived. But couldn't the matter be turned around and radically reversed? For one concerned with displacement in general, it is important to understand whether *différance* contains a deflected allusion to masturbation; the secret of secrecy that belongs to the work. Under the aegis of eros, the erotic zone replete with phantoms, what are the operations of the (masturbatory) *différance*. You write how it secretes the life, as semen, so that the grammatological insertion of *différance* by putting it in writing disseminates the *gramma* iterating throughout. Is there any use going on *in writing* with *différance* or is putting it in writing a cop-out to effectivity? The only choice by which to inscribe difference, with the audible on mute? The answer isn't difficult. A mute voice to accompany the inscription of *différance* is the linchpin of your thought. It says the mute 'a' without telling it. There is still room to wonder about the 'family scene' of eros. The full account of the relation between the mute 'a' and the oedipal transformation, the patricide, it still outstanding. I don't grasp the obverse in that you invert the killing (father kills son rather than the other way) other than from a disregard for philosophical transmission, that is, inherited debt.

Perhaps your analysis of Kierkegaard's Abraham holds a clue. The story is one of sacrifice, gifting a most precious possession. Ordinarily, sacrifice belongs to an economy of exchange. You argue that singularity—Abraham's irreplaceability in relation to God who commands sacrifice—redefines the meaning. Instead, sacrifice must entail absolute loss, dissymmetry, and nothing in return. An extreme view that requires a negativity that devours whatever sacrifice, in its generosity, would give. But certainly also, a radical emptiness that invites a replenishment by excess, which is the crux of your thought on hospitality. This brings me to ask whether *différance* also *is* sacrificial, Abrahamic sacrifice, or perhaps an inversion of (reversion to) sacrifice that is still sacrifice. To mark things as spatially or temporally different from one another, non-difference, the undifferentiated ('bad' infinity) necessarily is sacrificed absolutely. Presiding over the altar of the proto-same, *différance* 'kills' the non-epoch, and delivers it over to manifest being or phenomenal reality, and 'gets' nothing in return. Nothing is emptied by *différance* and *différance* 'signifies' by depositing a trace in each thing differentiated. The trace is not *différance* itself since *différance* is without ipseity, way beyond the verge of not being, and most importantly, is no part of audible speech. There, *différance* is sacrifice that has made a gift of what would be itself if it could be. Only the inner voice, the voice that speaks vocables to the inner ear, can read, giving voice sufficient to hear the mute 'a.' Hear as it were. Hear in quotation marks to signify the phantomization of hearing. On mute, the audibles have been sacrificed and the sacrifice leaves nothing in return. *Différance* always already rises from the ashes.

Only the reader who 'hears' *différance* is sensitive to the voice on mute, and vice versa. This would seem to repeat the classical formula, as you derive it:

> Thought obeying the Voice of Being is the first and the last resource of the sign, the difference between *signans* and *signatum*. There has to be a transcendental signified for the difference between signifier and signified to be somewhere absolute and irreducible. . . . The sign and divinity have the same place and time of birth. The age of the sign is essentially theological. . . . The *arche*-word is understood, in the intimacy of self-presence, as the voice of the other and as commandment.[25]

You then proceed in a magisterial tone about initialization of the mute. "I shall speak then of a letter—the first one, if we are to believe the alphabet and most of the speculations that have concerned themselves with it."[26] A formula for divine or objective reason, consciousness is conceived as a mediumistic vehicle for articulation of phonic material that must necessarily be contaminated, in this case, with the mute 'a.' Thus, "the attention we give it beforehand will allow us to recognize, as though prescribed by some mute irony, the inaudible but displaced character of this literal permutation."[27] Thought then is the burnt offering in voice's sacrifice of its own audibility, when it gives absolutely away its audibles. From now on, reason's voice must be muted, not heard, a ghost of its former self. Could it be that the motive is a thanatopic impulse that holds the gift of death supreme?

You've identified the birthplace of the sign (God), but the death site seems equally important since it inscribes one in the book of life (equally, death). The matter of the 'two's' is most basic to your version of nondualism. Saussure's theory of language posits a linguistic unit composed of both a sensible and an intelligible particle. The sign has a transcendental, conceptual component and an empirical, experimental one. When meaning is thus considered, one aspect is always involved in conjuring the other, the concept, the sound, or the audibility the signification. Surely, ghosting begins here, at the division, its *arche*; whoever orders the division conjures the possibility of the ghost, which is a ghost. Let the conjuring begin! To trace the division to the anterior is to recover the unrecoverable 'essence' of making a difference, namely *différance*. It is tempting to say, therefore, that *différance*, is a proto-ghost that it begins by coming back, a *revenant*. Wherever the sign is—a signifier signifying a signified—there too is the ghost. This equity means, moreover, that it is incorrect to blame the 'transcendental signified' for the *Ab*-phenomenon of phantomization. Spectrality is not the simple result of the non-existence of self-presence but of the complex duality of language.[28]

Différance suggests an obsession of yours (Kierkegaard's, of thought's love of the unthought): a passion to go straight to the other where there is no going. The mute 'a' is a passage to *différance* by way of a scandal's 'mute irony.' The fact is that a lacuna exists in Saussure's account of meaning, and you exemplify it by a unique and singular signifier, one that lacks all signifieds, transcendental or otherwise. Does the concealment have to do with deferred obedience? That which would be signified cannot be; due to the lack of phonic differentiation between the words *difference* and *différance*, it is already taken up. The 'a' in *différance* is, in the French language, mute. Nothing is left either logically, phonically, or linguistically to be signified by the signifier that lacks a voice. The lack is absolute and singular. It is in fact constituted by a ghost sign, the sign for a missing signified, missing because it must be. The missing sign is a ghost, no? Totally uncanny in the way of the absent one, excluder and excluded, it haunts the presence of the sign of each and every signification. The implication is that whatever presence is, is really the ghostly absence of a presence that was, is, and will be never there, an awareness of the signified missing that never crosses the threshold but continues to tease and lure.

The lure is the trace that can never be brought to fullness, is inherently impoverished, an almost indefectible gloss of nothing, the excluded of a never-completed process of finding a way back. The lure is an allure, the passion involving a murder, in this case, of the father, logos, voice. It is perhaps the passion of passions, or the passion more passive than passive, as Levinas writes. It follows that the lure is almost always taken, since hermeneutics never forsakes its love of novelty. Now if mourning is directed toward the trace of the absent presence, then all work is of mourning. Always one mourns what is not there, the exclusion. In the exclusion, moreover, is an eternal return. The exclusion that never will be included will, antinomously, come back. The formulation alone might recall the *revenant*. The dead and gone, the excluded, fill the lacuna in the semiological field that is fated to be endlessly replicated, a fate that is non-local.

The mourning is not limited to a dead past in light of how it extends to the future. One mourns not only the past, born and unborn—unborn Marranos—who will kill the father, but ones unborn never to be or have been born. Paradox: when the patrimony of voice is murdered, the unconceived belong to what is to come, even if it has already come. And not only because this conversation takes place. In the mourning of absolute loss—voice of discourse—the adventure of the trace begins, if it has an *arché*. Isn't the adventure the ash of the memorial, the embers of the eternal lamp that keeps the Ark, the never-extinguished faith of the never-extinguished absence, passing one moment to the next by witness and transmission. And you add the thought that "the engagement to keep secret is a testimony."[29] Did you mean that *différance* is *the witness that never appears*, the witness that is non-witness, vacated, lapsed, and no longer reliable? Yet witness nonetheless. Yes, a witness that can't reliably record, keep a record, or resort to any archiving device (science, technoscience, tele-techno-science), in order to archive what the non-witness witnessed—which would require excessive archiving. What would such an archive look like? Would it have a special encoding device for repression (since 'everything' and 'nothing' are the same), one known only to security, if there? Would such a witness make the barest difference, offer the weakest testimony, and attest to the very least degree—but still as witness? In any event, the archive in question would be a ghost archive, heteronomous, metaphorical, an errancy. This is the long way back to 'deferred obedience'—putting off obedience by putting it in writing, encoding the ghost voice—the obedience to the ghost. You seem in search of the key to the ghost archive and to the voice-reading what the archive puts in writing. Location: the unconscious, if you read below the threshold and the ghost that frequents there. That is another issue. But it is related to your secret secrecy, your way of saying without telling. One that produces scandal by a scandalous withholding to excess so that nothing or everything shows. No phenomena without the apparitional. No putting it in writing without the ghost voice of the dead logos. But still, a fan dance, with grand dissimulation, a display of nothing being shown, showing no pretense in showing nothing but making a great deal out of it. A spectral tattoo in the voice, so that it is acoustically speckled in body.

Philosophically, nihilism is the only position to avoid, in light of a fundamental respect for the other. The fidelity to trauma and repeated traumatization provides exposure to that. (Not to talk about other avoidance.) Fidelity blends with justice, another instance of 'stoic logic.' Several different impertinences unfold, but first is the principled obedience to the plenitude of empirical content, experience in general. "Do not seek to have events happen as you want them to, but instead want them to happen as they do happen, and your life will go well." Before deriving freedom from necessity which grounds subjectivity, stoic logic has to tailor desire to the same. It begins with an epoch of surveillance, under the sign of Heidegger's ontological difference once again. Does the spiritual basis of *différance* lie there, in the classical epoche? It isn't a big deal to say that *différance* is shaped by it. To want a different *différance*, that is, to want *différance* to be otherwise in any respect is to be in agreement with it, which is impossible and in contradiction to the stoic epoche. To find imperturbability (*ataraxia*), none other might be needed. Perhaps that paradox of desire, a volitional aporia, is another point of insistence to *différance*. *Différance* neither wants or does not want the same, and wants both to want to be and not want to be different. The *terstis* and the *testis*, the witness who never appears and never absents, again phantomize themselves into very heavy roles.

It is important to know just how far to press stoic logic. Perhaps the most accessible work is there at the origin of classical ethics, where mourning is a possibility already defeated before its conception as a mourning in the transcendent mode. A sublime mourning mourned not because of a known outcome, but because of its necessity. The most eminent necessity that trumps all: that is the *telos* of stoic reasoning on death, whose inspiration (expiration) extends the epoche farther back and reduces it to irreducibility. The rest of the philosophical machine is built on that foundation, including the 'ethics of deconstruction.' In fact the ethics of deconstruction so squarely fits the footprint that there is room for nothing else. Stoic logic classically situates the epoche in the compartment between the gift of life and the impressions given of it. The first is conscious of the second. It is evanescent, 'deconstructive' consciousness that never is present on either side of the equation, yet is able to pronounce the word "God" perhaps because it already bears his signature. The first watches the second that, looking outward, cannot look back and, therefore, is not further reducible. The second that feels there is "nothing to be done," with the infinite resignation of a Kierkegaardian knight. This is a fundamental derivation from stoic logic, however reinscribed as a transcendental epoche. In its 'linguistic' form, mourning mourns the signifier that lacks all signifieds. Not mortality to be mourned but a trace of transcendental absence, death to manifestation, surrender to concealment, achronicity to history. Parenthetically, that which would be signified produces a chain always exceeded by a trace that moves ghostlike everywhere. Supplementary to the classical account, *mourning is the work of remembrance* here too in an updated chapter of stoic logic. Since Epictetus, the work of mourning in all aspects must mourn an impossibility of possibility, seen as the relentless destruction of finitude. In the case of *différance* and the mute 'a,' it is an impossibility of a possible signification, a meaning that never could have been. One mourns the necessary incompleteness of the linguistic field, the other that cannot be included—in short, finitude. Remembrance of the limit and its delimitation: ultimately, mourning interjects the *mysterium tremendum* and its shattering, which at the same time can be gentle violence, opening the door to hospitality. As you once said, "Infinite *différance* is finite."

There is yet more to the 'a' on mute of *différance*, and the whole mutant chain of muteness, mutedness, mutationality, and ending with mutancy or mutantness. There is the meaning of that singular quality in you that can serve as an insistence or repetition of an archetype that never will have existed. Certainly this requires a tone of voice, a vocality or vocerificity, that is in your name, which is said iteratively. To hear that in the voice-reading as it is put in writing, immanent to the text, is to hear the voice that keeps you. At the very least, in memorialization. For all its muteness is not silence, so let it be witness. The mute 'a' stands also for attestation, taking part by not taking part. Levinas shows that the witness is the heart of the moral essence, the one without a second to observe. He who is first killed, the first killed son, the son the Jew would kill and say he didn't.

The mute that is unheard because it is inaudible and non-phonic, but whose undetectable presence is everywhere, as if it remained a perpetual possibility (of hearing), never a rumble, crash, clack, swish, hiss, or even a tintinnabulation. A ghost possibility that haunts otology and the ear as well as ontology and the real, which designates the phantom as unread, which is what its reality really is, that is, unreal—so unreal that the inscription of it makes it real. It is that selfsame unreal that is written about, as I write here to you, Jacques, the representation of unreal things, ghosts of reason that have always haunted it as antinomy, paralogism, transcendental illusion, and others of Kant's incredible monstrosities. Symptoms of an obsession that haunts the real, never showing themselves other than as a spectral illness that is simulated. Simulated but not unreal; not real either. Some such route takes Kant to the transcendental imagination, replicator of spectral devices, unless the replicator itself is replication—ghosts either way. The ghosts don't exit: is this, Jacques, an obedience to the 'a' on mute in *différance*? Once conjured by a word, they stay as long as *différance* is written in the language. Nor would they leave even if the word were effaced since such conjuration once set motion has its own life.

The mute 'a' traces (as a verb) the body of sound on mute, an utterly interior constant repetition, a basal note of subaudible vibration—a drone of absence. It is the incorporeality of sonicness or the sonicness of incorporeality. In either case, either as the *corps objectif* or *corps sujetif*, it doesn't lend itself to demarcation, marking, remarking—or scarring. As you once suggested, unlike the breath, it produces only a silent pneumology or pneumo-theology. To draw the science out farther, the 'a' is a simulation of breath peculiar to inner reading and is as necessary as respiration is to the voice of the lecturer. Simulation is a metaphoric displacement that tries to indicate the direction of meaning.

In many ways, the 'a' is the exemplar of the performative in meaning. It performs the signification of 'saying without telling.' What it says 'means' but doesn't tell what it means. What needs to be told in the telling, a *bon mot*, is 'said' by putting it in writing, and the transcendental illusion thereby safeguards by performance. This remains the preferred mode of transmission by the lineage of the secret. *The* secret: as you notice, "God is the name of the possibility I have of keeping a secret that is invisible from the interior but not from the exterior."[30] The first telling lesson purposes to sagely hide it, since its exposure is impossible to bear, and in the concealment the avoidance of mourning commences. It teaches a self-protection for which there is no known password.[31]

There stands the mute with his tongue cut out, a mutilated mute, suffering a distortion or diminution, a social outcast, without a spoken language, as you say it was for you. It is noteworthy that this mute, besides the tongue, has the foreskin removed, a crime that left you marked, no, you felt barbarically mutilated, with a scar of identity—racial, ethnic, liturgical, monotheistic—not only your own. The Jew, and thereupon, the naming of a secret name inscribed in flesh, is a secret that keeps its name secret by remaining bent on its articulation. The Jew and his unnamable secret is atoned by him in a *language meant to keep the secret secret*. An expiation that has to do with life and eros and also, "a structural disproportion or dissymmetry between the finite and responsible mortal on the one hand and the goodness of the finite gift on the other hand."[32] The fear and trembling that anticipates the *mysterium tremendum* initializes the sacrifice that defines stoic logic, the epoche. A counter-current to 'Western metaphysics.' There, a passage between the transcendental and the empirical, a passage that subtly marks the erotic, can be reopened. The erotic *daemonium* clandestinely works, plying the space between the two's. (This is the incorporation for which you and Patocka directly reproach Plato.) The function of eros is central to putting it in writing that your text, mutilated, homeless (*unheimlich*, no body, no identity of its own) performs an erotic inquiry. The erotic is in essence the insistent movement between, forth and back, to and fro, up and down, in oscillation, even, uneven—but always a failed attempt at being a messenger, a third, *tertis*. It operates in the service of the transcendental imagination, extolling "the beauty of the beautiful . . . memories of death." As an inheritance, "it leaves only its erotic simulacrum, its pseudonym in painting, its sexual idols, its masks of seduction: lovely impressions."[33] In either case, eros is the ghostly frequency of visitation. It could, up to a point, be mutely chanted.

I'm starting in again, that Jewish joke at the beginning of "Hostipitality." It's strange, Jacques, a presentation of the most profound thought in a work as an amusement. How you play with *différance*, introduce it as a play, and delight in the 'a' of an an-acoustical, a-phonic, non-phonetic, and almost audible laugh. It takes a while to see how the humor displaces the point until later. The joke defers the idea. Another point for Freud: how a joke can throw the reader off the scent. It thus shields, hides, protects, and keeps private what is on the verge of being public, however it requires secrecy of secrets. The impossibly thin skin of the ethical sensitivity; reticence to excess. The secret of *différance* is hidden well; after all, in the possible difference a mute 'a' can make. Differing 'as such' exists only in a paradox: differing cannot differ without being different—what blocks *différance* from existence. The conclusion—there is nothing to be found—jolts just because each step in the argument leads one to expect a soft landing . . . until the final crash. The other, ethically speaking, lies in exile, and suffers trauma and non-readjustment. *The other: the signifier without a meaning.*

The awareness of a phantom that frequents language, outside focal consciousness, includes the imminence of the guest. Being beyond, *au-delà*—by definition lacking all signifieds—the other remains outside, an alien. The two, the phantom awareness and the other, have many important crossings, and one is where the thaumaturgical and the ethical meet. In most approaches to the ethical, the phantom is conjured away, spirited below, killed (as in kill a light), deadened, or repressed—all by virtue of the conjuring power it has had bestowed on it. Your *différance* strains unsuccessfully against neutering ethics. *Différance* is the sign under which both conjuration and generosity reign. Both ethical *tour de force* and as bewitchment over language are practiced under it. Even given their co-origination, the question of conflict arises. Isn't a master of ghosts necessarily a master also of conjuring, abjuring, and perjuring, and hardly exhibits ethical values? An ancient question—since Plato's noble lie—for moral reasoning. Can the gift of ethics be found trustworthy if it arises from corruption, alchemically? Must it command sacrifice and impossibility? Is it possible that protection against the excessive exposure to the glare of the guest is absolutely needed for survival?

The ghost always comes back to the scene, which is the scene of putting it in writing. It frequents the writing because it is most nearly haunting there, in its site of visitation. By mere mention (*"Enter, ghost"*), the ghost returns with a definite inheritance including the past earlier than all pasts, before representation, the Paleolithic. The deeper inheritance, heavier debt, and initializing traumatization that marks reading, writing, and *hote*-ing, is the first inscription, not chronologically but nomologically, as epitomized alphabetically—the letter 'a.' First in law, first in language, it subsequently gives rise to all lesser laws. Through them, it conjures a place of dwelling, in Heidegger's terms, a refuge but also an exile, a solitary confinement, 'on death row.' There, it learns that the deferred is in truth the mark of death, whether in writing as buffered (spacing) or postponed, perhaps retrograde (timing). The written text, therefore, must include an apparition that is homeopathically effective in warding off the death phantom. That which creates the scene is necessarily mute. To conjure death away, as the saw goes, "As long as there are ghosts, there is no death." All the same, it must break the xenophobic attitude and open the door to trauma of the other. The question is, in its call to remembrance and memorialization, must it interrupt the conjuration? Here is another question of the crossing lines.

Having veered, nonetheless, I feel deeply about your discovery of a wounding in language. Our language, the voice reading with the voice writing, is wounded. A possibility but more; the wound has already occurred as a poisoning. It's without remedy and without cure since once introduced, the aberration persists and the body of language, which includes voice, is toxic and doomed. The cause, the pathogen or agent, is inaccessible through language as a result of the inventor's ingenuity. It is made to appear exterior but the concept of exteriority is itself a product of language and predication. It may even be delusionary and uncertain. Your solution is to put it neither beyond language nor *au-delà*, but within the tender tissue, the sensitive integument, that gives language an intimation of a body, empiricism and the world. It is a brave choice of site of the 'a' on mute, that irritates as in a phantom limb. It remains to ask you what could be the purpose of inflicting a mortal wound on language? I risk a speculation on another element of 'stoic logic.' That the wound is a 'reminding factor' for a work on a hospitality so radical that it would welcome the other that owes no allegiance or gratitude, and has zero debt. To become hostage to that hospitality is to choose *in the name of justice and mourning. The surrender to the radically unmet other is a mourning for life surrendered, gifted to death, if one names it that.* Woundedness—both cause and result of the work—remains devotion, promise, and faith. One more question: is it done to contest that the wound is real, but that simulation is a difference that makes no difference, and thereby draws the limit to hospitality?

To awaken unto what, would you say? To *philosophia*, you say, as the dream of empiricism fades and consciousness dawns. That is to work in a language wounded and brutally disruptive, toward release of repression by death. The release could equally figure in birth and death, birth of what survives death, the survivor. That inscription on the soul's memory, the concept of immortality. That streak of Platonism or Pythagoreanism invisibly is put in writing as a work of survival. Epitaphial. To put a road to immortality in writing, to work the reading voice to the pitch: introducing infinities and absolutes on every note. Arousing indeterminacy, co-origination, and impermanence, painfully disruptive memories, of trauma and shock—in divers modalities. Immortality is not played out as endless space (Bergson), but putting endlessness in writing as the text. Reinscription repeated gives proof to the name, ever at risk. A survivor, *sur vie*, at least continues to be written into the text, and thereby gifted with renewed life at each reading. The survivor able to survive as a voice heard by another person, read by another person. To be more precise, survival is the gift of the subvocal reading voice, a mute, that alone can affect the mute 'a' of *différance* and pronounce it 'truly' as inaudible. The 'a,' gift now in a theological sense, is always already presented to the voice, since it is the gift of the singular, and voice in its eminence in reading would be in the singular.

Tell me when it was for you. Someone could peruse *Circumfession* without success in uncovering, a secret encrypted among the hum of avowals. In "A Silkworm of One's Own," the whisper is more generous onstage, generosity itself:

> Already I'm getting ready, I am ready, I say to myself, I'm quite close to enjoying in peace, I'm already enjoying the turbulence and the burst cloud, the accepted self-evidence, the new finitude affirmed. What luck, this verdict, what feared chance: yes, now there will be for me worse than death, I would never have believed it, and the enjoyment here nicknamed "resurrection," that is, the price to pay for the extraordinarily ordinary life toward which I should like to turn, without conversion, for some time still, such an enjoyment will be worth more than life itself.[34]

Véraison you call it, and though the writing could be fabrication, it names a possibility as realization. Perhaps it names a truth about writing, perhaps even the one indicated here—paraphrased by Blanchot: "To write is to no longer put in the future a death always already past, but to accept that one must endure it without making it present and without making oneself present to it; it is to know that death has taken place even though it has not been experienced."[35] The truth, if it is that, doesn't belong to the farthest dream of empiricism. It is death for the undergoing *subjectum* whose voice enters the voice-reading without telling, indicating, expressing, or disclosing the gift. The saying (*le dire*) is a mantra, a repetition that doesn't arrive for voice to voice it. The secret is secret because writing itself has put poison in writing to render it illegible. After the act of poisoning, you couldn't tell if you most wanted to. But it is there, decipherable, how the voice-reading vociferates what is impervious to death. A repetitive subvocal drone of immortality.

Wanting the verdict gets in the way, that is clear. Wanting the verdict in: that sounds like time's revenge, the "it was" of Nietzsche, at work. Peace would seem in opposition to life's avenging itself on itself, frustration itself. Peace, *socius*, hospitality; the three components of justice. That the verdict is secret might be the realization itself. A secret that absolutely coincides with the world that it is a secret of, whose coincidence keeps the secret absolutely, is no secret at all. That must be the meaning of "ordinary," the ordinality of life, order, orderly, orderliness: the excess consumed by excessiveness. Life finitized and magnetized, leaving it attractive and open to view. The "mystical experience" of Wittgenstein, the solution that presents itself the moment when the problem dissolves.

When the secret will have been realized is an event that is unknowable because singular. It would come as the result of the work. In the meantime—now—writing is the wound that festers, the reading of which attests to the sickness unto death. It festers, moreover, because it utilizes wounded language, a language wounded in a peculiar way, spectrally, with a non-evadable wounding (a gadfly) that haunts writing as the hand of destiny. If it is an *au-delà* of language, it is not the absolute other. Instead, it is more like a representation of the nonrepresentable. It is to take a liberty and to call it "death," since it could as easily been named "God" or "nothing." All are portals out of language. The mute 'a' emanates from a point within the doorway, or perhaps the doorman or daemon just on the other side. Here is another unexplored, unpronounced element of eroticism in your thought—an eroticism of death. Freud says how the death drive drapes itself in things of great beauty and contrivance. There is nothing uncommon in the marriage of eros and thanatos, though unlike the Amor and Psyche mythomene, eros is likely to lose out in the partnership. It gives a special twist to your life-affirming yes, I will yes, of Joyce. The yes is that of hospitality and the guest, death; as you write, "when hospitality takes place, the impossible becomes possible but *as* impossible."[36]

Insistence is the crux of obsession, together with resistance and desistance. It is tempting to trace obsession (with Freud) back to a death eroticism because it would be another haunting, a haunting by the future. Obsession is never able to be completed and its ghost comes from the yet-to-come and never arrives there. There is an obsession in your writing that hinges on two different impossibilities that must hold a strong affinity for one another, the affinity "between the impossibility called death and the impossibility called forgiveness, between the gift of death and the gift of forgiveness as possibility of the impossible, possibility of the impossible hospitality."[37] Laced with death eroticism, bent on forgiveness, writing does not fit itself. Noncoincident, inadequate to itself, it is an excess that destroys a plenitude. Seeking obsessively a forgiveness it cannot gift itself, writing is a misfit, a disturbance that interrupts a sentence. As the disruption arrives from the to-come, time appears as insufficiency; this is its irredemption. It is confession and avowal forever aborted—the promise of a birth that eventuates in a phantom event.

Starting in again (the Jewish joke), returning to the deferral of obedience. Obeying seems encrypted in a primal attitude, the *hote*'s, guest *and* host, a pairing of the 'two's' named by a kind of Noah, yourself. Perhaps the exact arc of radical hospitality, the praxis of justice or justness, cannot be described, or perhaps it can be traced to the pledge (*gage*), found in an extended footnote in *Of Spirit*. There it is argued that before *any* question—ethical or ontological—an initializing affirmation, *yes*, must be given. The gift of avowal is akin to assenting to language, which is to say, thought, determination (*Bestimmung*), distinction, destination, and, therefore, interrogation. Until the initializing, there can be no going forward or moving backward (*retrait*)—parenthetically, the saying (*le dire*) and the unsaying (*le dedire*.) The identity of the donor is the one who never leaves his/her name, or leaves a false name.[38] Anonymity serves the gift of gifts, the gift of the pledge—pledgeability, the condition for making the gift possible—as Jewish law exemplifies, the highest donation is anonymous. In a way, for the phenomenologist the same movement is gifting, from anteriority to the anteriority of anteriority. Both state the priority of the condition and of conditionality, as alluded to first by Kierkegaard.

In the end, as we near it, to what (whom) is the deferral of obedience owed? Not the obedience itself (a different question) but the deferment. With the obedience, it must be owed or it wouldn't be obedience. With deferral, it is the opposite, not owed at all. The question is, is there a dative here, the *to whom* that is deferred? With obedience, it may be owed as to an inheritance, with a dative, owed to someone or something. One is born in debt, one owed absolutely also, by virtue of being born into possibilities already constituted. The *wound* is the mark of debt and writing levies greater debt by drawing on the primal one. *One is born into debt*, and putting it in writing attests to the increase in it. Nor is in the meaning of the debt that it ever is to be repaid. Perhaps it's right to agree that to render illegible the debt signified by an indelible mark is best. One learns by living with a wound and learning "stoic logic." It is as a "reminding factor," meant to remind that the deferral must be made, or the obedience, by necessity, will be enforced. In deferral, the work of mourning finds a place. In mourning the end to come, obedience to that end is spaced, postponed, made to wait. In putting the mourning in writing, death is left to abide, and an ephemeral immortality procedes. The wound is the mark that marks one in both ways, the absolutely mortal and absolutely immortal—the *pharmakon* in action.

Illegibility is when death *as such* is no longer readable, rubbed out—yet not any less present in its absence. It comes as both threat and promise. Threatening loss of meaning and pledging conquest of death's imminence, illegibility has arrived. It arrives in the crouch of the 'a' on mute, the immortal letter of incline. In the inherited wound, voice gains an obedience *owed in advance*. Like any thinker, I'm interested in what hides, the hidden, reasons for hiding, provenance of that reason, and of reason itself, and of ipseity. The top of the game is to where reason undoes itself and steps away, empties itself, and becomes the night, what never takes place, absolute stagnation or pure stasis—death of any coming-to-be from the to-come. But you hide it by showing how it rubs the decipherability away. The same strategy is deployed extensively and cannot be reproduced—not being subject to repetition, a version of hell that leads to the repetition phenomenon, having to repeat life, again reproduce it, because it has come back, with a debt unpaid, *the payment in advance*.

And lastly, it seems to follow from the two impossible gifts, death and forgiveness, that their impossibility is the gift, and their relation undeniable. Death is postponed in the act of putting it in writing, and it must be fore-given, given in advance. Writing is the payment in advance that pays off the debt by poisoning language with the inadmissible 'a' and bringing death there, here. In writing, it must be forgiven in advance that obedience to death is deferred, put off to another time. At least in the voice-reading, there is a prefiguration or adumbration of the work there, the subtle heart of mourning—a mourning that forbids mourning. May I imagine you found joy, in that voiced proximity whose saturation exceeds the excess of death, and outlives it, the survivor? Whose voice-reading as it is put in writing is able to attest to the conjuration of the undying, the phenomenon of which brings an impossible gift of holy hope.

Notes

Introduction

1. Emmanuel Levinas, *Totality and Infinity*, tr. Alphonso Lingus (Pittsburgh: Duquesne University Press, 1969), p. 269.
2. Hélène Cixous, *Portrait of Jacques Derrida as a Young Jewish Saint*, tr. Beverley Bie Brahic (New York: Columbia University Press, 2004), p. 9.
3. Jacques Derrida, *Specters of Marx*, tr. Peggy Kamuf (New York: Routledge, 1994), p. 28.
4. "Deconstruction is justice," simply put. Jacques Derrida, "Force of Law: The Mystical Foundations of Authority," in *Acts of Religion*, p. 243.
5. *Specters of Marx*, p. xviii.
6. Ibid., p. xix.
7. Jacques Derrida, *Archive Fever*, tr. Eric Prenowitz (Chicago: University of Chicago Press, 1996), p. 39.
8. Emmanuel Levinas, "The Trace of the Other," in *Deconstruction in Context*, ed. Mark C. Taylor (Chicago: University of Chicago Press, 1986), p. 349.
9. Idem.

Chapter 1. With the word I

1. Performative grammar applies to writing and speaking, and their reciprocals, reading and listening; but with the present study, the emphasis is on writing. The fault line of vocality to grammaticality, phonocentrism and logocentrism, runs tectonically throughout Derrida's writing, exposing the possibility of sudden seismic shifts in the grounding of discourse.
2. From *thaumazein*, wonder at the miraculous, the traditional source cited for philosophy, against which Derrida voices no skepticism. The term quickly bifurcates into the lower and the higher, the magical effect railed against

by Plato and directed toward the Sophists, and the awe felt in the face of the wholly other, or the *mysterium tremendum* of Otto and other emotivists.

3. The project of putting a conjuration in writing, similarly bifurcated into a magical and an ethical aspect, necessarily proceeds in writing, where the possibility of conjuring lies. The special potency of writing is recognized by Derrida; "For if such a conjuration seems welcoming and hospitality since it calls forth the dead, makes or lets them come, it is never free of anxiety." *Specters of Marx*, p. 108.

4. Augustine, Proust, Stendhal, Celan: the chain of confessional writing Derrida identifies as correctly giving the writer's signature in relation to the mark or inscription. Autobiography in this degree recognizes that the writer's privilege is to give entry to the voice of the other that puts it in writing through him, by an act of appropriation or expropriation. The I that writes trembles and puts the trembling in writing so that the writer's voice trembles with the words of the other, that is, God, for Augustine.

5. Shibboleths dear to the thought of Derrida, names that have been thaumaturgically imbued with the power to engender the exclusionary and totalizing logic of the traditional canon.

6. Joint, peg, pin, connector rod, nail, stitch: the series. It brings to mind an act to undo the binding or bond, the bounds, boundness, or boundary, and loosen the strictures, strictness, and re-striction: an absolution in the original meaning. An ab-solving force drives 'deconstruction' that is essentially religious without being religion.

7. "So by *oeuvre* I mean something that remains, that is absolutely not translatable, that bears a signature. . . . *oeuvre* is a manner (endogenous to some degree) of producing the conditions of legibility of that which has been produced." Jacques Derrida and Maurizio Ferraris, *A Taste for the Secret*, tr. Giacomo Donis. Ed. Giacomo Donis and David Webb (Cambridge, England: Polity, 2001), pp. 14–15.

8. Does the concept of line derive from an authentic relation to a death of "my own," as Heidegger argues? Or does the porosity of the border refute the derivation as well as the possibility of defining what is "proper to me" in this regard, and leave "my death" without a signifier, as Derrida contends. See *Aporias*, tr. Eric Prenowitz (Chicago: University of Chicago Press, 1996).

9. To echo something Derrida once wrote about Roland Barthes, the ghost of Derrida that has been put in writing by me (he nor I completely *in* it) is one who would smile in writing now. Does this speak of a conjuring?

10. "Structure, Sign, and Play," in *Writing and Difference*, tr. Alan Bass (Chicago: University of Chicago Press, 1978), p. 280.

11. Leibniz first formulated the requirement, dating back to Parmenides, as the identity of indiscernibles. *Différance* strives to break the lawfulness of the requirement and would argue that the set of indiscernible pairs is empty, that no two things are the same, that is, if they can be given distinct numbers. On the other hand, indiscernibility identifies the empty set, being a property (if that) common to all 'members' of the set. It is the absolute erasure of marks of distinction that does not at the same time result in a homogeneity.

12. *Of Grammatology*, tr. Gayatri Chakravorty Spivak (Baltimore: The Johns Hopkins University Press, 1974), p. 70.

13. "Is an experience possible that would not be an experience of the aporia? . . . [D]econstruction is explicitly defined as a certain aporetic experience of the impossible." *Aporias*, p. 15. As a project, deconstruction unearths the aporia—"when 'nothing is possible' is true"—in thinking a thought to the end and thus is essential performative, performing the experience of impossibility. Geoffrey Bennington summarizes the 'strategy' "as the attempt to think through the relationship between the singularity of the singular case and the generality of the universality of the structure which makes it (im)possible—on the one hand allowing the singular to be marked or recognized as singular and on the other tending to lose that singularity in the very structures thus brought out." "Double Tonguing: Derrida's Monolingualism" see www.usc.edu/dept/comp-lit/tympanum/4/khora.html.

14. To which chain, John Llewelyn would add the link, teaching: "In his very philosophizing about what is beyond being, the author is responding to an ethical call in the face to face with his reader. His reader is therefore, ethically speaking, at that moment his *magister*, his teacher and master." *Appositions of Jacques Derrida and Emmanuel Levinas* (Bloomington: Indiana University Press, 2002), pp. 11–12. The relation of the reader's voice to the writing occupies much of the subsequent analysis of this project.

15. Heidegger invests the work with the signature that in the reading of it, its legibility is used up and left in ruins. See "The Origin of the Work of Art," in *Poetry, Language, Thought*, tr. Albert Hofstadter (New York: Harper and Row, 1971), pp. 17–87.

16. It is important to avoid assuming that the problem is solvable. The distinction between the voice reading and the writing voice, and between the author's and the reader's may be undecidable. In another context, Derrida suggests as much: "I no longer hear your voice. . . . I have difficulty distinguishing it from mine, from any other . . ." "At this very moment," in *Rereading Levinas*, ed. Robert Bernasconi and Simon Critchley (Bloomington: Indiana University Press, 1991), p. 11.

17. *The Gift of Death*, tr. David Wills (Chicago: University of Chicago Press, 1994), p. 92.

18. One would need to investigate the implications of the concept of trembling in Derrida's source, Hegel: "The remaining ideal sense of hearing. This is in signal contrast to the one just described. Hearing is concerned with the tone, rather than the form and color of the object, with the vibration of what is corporeal; it requires no process of dissolution, as the sense of smell requires, but merely a trembling of the object, by which the same is in no wise impoverished. This ideal motion, in which through its sound what is as it were the simple individuality the soul of the material thing expresses itself, the ear receives also in an ideal way, just as the eye shape and color, and suffers thereby what is ideal or not external in the object to appear to what is spiritual or non-corporeal." G. W. F. Hegel, *The Philosophy of Fine Art*, tr. F. P. B. Osmaston (London: C. Bell and Sons, 1920), 1: 206.

19. *Aporias*, p. 32.

20. *Being and Time*, tr. Joan Stambaugh (Albany: State University of New York Press, 1996), §7, p. 34.

21. Nietzsche's point that forces cannot be adequately named establishes one pole of *différance*, in that there will always be a remainder, an excess, that isn't in the scope of a name since it differs from anything named. "Now force itself is never present; it is only a play of differences and quantities. There would be no force in general without the difference between forces . . ." Jacques Derrida, "*Différance*" in *Speech and Phenomena*, tr. David Allison (Evanston: Northwestern University Press, 1973), p. 148. The play of excess, the left-over, unused, wrung-out, expelled, is acoustical aura in which sounds of the ghost, ghost-sounds, are overheard.

22. Death "reveals itself as something which knows no measure at all, no more or less, but means the possibility of the measureless impossibility of existence." *Being and Time*, §53, p. 242. It is the empty possibility, possibility hollowed, nothing left to take place, traceless night that brings on the tremor. The tremor that is life responds to the extremity, exterminability, and externality (terms that Derrida challenges) of that possibility.

23. Diderot: "I write without seeing. I came. I wanted to kiss you and then leave. . . . This is the first time I have ever written in the dark. Such a situation should inspire me with tender thoughts. I feel only one, which is that I do not know how to leave this place." Letter to Sophie Vollard, June 10, 1759, in Denis Diderot, *Diderot's Early Philosophical Works*, tr. and ed. Margaret Jourdain (Chicago: The Open Court Publishing Company, 1916), p. 155–156.

24. In *The Gaze of Orpheus*, tr. Lydia Davis (Barrytown, NY: Station Hill Press, 1981), pp. 21–62. Critchley, in *Very Little . . . Almost Nothing: Death, Philosophy, Literature* (London: Routledge, 1997) gives a more extended analysis of Blanchot's *il y a*, and contends that Blanchot's main thesis on writing is the other night, "the profoundly dark point towards which art, desire, death, and the night all seem to lead." *Very Little . . . Almost Nothing*, p. 99.

25. *The Space of Literature*, tr. Ann Smock (Lincoln: University of Nebraska Press, 1982), p. 169.

26. Cf. *Aporias*, pp. 61–62, 70–71, especially "we will have to ask ourselves how a (most proper) possibility as impossibility can still appear *as such* without immediately disappearing, without the 'as such' already sinking beforehand and without its essential disappearance making *Dasein* lose everything that distinguished it—both from other forms of entities and even from the living animal in general, from the animal." The *as such* has been incorporated, and as Llewelyn observes, "incorporation is cryptography. It encrypts the lost object whose loss it pretends not to acknowledge, by hiding it in a tomb that is simultaneously inside and outside the self that has the gaol of introjection for its goal." *Appositions*, p. 48.

27. Worth noticing is Derrida's opposition to a "strong, indeed barely repressible, temptation to consider the growing predominance of the formal function of the copula as a process of falling, an abstraction, degradation, or emptying of the semantic plenitude of the lexeme 'to be' . . ." "The Supplement of the Copula," in *Margins of Philosophy*, tr. Alan Bass (Chicago: University of Chicago Press, 1982), p. 203.

28. *The Work of Mourning*, tr. Pascale-Anne Brault and Michael B. Naas (Chicago: University of Chicago Press, 1978), p. 159.

29. Ibid., p. 160.

30. Ibid., pp. 41–42.

Chapter 2. The book begins

1. In an analysis of Hegel's rich discussions on prefaces, Derrida writes, "*Written* prefaces are phenomena external to the concept, while the concept (the being-abreast-of-itself of absolute logos) is the true *pre-face, the essential predicate* of all writings." "Outwork," in *Dissemination*, tr. Barbara Johnson (Chicago: University of Chicago Press, 1981), p. 15. *Pari passu*, the chapter that follows the one before it.

2. Not only the ghost but also God, as Llewelyn writes, "Iterability is another name for what theology calls God." *Appositions*, p. 30.

3. This line of reasoning needs to be juxtaposed with Derrida's analysis of the inner voice: "The voice is *heard* (understood). . . . It is the unique experience of the signified producing itself spontaneously, from within the self, and nevertheless, as signified concept, in the element of ideality or universality. The unworldly character of this substance of expression is constitutive of this ideality. This experience of the effacement of the signifier in the voice is not merely only illusion among many—since it is the condition of the very idea of truth. . . . This illusion is the history of truth and it cannot be dissipated so quickly." *Of Grammatology*, p. 20.

4. "Plato's Pharmacy," in *Dissemination*, p. 111.

5. Cf. Blanchot in "Literature and the Right to Die," in *The Gaze of Orpheus*: "The danger of writing for others is that the others will not understand your voice, but the voice of another, a 'real' voice, profound and disturbing like truth." As Derrida makes clear, the voice reading must bear the acoustic signature of the writer of the work, and that that voice, eternally tremulous, is the voice put in writing by the one who writes.

6. "Plato's Pharmacy," p. 111.

7. Saussure: "I propose to retain the word *sign* (*signe*) to designate the whole and to replace *concept* and *sound-image* respectively by *signified* (*signifié*) and *signifier* (*significant*)." *Course in General Linguistics*, ed. Charles Bally and Albert Sechehaye in collaboration with Albert Riedlinger, tr. by Wade Baskin (New York: McGraw-Hill, 1959), p. 67.

8. The essential relation between the performative philosopheme and repetition is guaranteed by an idealism, that of phenomenology. It becomes the work of deconstruction to 'articulate' the logic, viz. "of spectrality, inseparable from the idea of the idea (of the idealization of ideality as effect of iterability), inseparable from the very motif (let us not say the idea) of deconstruction." *Specters of Marx*, p. 175n.

9. "Plato's Pharmacy," p. 111.

10. *Symposium* 215d. Plato writes of speaking, that is, puts it in writing performatively so that once the reading is voice, the 'spell' is enacted in the scene.

11. "Structure, Sign, and Play," in *Writing and Difference*, p. 279.

12. "Conversations along a Country Path," *Discourse in Thinking* (New York: Harper, 1964), p. 65.

13. Eschatology supposes the existence of a border to be crossed, the end, viz., of philosophy: a silence, a coming night. The question of the borderless border whose crossing undoes itself is raised, according to Derrida, by the grand assumer of border crossings, up to the absolute, Hegel. "But is not Hegel the one who wanted to think the unilaterality of the border and thereby show that one is always already on the other side of the here?" *Aporias*, p. 55.

14. *The Post Card*, p. 260.

15. Borrowed from German Idealism (but not only German Idealism, idealism as a genre), the identity is defined in the equation "I = I." Where the equation fails to hold, 'logic' no longer follows a protocol defined by a law of exclusion (of the middle), the inequity becomes a spectral spillway of the discrepancy or noncoincidence that results.

16. *The Post Card*, p. 270.

17. This means that the ghost has no predecessor, in a logic sense, no ancestry, and inhabits a time that goes backward, in which the last event is the first of a sequence. Ghost-time is anti-eschatological, a recurrence of the *arche*, that in its recommencement has already used time up. Its intersection with living time, the time of living and of the non-living, is ephemeral, is ephemerality itself, barely available to the glance.

18. The stillborn death of the reading voice, its fall back into silence, is for Hegel the sound of the animal voice. "In the voice, meaning turns back into itself: it is negative self, desire. It is lack, absence of substance in itself." *Jenenser Realphilosophie II, Die Vorlesungent von 1805–1806*, ed. J. Hoffmeister, Leipzig, 1931, p. 161. Cited in Agamben, *Language and Death: The Place of Negativity*, tr. Karen E. Pinkus with Michael Hardt (Minneapolis: University of Minnesota Press, 1991), p. 45.

19. *The Post Card*, p. 262.

20. *Aporias*, p. 60.

21. A connection between the ghost voice and animal voice is apparent from Hegel's comment, "Every animal finds a voice in its violent death; it expresses itself as a removed-self." Agamben, *Language and Death*, p. 60.

22. The relation is highly nuanced and nonliteral and must include the possibility of the nonrelational, the failed relational, the absconded relational, and so on. As in *The Post Card*, "the postal principle, that a letter can always not arrive at the destination," p. xix. Analogously, the master may not come, there may be nothing to write, and the son may be disowned.

23. "Plato's Pharmacy," p. 122.

24. Ibid., p. 123.

25. *Crito*, 53e.

26. "Philosophy consists of offering reassurance to children. That is, if one prefers, of taking them out of childhood, of forgetting about the child, or,

inversely, but by the same token, of speaking first and foremost for that little boy within us, of teaching him to speak—to dialogue—by displacing his fear of his desire." "Plato's Pharmacy," p. 122.

27. Ibid., p. 128.
28. Ibid., p. 145.

Chapter 3. To be read

1. Perhaps charged with a Nietzschean force rather than referential meaning. As Derrida insists, "There would have to be a writing that performs, but with a performative without presence (who has ever defined such a performative?), one that would respond to his, a performative without a present event, a performative whose essence cannot be resumed as to presence." "At this very moment," in *Re-Reading Levinas*, p. 35.

2. *Specters of Marx*, p. 51. Peggy Kamuf has a slightly different interpretation of Derrida's performative intentions in *Specters*. See "The Ghosts of Critique and Deconstruction," www.usc.edu/dept/comp-lit/tympanum/2/.

3. "At this very moment," p. 35.

4. "Plato's Pharmacy," p. 152.

5. Ibid., p. 110.

6. Secrecy is not a prehension (com-prehension, ap-prehension) since it isn't a holding or keeping, since there is nothing to grasp. Here, "the gift is precisely what must not present itself. In this sense it is never given, it must not be given as something, nor by someone." *A Taste for the Secret*, p. 34.

7. The inner circuit of voice reading, writing read, voice heard exemplifies, in classical terms, the soul speaking to itself, the language of ipseity. For Heidegger, it is "Though obeying the Voice of Being." "What is Metaphysics?" in *Existence and Being* (Chicago: Henry Regnery, 1949), p. 360. As a model, it has repressed alterity, since the language of language is to express the same, self. The acoustics of the other then must be included in the register of the inner circuit. To raise the question of the other-than-sound is to ask about the other's appearance in the voice reading: the ghost.

8. A further corollary, anti-eschatological in nature, that there will be no end to reading the writing, at which the writing will have been perfectly read. No unique signification or singular meaning either awaits the elect reader. The radical substitutivity of putting voice to readings contests the idea of a true reading, and perhaps a prioritizing of the voicings, since the value-conferring 'event' can strike anywhere.

9. *Specters of Marx*, p. 101. The "visor effect" is an obsession with Derrida: "the visor effect: we do not see who looks at us." Ibid., p. 7. It is a trope for egology also, as in Levinas who considers it the ring of Gyges, that renders the bearer invisible to others and able to harm that way. But it also is a trope for the eye of God, according to the Abrahamic religions, "the one who, in absolute transcendence, sees me without my seeing, holds me in his hands while remaining inaccessible." *The Gift of Death*, p. 40.

10. *Specters of Marx*, p. 196n.

11. Ibid., p. 126. Furthermore, the ghost body is produced "by incarnating the latter in another artefactual body, a prosthetic body, a ghost of spirit, one might say a ghost of a ghost." Idem.

12. In a similar vein, Derrida notes, "In order to be absolutely foreign to the visible, the invisibility would still inhabit the visible, or rather, it would come to haunt it to the point of being confused with it, in order to assure, from the specter of this very impossibility, its most proper essence." *Memoirs of the Blind*, tr. Pascale-Anne Brault and Michael Naas (Chicago: University of Chicago Press, 1993), p. 51.

13. Cf. "The *phainesthai* itself (before its determination as phenomenon or phantasm, thus phantom) is the very possibility of the specter, it brings death, it gives death, it works at mourning." *Specters of Marx*, p. 135. Also, "What is a phenomenology is not a logic of the *phainesthai* and of the phantasm, therefore of the phantom." Ibid., p. 122.

14. Thus is it possible to ask whether the phenomenological reduction is inherently onto-theological, that is, Christian, and whether therefore Hegel's version of phenomenology is more ancient. Derrida notices that "all phenomenology is a phenomenology of spirit (let us translate here: phenomenology of the specter) and that, as such, it cannot hide its Christian vocation." Ibid., p. 133.

15. Ibid., p. 136.

16. Redemption is tantamount to purification, in this case, of the impurities of the ghost. Spirit is necessarily impure ("the essential contamination of spirit by specter," ibid., p. 113), in need of a Hegelian *Aufhoben* to delete the impurities of sense certainty. Deferral in the face of death constitutes the final grounds of deferred obedience or any deferred action, *Nachtraglichkeit* or *après coup*.

17. *Of Spirit*, tr. Geoffrey Bennington and Rachel Bowlby (Chicago: University of Chicago Press, 1989), p. 14.

18. *Specters of Marx*, p. 133.

19. The further implication is that the "repetition compulsion . . . remains indistinguishable from the death drive." *Archive Fever*, p. 12. Beyond that is the intercession of the teleological itself: "Teleology organizes the return of the old, the oldest, the farthest away, of the 'potentially' most archaic," that is, the same death drive. *The Post Card*, p. 369.

20. Regarding the apprehension, Derrida writes that is driven by "the logic of this fear of oneself. . . . The ipseity of the self is constituted there." *Specters of Marx*, p. 145.

21. Derrida is quite explicit here: "The conjuration is in mourning for itself and turns its own force against itself." Ibid., p. 116.

22. Ibid., p. 9.

23. On the function of the proper name in the work, Derrida writes, "It will slowly decompose, taking its time, in the course of a work of mourning in which, achieved successfully in spiritual interiorization, an idealization that certain psychoanalysts call introjection, or paralyzed in a melancholic pathology (incorporation),

the other as other will be kept in guard, wounded, wounding, impossible utterance." "At this very moment in this work here I am." *Re-Reading Levinas*, p. 44.

Chapter 4. With the voice

1. "Plato's Pharmacy," p. 105.

2. The dream is that of empiricism, the worry of Derrida's that is constantly on his mind. In that sense, the deepest of his writing is under the spell of not having quite left the exterior and not quite having found the interior, in the logos. While he rejects the faith of a Kierkegaard or Levinas, who locate it in exteriority, he does not reject faith per se, but in relocating exteriority within as the trace. Faith concerns the justness of the law, the Law, and one's appearing before it, like Kafka, a trembling by which the ethical is surpassed. While Levinas would say that it involves the eminent, Derrida places it in the mysterious workings in the text, which appear putting it in writing. It concerns being faithful—fidelity—to the appearance of the incomprehensible, the ghost.

3. When truth is seen as the teleology of classical ontology, the truth of presence, then the passing of that ontology, the end of its history, is necessary for the 'proper' work of mourning. What engenders mourning cannot be mourned for it is nothing but an inherent breakdown mechanism, like Hegel's seed of autodestruction, as real as the *conatus*. Derrida writes, "Do one's mourning for truth, don't make truth one's mourning, and the mourning of ipseity itself, but (or therefore) without wearing or making anyone else wear mourning and without truth ever suffering itself, I mean truth-in-itself, if there ever was any." "A Silkworm of Its Own," in *Acts of Religion*, ed. and tr. Gil Anidjar (New York: Routledge, 2002), pp. 325–326.

4. Freud, *A General Course in Psychoanalysis*, tr. Joan Riviere (New York: Washington Square Press, 1935), p. 442.

5. A tense of weighty important, "the future anterior, here indeed, will have designated 'within' language that which remains most irreducible to the economy of Hegelian teleology and the dominant interpretation of language." And: "Its future anteriority will have been irreducible to ontology." "At this very moment," p. 37. In a way, it is the tense proper to *différance*.

6. *Poetry, Language, Thought*, p. 199.

7. Plato, *Apology*, tr. G. M. A. Grube (Indianapolis: Hackett, 1975), 39c.

8. The 'surplus always exterior to the totality' is an index of a commandment to respect the absolute other, the Platonic beyond-being. In such a system (if it is that), the exterior infects and inflects the interior—by the logic of supplementarity. No internal immunity, insularity, or isolation exists. The permeable agents that invade inside and outside, overriding limits, are the phantoms. Their quasi-ontological status identifies their unique commerce back and forth in a movement reminiscent (and not merely reminiscent) of Plato's *daemonia*.

9. *Being and Time*, p. 319.

10. Ibid., p. 331.

11. "Language," in *Poetry, Language, Thought*, p. 198.

12. Ibid.

13. A full investigation would require knowing the differences between the alien voice, animal voice, and natural voice in order to isolate the effect of the specter's grip on vocality. For a discussion of natural and animal voice, see Giorgio Agamben's discussion of Hegel, in *Language and Death* (Minneapolis: University of Minnesota Press, 1991), "The fifth day," pp. 41–49.

14. "Force of Law: The 'Mystical Foundation of Authority,'" in *Deconstruction and the Possibility of Justice*, ed. Drucilla Cornell, Michel Rosenfield, and David Grey Carlson (London: Routledge, 1992), p. 24.

15. See Heidegger's discussion of *Gestellung* in "The Origin of the Work of Art," in *Poetry, Language, Thought*, pp. 15–88.

16. "Language," p. 199.

17. "Envois" in *The Post Card*, p. 56.

Chapter 5. Reading itself

1. Certainly the mute or muted voice, leaning on the trope of audibility, derives from a comment of Derrida's on the 'third': "The unheard difference between the appearing and the appearance (between the 'world' and 'lived experience') is the condition of all other differences, of all other traces, and it is already a trace." (*Of Grammatology*, p. 65.) The weight of this admission is to emphasize the acoustical primary of the trace, to locate its primary site within the audible field.

2. It is their outlaw nature that produces the fright in their appearance. "The conjuration is anxiety for the moment it calls upon death to invent the quick and contain the new, to summon the presence of what is not yet there." *Specters of Marx*, p. 109.

3. Cf. the relation between heteronomous law and the oath: "In the incoercible difference the here-now unfurls . . . it is the precipitation of an absolute singularity in imminence and in urgency; even if it moves toward what remains to come, there is the pledge." Ibid., p. 31.

4. *A Taste for the Secret*, p. 60. For an overview of the relation between citation and spectrality, see Julian Wolfrey, "Citation's Haunt: Specters of Derrida," *Mosaic* (Winnipeg), March 2002.

5. *A Taste for the Secret*, p. 76.

6. In this regard, Derrida writes that "it is in order to destroy, so that nothing is preserved except an illegible signpost, or even a snapshot, nothing that has deserved, or allegedly deserved, preservation." *The Post Card*, p. 32.

7. In analysis of Kierkegaard's understanding of the ethical, Derrida suggests aporetically, "it is as if absolute responsibility could not be derived from a concept of responsibility and therefore, in order for it to be what it must be it must remain inconceivable, indeed unthinkable: it must there be irresponsible in order to be absolutely responsible." *The Gift of Death*, p. 61.

8. Levinas draws the connection with transcendence: "Transcendence, the beyond of essence which is also Being-in-the-world, requires ambiguity: a flickering of meaning which is not only a chance certainty, but a frontier both ineffaceable and finer than the tracing of an ideal line." *Otherwise Than Being or Beyond Essence*, tr. Alphonso Lingis (The Hague: Martinus Nijhoff, 1981), p. 152.

9. Cf. "The concept of responsibility, like that of decision, would thus be found to lack coherence or consequence, even lacking identity with respect to itself, paralyzed by what could be called an aporia or an antinomy." *The Gift of Death*, p. 84. Responsibility itself is a phantom concept that calls up the ghost and 'teaches' the undecidable issue of presence in life.

10. *De Anima* 450b.

11. Ibid., 451a.

12. For Kant, presentation presupposes representation and the a priori ground of a unitary presence resides in "a pure transcendental synthesis of imagination as conditioning the very possibility of all experiences." *Critique of Pure Reason*, A102, tr. Norman Kemp Smith (London: MacMillan, 1950), p. 133.

13. *Archive Fever*, p. 36. The chain of memory, the future, and uncanniness are closely connected to Derrida's messianism or messianicity and its prophetic voice.

14. Ibid.

15. Ibid., p. 90.

16. Derrida pronounces it the lesser violence, choice of which takes precedence over the night of prelingistic chaos. See "Violence and Metaphysics," *Writing and Difference*, pp. 147ff.

17. *Apology* 39c.

Chapter 6. Words 'I' write

1. The work is related to performance or the performative, and is thus dependent on what Derrida calls "the originary performativity . . . whose force of rupture produces the institution or the constitution, the law itself . . ." *Specters of Marx*, p. 31. Regarding the essential incompleteness of the work, Levinas writes, "The work is always, in a certain sense, an abortive action. I am not entirely what I want to do. Thus there lies open an unlimited field of investigation for psychoanalysis or sociology, which apprehends the will on the basis of its apparition in the work, in its behavior, or in its product." *Totality and Infinity*, p. 228. Cf. "The work, thought radically is indeed a movement from the Same toward the other which never returns to the Same." *En decouvrant l'existence avec Husserl et Heidegger* (Paris: Vrin, 1967), p. 191; my own translation.

2. An abundant secondary literature is available on the theme. See especially Gerald L. Brun's *Heidegger's Estrangements* (New Haven: Yale University Press, 1991), pp. 11–26. On the relation of French thought to Heidegger, Ethan Kleinberg, *Generation Existential* (Ithaca: Cornell University Press, 2005) and

Samuel Moyn, *Origins of the Other* (Ithaca: Cornell University Press, 2005). On the relation of Heidegger's politics and philosophy, see Richard Wolin, *The Politics of Being: The Political Thought of Martin Heidegger* (New York: Columbia University Press, 1990), Tom Rockmore, *On Heidegger's Nazism and Philosophy* (Berkeley: University of California Press, 1992), and Hans Sluga, *Heidegger's Crisis: Philosophy and Politics in Nazi Germany* (Cambridge: Harvard University Press, 1993).

3. Cf. "This disclosedness of beings is the violence that humanity has to surmount in order to be itself first of all—that is, to be historical in doing violence in the midst of beings." *Introduction to Metaphysics*, tr. Gregory Friend and Richard Polt (New Haven: Yale University Press, 2000), p. 167.

4. And it is to place the originary violence *sous rature*, to commit it to language violently in a manner as to leave no legible record of the act.

5. *Totality and Infinity*, p. 21.

6. *Otherwise Than Being*, p. 100.

7. *Of Spirit*, p. 109.

8. Ibid., p. 24.

9. Idem.

10. Idem.

11. "Plato's Pharmacy," p. 162.

12. "Plato's Pharmacy," p. 103. Likewise in any opposition, one term must be external to and exclude the other.

13. *Différance* is the incomprehensible and rubs comprehensibility out in its appearance. But the extinction is not a simple negation but the negation of negation (*negatio negationis*). "This incomprehensibility, this rupture of logos, is not the beginning of irrationalism but the word or inspiration which opens speech and then makes possible every logos or every rationalism." "The Cogito and the History of Madness," in *Writing and Difference*, p. 98.

14. Experience or empiricism is the oneiric phantom of philosophy, canonical or radically deconstructive, the dream that wakes to remember philosophy. Derrida writes, "Hegel says somewhere, empiricism always forgets, at the very least, that it employs the words to be. Empiricism is thinking by metaphor without thinking the metaphor as such." "Violence and Metaphysics," p. 139.

15. "Plato's Pharmacy," pp. 103–104.

16. But also the ethical consciousness, that is, conscience, in its aspect of humility. Levinas writes that it, "rather than signifying a knowledge of self, is a self-effacement or discretion of presence. Bad conscience: without intentions, without aims, without the protective mask of the character contemplating himself in the mirror of the world, self-assured and affirming himself." "Non-intentional Conscience," in *Entre Nous* (New York: Columbia University Press, 1998), p. 129.

17. *The Gift of Death*, p. 92.

18. For the connection between scholastic thought, medievalism, and French post-structuralism, see Bruce Holsinger, *The Premodern Condition: Medievalism and the Making of Theory* (Chicago: University of Chicago Press, 2005), esp.

pp. 114–152; and Kathleen Biddick, *The Shock of Medievalism* (Durham: Duke University Press, 1998).

19. *The Gift of Death*, p. 92.

20. Cited in Levinas, "Hermeneutics and the Beyond," in *Entre Nous*, pp. 74–75. Cf. "One must give without knowing, without knowledge or recognition, without *thanks* (*remerciement*): without anteing, or at least without any object." *The Gift of Death*, p. 112.

Chapter 7. A ghost

1. The Platonic strategy of substitution and incorporation is detailed in Jan Patochka, *Plato and Europe*, tr. Petr Lom (Stanford: Stanford University Press, 2002).

2. Cf. "This radical alterity, removed from every possible mode of presence, is characterized by . . . delayed effects. In order to describe them, in order to read the trace of 'unconscious' traces, the language of presence or absence, the metaphysical speech of phenomenology, is in principle inadequate." "*Différance*" in *Speech and Phenomena*, p. 162.

3. And the double restitution of philosophy, philosophy restored to justice, involves what Derrida describes as "this epiphany of a certain non-light before which all violence is to be quieted and disarmed." "Violence and Metaphysics," in *Writing and Difference*, p. 85.

4. "The Cogito and the History of Madness," in *Writing and Difference*, p. 62.

5. But does this imply a historiography that is linear and progressive, whereas "if repetition is thus inscribed at the head of the future to come, one must also import there in the same stroke, the death force, the violence of forgetting . . ." *Archive Fever*, p. 79.

6. *Apology* 31a.

7. Hence, the salient issue: "Is it not true that the logic of after-the-fact, which is not only at the heart of psychoanalysis, but even, literally, the sinew of all 'deferred' obedience, turns out to disrupt, disturb, entangle forever the reassuring distinction between . . . the past and the future . . . ?" *Archive Fever*, p. 80.

8. Ibid., p. 39.

9. Cf. "one has to realize that the ghost is there . . . before its first apparition." *Specters of Marx*, p. 163.

10. As Derrida notices elsewhere, "Renon and Nietzsche, for example, refer to respiration as the etymological origin of the word Being . . ." "Violence and Metaphysics," p. 139.

11. *Aporias*, p. 43.

12. Ibid., p. 22.

13. Derrida writes, "'traumatism': the non-symbolizable wound that comes, before any other effraction, from the past anterior of the other. A terrifying wound, a wound of life, the only one that life opens up (*fraye*) today." "At this very moment," p. 43.

14. "What Is the Phenomenon?" in *Plato and Europe*, pp. 15–38.
15. *Of Grammatology*, p. 60.
16. *The Gift of Death*, p. 27.

Chapter 8. Writing itself

1. Hegel, *Jenenser Realphilosophie* II . . . p. 161; cited in Agamben, *Language and Death*, tr. Karen E. Pinkus with Michael Hardt (Minneapolis: University of Minnesota Press, 1991), p. 45.
2. *Being and Time*, §47, p. 284.
3. Ibid.
4. Ibid., §57, p. 320.
5. "Non-intentional Consciousness," in *Entre Nous*, p. 132; translation modified.
6. Levinas, *God, Death, and Time*, tr. Bettina Bergo (Stanford: Stanford University Press, 2000), p. 53.
7. Ibid., p. 22.
8. Ibid., p. 16.
9. Cf. "When I testify, I am unique and irreplaceable." *Demeure* in Blanchot, *The Instant of My Death*/Derrida, *Demeure*, tr. Elizabeth Rottenberg (Stanford: Stanford University Press, 2000), p. 40.
10. Levinas, *God, Death, and Time*, p. 12. Translation modified.
11. The possibility of testimony supposes an 'instant' that is exemplary and therefore divided in itself. It must be both unique ("it happen exactly this way") and reproducible ("I am telling exactly what happened"). See *Demeure*, pp. 35ff.
12. *The Work of Mourning*, p. 200.
13. Exodus 33:20. "Thou canst not see my face: for this shall be no man see me and live . . ."
14. *The Work of Mourning*, p. 44.
15. Ibid., p. 160.
16. Ibid., pp. 41–42.
17. Heidegger's supposition of a hard line between living and death falls under question. The same idea, the impossibility of the possibility of *Dasein*, can be used to expose the inauthenticity that from the very start contaminates *Dasein*'s appropriation of self. The logic of contamination, always at work as the entropy of the grammatical world, consists of the steady deterioration of check points between terms. See *Aporias*, pp. 62ff.
18. Ibid., p. 78. Cf. "Is an experience possible that would not be an experience of the aporia?" p. 15.
19. In the case of autobiographical writing, this thought engages "an 'I' that is structured by the alterity within it, an 'I' that is itself in a state of self-deception, of dislocation." *A Taste of the Secret*, p. 84.
20. Cf. "the experience of the secret is, however contradictory it may seem, a testimonial experience." *Demeure*, p. 32. Cf. "As to this so enigmatic value of

attestation, or even of exemplarity in witnessing, here is a first question, no doubt the most general. What is happening when someone comes to describe a supposedly singular 'situation' by veering witness to it in terms which go beyond it, in a language the generality of which takes on a value which is in some sense structural, universal, transcendental, or ontological?" *Monolingalism of the Other, or the Prosthesis of Origin*, tr. Patrick Mensah (Stanford: Stanford University Press, 1998), pp. 19–20; translation modified by Geoffrey Bennington.

21. *Specters of Marx*, p. 113.

22. *The Writing of Disaster*, tr. Ann Smock (Lincoln: University of Nebraska Press, 1986), p. 65.

23. Cf. "where there appears the desire and power to render absolutely invisible and to constitute within oneself a witness of that invisibility, that is the history of God and of the name of God, as the history of secrecy, a history that is at the same time the secret and without any secrets." *The Gift of Death*, p. 109.

Chapter 9. Into the Book

1. Cf. "The trace must be thought before the entity. But the movement of the trace is necessarily occulted, it produces itself as self-occultation." *Of Grammatology*, p. 47.

2. Two further questions follow suit. On the one hand, is the transcendental imagination irreducible? On the other, is the (transcendental) epoche able to suspend the operation of it? Both inquiries belong to a full elaboration of another 'regional' phenomenology.

3. *Circumfession*, period 4, p. 22.

4. The trace provides no foundation, no "transcendental signified," and in fact is an anti-transcendental signified. Cf. "the transcendental signified, which, at one time or another, would place a reassuring end to the reference from sign to sign" is not situated in the trace, which is no site at all. *Of Grammatology*, p. 49.

5. Cixous associates the mute vowel with the feminine in French: "Always that French feminine *e* at the end, smuggled in, opening him to others, and time and again to this woman's voice vying with him for death [*la mort*] . . ." Hélène Cixous, *Portrait of Jacques Derrida as a Young Jewish Saint*, tr. Beverley Bie Brahic (New York: Columbia University Press, 2004), p. 24.

6. That is, the voice of the ghost necessarily interrupts Voice, here capitalized to signify the classical concept, which Derrida characterizes as follows: "the beginning arche-word is understood, in the intimacy of self-presence, as the voice of the other and as commandment." *Of Grammatology*, p. 17.

7. *The Work of Mourning*, p. 36.

8. Ibid., p. 21.

9. *Memories for Paul de Man*, tr. Cecile Lindsay, Jonathan Culler, and Eduardo Cadava (New York: Columbia University Press, 1986), p. 34.

10. That this strong contestation of Levinas's ethics is carried by Derrida throughout his treatment of ethical subjectivity and its subject. The inheritance

of Levinas's ethical proclivities is discussed at length in Kleinberg, *Generation Existential*.

11. *The Work of Mourning*, pp. 32–33.
12. Ibid., p. 150.
13. Ibid., p. 34.
14. Cf. "Inheritance is never a given, always a task." *Specters of Marx*, p. 54. In a similar context, Derrida cites Holderlin as writing that man "bears witness to having inherited what he is."
15. Cf. "ethics is also the order of and respect for absolute singularity, and not only that of generality or of repetition of the same." *The Gift of Death*, p. 84.
16. Cf. "What is it that makes us tremble in the *mysterium tremendum*? It is the gift of infinite love, the dissymmetry that exists between the divine regard that sees me, and myself, who doesn't see what is looking at me; it is the gift and endurance of death that exists in the irreplaceable, the disproportion between the infinite fit and my finitude, responsibility, as culpability, sin, salvation, repentance, and sacrifice." Ibid., pp. 55–56.
17. Ibid., p. 60.
18. "A Silkworm of One's Own," in *Acts of Religion* p. 322. A page before, Derrida writes, "The avowal itself was the fault, voila the sentence, voila the judgment, another verdict and one miraculously contemporaneous with the one awaiting me, the sentence of a text which thereby turns out to be the most innocent, but also the most cleverly calculating . . ."
19. Cf. "The first effect or first destination of language therefore involves depriving me of, or delivering me from, my singularity." *The Gift of Death*, p. 60.

Speaking with the ghost

This conversation is recorded in deference to Yosef Hayim Yerushalmi's "Monologue with Freud," in *Freud's Moses* (New Haven: Yale University Press, 1991), with Derrida's own assessment of it in *Archive Fever* as a supplement. Additional material marginal to spectral conversation is found in Avital Ronell, *Dictations: On Haunted Writing* (Lincoln: University of Nebraska Press, 1986).

1. *The Work of Mourning*, p. 56.
2. Cf. "as I venture a few remarks which, obedient in turn, I will group under the title of 'deferred obedience'." *Archive Fever*, p. 60.
3. Actually, you go much farther along the same line when you write, "no responsibility to a given word, a sworn faith, without a pledge, without an oath, without some sacrament or *ius iurandum*." "Faith and Knowledge," in *Acts of Religion*, p. 64.
4. Martin Srajek argues that you borrow the concept of truth from the neo-Kantian Hermann Cohen. See *In the Margins of Deconstruction* (Pittsburgh: Duquesne University Press, 1998), especially chapter 7.

5. You mention this fact in *The Post Card*, p. 80, when you note, "I write while concealing every possible divulging of the very thing which appears to be published."

6. In "White Mythology," in *Margins of Philosophy*, especially pp. 230–245. Aristotle's aphoristic "To produce a good metaphor is to see a likeness" (*Poetics* 1459a 7–8) is a thaumaturgical formula.

7. That is, Hegel's teleological hierarchy of writings that places alphabetic phonetics at the peak, and the first letter on top. Your citation of him: "Alphabetic writing is on all accounts the more intelligent." Hegel, *Philosophy of Nature* (part 2 of *Encyclopedia of the Philosophical Sciences*), tr. William Wallace (Oxford: Clarendon Press, 1971), sec. 459.

8. And you continue: "any discourse . . . on this alteration, this graphic and grammatical aggression, implies an irreducible reference to the mute intervention of a written sign." *Positions*, tr. Alan Bass (London: Athlone, 1981), p. 8.

9. But it isn't the only example of phonic or phonetic mutism in your corpus. Other favorites include *plus d'un* and *sauf le nom*. Toxicity of the *bête noir* of translators.

10. *Archive Fever*, p. 42.

11. "Plato's Pharmacy," pp. 81–82.

12. You aptly compare the process to the muteness of Freud's death drive: "It is at work, but since it always operates in silence, it never leaves archives of its own. It destroys in advance its own archive, as if that were in truth the very motivation of its most proper movement." *Archive Fever*, p. 10.

13. "What gives me my singularity, namely, death and finitude, is what makes me unequal to the infinite goodness of the gift that is always the first appeal to responsibility. Guilt is inherent in responsibility because responsibility is always unequal to itself: one is never responsible enough." *The Gift of Death*, p. 51.

14. *Archive Fever*, p. 78.

15. Or, as you otherwise put it, "would the event of revelation have consisted in revealing revealability itself, and the origin of light, the originary light, the very invisibility of visibility?" "Faith and Knowledge," in *Acts of Religion*, p. 55.

16. *Memoirs of the Blind*, p. 45.

17. So, intricately entwined in writing difference are the matters of expiation, debt, and responsibility. *Différance* should not be conceived as a purely linguistic or conceptual strategy. It is primarily ethical. As you put it, "it is on the basis of this gaze that singles me out that my responsibility comes into being." *The Gift of Death*, p. 91.

18. You acknowledge a related idea when you write, "By tying testimony both to the secret and to this instant, by saying at this very instant at this very instant, I would like to announce a singular testimonial alliance of the secret and the instant, namely, that which in the indivisible unicity of the instant is temporalized without being temporalized permanently." *Demeure*, p. 27.

19. "A Silkworm of One's Own," p. 321.

20. Another clue regarding the source of *différance*: "Because of this passion, which is not active, is not simply passive either, the entire history without history of the middle voice . . . is opened in passion. If a *différance* can only be written in the grammar of a certain middle voice, even if it cannot be confirmed by such a historical grammar, one might be able to reduce '*différance*' to another name for 'passion.'" *Demeure*, p. 27.

21. "Hostipitality," in *Acts of Religion*, p. 360.

22. *Archive Fever*, p. 87.

23. Cf. "As a promise to make true . . . where the witness must be irreplaceable alone, where the witness alone is capable of dying his own death, testimony always goes hand in hand with at least the possibility of fiction, perjury, and lie." *Demeure*, p. 27.

24. *The Gift of Death*, p. 68.

25. *Of Grammatology*, pp. 14, 17, 20.

26. "*Différance*," in *Speech and Phenomena*, p. 131.

27. Ibid.

28. You seems to recognize this when you note, "This does not mean, by simple inversion, that the signifier is fundamental or primary. The 'primacy' or 'priority' of the signifier would be an expression untenable and absurd to formulate illogically within the very logic that it would legitimately destroy. The signifier will never by rights precede the signified, in which case it would no longer be a signifier and the 'signifying' signifier would no longer have a possible signified." *Of Grammatology*, p. 324, note 9.

29. *Demeure*, p. 32.

30. *The Gift of Death*, p. 108.

31. The secret of muteness derives from the source that you indicate but in ways is obverse to what you report: "The maintenance of the rigorous distinction—between the *signans* and the *signatum*, the equation of the *signatum* and the concept, inherently leaves open the possibility of thinking a concept signified in and of itself, a concept simply present for thought, independent of a relationship to language, that is of a relationship to a system of signifiers." *Positions*, tr. Alan Bass (London: Athlone, 1981), p. 19.

32. *The Gift of Death*, p. 51.

33. *Archive Fever*, p. 11.

34. "A Silkworm of One's Own," in *Acts of Religion*, p. 352.

35. Blanchot, *The Writing of Disaster*, tr. Ann Smock (Lincoln: University of Nebraska Press, 1986) p. 65.

36. "Hostipitality," p. 387.

37. Ibid.

38. On the impossibility of establishing absolute authorship: "The name of a philosophical subject, when he says I, is always, in a certain way, a pseudonym." "Violence and Metaphysics," p. 110.

Bibliography

Works by Derrida

Acts of Literature. Ed. Derek Attridge. New York: Routledge, 1992.

Acts of Religion. Ed. Gil Anidjar. New York: Routledge, 2002.

Aporias: Dying—Awaiting (One Another at) the "Limits of Truth." Tr. Thomas Dutoit. Stanford: Stanford University Press, 1993.

Archive Fever: A Freudian Impression. Tr. Eric Prenowitz. Chicago: University of Chicago Press, 1996.

"At this very moment in this work here I am." In *Re-Reading Levinas*. Ed. Robert Bernasconi and Simon Critchley. Bloomington: Indiana University Press, 1991.

Circumfession. In *Jacques Derrida*. *Derridabase*, by Geoffrey Bennington, and *Circumfession*. Tr. Geoffrey Bennington. Chicago: University of Chicago Press, 1993.

Demeure. In *The Instant of My Death*, by Maurice Blanchot, and *Demeure*. Tr. Elizabeth Rottenberg. Stanford: Stanford University Press, 2000.

Dissemination. Tr. Barbara Johnson. Chicago: University of Chicago Press, 1981.

The Ear of the Other: Otobiographies, Transference, Translation; Texts and Discussions with *Jacques Derrida*. Tr. Peggy Kamuf. Lincoln: University of Nebraska Press, 1985.

Edmund Husserl's Origin of Geometry, *An Introduction*. Tr. J. P. Leavey Jr. New York: Harvester Press, 1978.

"Geschlecht II: Heidegger's Hand." Tr. John P. Leavey Jr. In *Deconstruction and Philosophy: The Texts of Jacques Derrida*. Ed. John Sallis, pp. 161–196. Chicago: University of Chicago Press, 1986.

The Gift of Death. Tr. David Wills. Chicago: University of Chicago Press, 1994.

Glas. Tr. J. P. Leavey Jr. and Richard Rand. Lincoln: University of Nebraska Press, 1990.

Margins of Philosophy. Tr. Alan Bass. Chicago: University of Chicago Press, 1982.

Memoirs of the Blind: The Self-Portrait and Other Ruins. Tr. Pascale-Anne Brault and Michael Naas. Chicago: University of Chicago Press, 1993.

On the Name. Ed. Thomas Dutoit. Tr. David Wood, J. P. Leavey Jr., and Ian McLeod. Stanford: Stanford University Press, 1995.

Of Grammatology. Tr. Gayatri Chakravorty Spivak. Baltimore: The Johns Hopkins University Press, 1974.

Of Hospitality. Tr. Rachel Bowlby. Stanford: Stanford University Press, 2000.

Of Spirit: Heidegger and the Question. Tr. Geoffrey Bennington and Rachel Bowlby. Chicago: University of Chicago Press, 1989.

Philosophy in a Time of Terror: Dialogues with Jürgen Habermas and Jacques Derrida. Ed. and tr. Giovanna Borradori. Chicago: University of Chicago Press, 2003.

Positions. Tr. Alan Bass. London: Athlone, 1981.

The Post Card: From Socrates to Freud and Beyond. Tr. Alan Bass. Chicago: University of Chicago Press, 1987.

Rogues: Two Essays on Reason. Tr. Pascale-Anne Brault and Michael Naas. Stanford: Stanford University Press, 2005.

Specters of Marx: The State of the Debt, The Work of Mourning, and the New International. Tr. Peggy Kamuf. New York: Routledge, 1994.

Speech and Phenomena, and Other Essays on Husserl's Theory of Signs. Tr. David B. Allison. Evanston, Ill.: Northwestern University Press, 1973.

A Taste for the Secret. Jacques Derrida and Maurizio Ferraris. Tr. Giacomo Donis. Ed. Giacomo Donis and David Webb. Cambridge, England: Polity, 2001.

The Work of Mourning. Tr. Pascale-Anne Brault and Michael B. Naas. Chicago: University of Chicago Press, 2001.

Writing and Difference. Tr. Alan Bass. Chicago: University of Chicago Press, 1978.

Works by Levinas

Collected Philosophical Papers. Tr. Alphonso Lingis. The Hague: Martinas Nijhoff, 1987.

Emmanuel Levinas: Basic Philosophical Writings. Ed. Adriaan T. Peperzak, Simon Critchley, and Robert Bernasconi. Bloomington: Indiana University Press, 1996.

Entre Nous: Thinking-of-the-Other. Tr. Michael B. Smith and Barbara Harshav. New York: Columbia University Press, 1998.

Existence and Existents. Tr. Alphonso Lingis. The Hague: Martinas Nijhoff, 1978.

God, Death, and Time. Tr. Bettina Bergo. Stanford: Stanford University Press, 2000.

Otherwise Than Being or Beyond Essence. Tr. Alphonso Lingis. The Hague: Martinas Nijhoff, 1981.

Outside the Subject. Tr. Michael B. Smith. London: Athlone, 1993.
Time and the Other. Tr. Richard A. Cohen. Pittsburgh: Duquesne University Press, 1987.
Totality and Infinity: An Essay on Exteriority. Tr. Alphonso Lingis. Pittsburgh: Duquesne University Press, 1969.

Other Works

Agamben, Giorgio. *The Coming Community.* Tr. Michael Hardt. Minneapolis: University of Minnesota Press, 1993.

———. *Language and Death: The Place of Negativity.* Tr. Karen E. Pinkus with Michael Hardt. Minneapolis: University of Minnesota Press, 1991.

Bennington, Geoffrey. "Double Tonguing: Derrida's Monolingualism." From www.usc.edu/dept/comp-lit/tympanum/4/khora.html

Bernasconi, Robert. "Deconstruction and the Possibility of Ethics." In *Deconstruction and Philosophy: The Texts of Jacques Derrida.* Ed. John Sallis, pp. 122-141. Chicago: University of Chicago, Press, 1986.

———. "Whose Death is it anyway? Philosophy and the Cultures of Death." From www.usc.edu/dept/comp-lit/tympanum/4/khora.html.

Blanchot, Maurice. *The Gaze of Orpheus.* Tr. Lydia Davis. Barrytown, N.Y.: Station Hill, 1981.

Brun, Gerald L. *Heidegger's Estrangements: Language, Truth, and Poetry in the Later Writings.* New Haven: Yale University Press, 1989.

Caputo, John. *Against Ethics: Contributions to a Poetics of Obligation with Constant Reference to Deconstruction.* Bloomington: Indiana University Press, 1993.

———. *The Prayer and Tears of Jacques Derrida: Religion without Religion.* Bloomington: Indiana University Press, 1997.

———. "Instants, Secrets, Singularities: Dealing Death in Kierkegaard and Derrida." In *Kierkegaard in Post/Modernity.* Ed. Martin Matustik and Merold Westphal, pp. 216–238. Bloomington: Indiana University Press, 1995.

Cixous, Hélène. *Portrait of Jacques Derrida as a Young Jewish Saint.* Tr. Beverly Bie Brahic. New York: Columbia University Press, 2004.

Critchley, Simon. "'Bois'—Derrida's Final Word on Levinas." In *Re-Reading Levinas.* Ed. Robert Bernasconi and Simon Critchley, pp. 162–190. Bloomington: Indiana University Press, 1991.

———. *The Ethics of Deconstruction: Derrida and Levinas.* Oxford: Blackwell, 1992.

Dick, Kirby, and Amy Ziering Kofman. *Derrida: Screenplay and Essays on the Film.* New York: Routledge, 2005.

Freud, Sigmund. *A General Introduction to Psychoanalysis.* Tr. Joan Riviere. New York: Washington Square Press, 1952.

———. *Moses and Monotheism*. Tr. Katherine Jones. New York: Random House, 1939.

———. *The Uncanny*. Tr. David McLintock. New York: Penguin, 2003.

Gasche, Rodolphe. "Infrastructures and Systematicity." In *Deconstruction and Philosophy: The Texts of Jacques Derrida*. Ed. John Sallis, pp. 3–20. Chicago: University of Chicago Press, 1986).

Handelman, Susan. "Jacques Derrida and the Heretic Mereneutic." In *Displacement: Derrida and After*. Ed. Mark Krupnick, pp. 98–129. Bloomington: Indiana University Press, 1983.

Hegel, G. W. F., *Phenomenology of Spirit*. Tr. A.V. Miller. New York: Oxford University Press, 1977.

Heidegger, Martin. *Being and Time*. Tr. Joan Stambaugh. Albany: State University of New York Press, 1996.

———. "Building Dwelling Thinking." In *Poetry, Language, Thought*. Tr. Albert Hofstadter, pp. 143–162. New York: Harper and Row, 1971.

———. *Identity and Difference*. Tr. Joan Stambaugh. New York: Harper and Row, 1969.

———. *Introduction to Metaphysics*. Tr. Gregory Fried and Richard Polt. New Haven: Yale University Press, 2000.

Kamuf, Peggy. "The Ghosts of Critique and Deconstruction." From www.usc.edu/dept/comp-lit/tympanum/2/

Kleinberg, Ethan. *Generation Existential: Heidegger's Philosophy in France 1927–1961*. Ithaca: Cornell University Press, 2005.

Lacan, Jacques. *Ecrits*. Tr. Bruce Fink. New York: Norton, 2004.

Lawlor, Leonard. *Thinking Through French Philosophy: The Being of the Question*. Bloomington: Indiana University Press, 2003.

Llewelyn, John. *Appositions of Jacques Derrida and Emmanuel Levinas*. Bloomington: Indiana University Press, 2002.

Lowe, Walter. *Theology and Difference: The Wound of Reason*. Bloomington: Indiana University Press, 1993.

Moyn, Samuel. *Origins of the Other: Emmanuel Levinas between Revelation and Ethics*. Ithaca: Cornell University Press, 2005.

Ronell, Avital. *Dictations: On Haunted Writing*. Lincoln: University of Nebraska Press, 1986.

Srajek, Martin. *In the Margins of Deconstruction: Jewish Conceptions of Ethics in Emmanuel Levinas and Jacques Derrida*. Pittsburgh: Duquesne University Press, 1998.

Taylor, Mark C. *Tears*. Albany: State University of New York Press, 1990.

Wolfrey, Julian. "Citation's Haunt: Specters of Derrida." *Mosaic* (Winnipeg), March 2002.

Yerushalmi, Yosef Hayim. *Freud's Moses: Judaism Terminable and Interminable*. New Haven: Yale University Press, 1991.

Index

'a': attestation and, 111; of *différance*, 11, 115; first, 114; ghost, 94; inadmissible, 118; mute, 94, 100, 105, 106, 107, 108, 111, 113, 115, 116, 118; as simulation of breath of inner reading, 112; unheard, 95

alterity: deconstruction and, ix; *différance* as guarantor of respect for, 2; as irreplaceability, 78; law of, 91; recursive, x; temporal, ix; vibratory, 27

amnesis: and forgetfulness of order of things, 52; onset of, 35

anti-Semitism, 52

Apology (Plato), 61

apophasis: preservation of secrecy of secret by, 2

aporia: afflicting identity with ambivalence, 8; circumvention of, 6; between contrivance and authenticity, 89; of death, 60; death at, 75; deference to, 76; deferral of, 76; defining, 7; of desire, 68; of the ear, 56; of the *episteme*, 57; experience of, 121*n*13, 132*n*18; first, 97; inability to be directly heard, 76; of knowledge, 50; logos as, 22; as parasite of experience, 75; as sacrifice, 104; of survival, 83; and work of mourning, 13

apparition: of the apparition, 30; effects of, 19; and insecurity with presence, 21; of truth, 29

apprehension: emotional basis for, 19

arche, 13; as commandment, 21; as commencement, 21; existence and, 93; function as rule of exclusion, 12; origin of, 35; and protocols of responsibility, 21

Archive Fever (Derrida), 21

archives: death drive and, 101; derangement of, 90; destruction of, 101; expression of repressed contents of, 48; function of, 21; oracular voice of, 48; supplementation and, 52; totality of, 101

Aristotle, 94; and memory, 47; on triangle of ghost/dream, death, 10

attestation, 58

awareness: of phantom frequenting language, 113; self, 99; that refuses awareness, 53; trace of, 69

Barthes, Roland, 13, 120*n*9

Being: apparitions of, 9; of the being, 8; identity as essence of, 7; as individualization, 30; insouciance of, 46; in-the-world, 129*n*8; knowledge of, 35; mortal, 31; and nonbeing, 2; nothingness

Being (*continued*)
  as, 11; as outcome of *polemos*, 52–53; possible, 9; potentiality for, 30, 62; precedence over actual being, 30; repose of, 18; as spiritualization proper, 30; as such, 94; totality of, 39; *ur*-ghost of, 97; violence of, 52; voice of, 107; as war to philosophical thought, 53
Being and Time (Heidegger), 31, 39, 40, 54
being-there, 9, 11
Blanchot, Maurice, x, 11, 20, 76, 77, 115; "Literature and the Right to Death," 10; Orphic hermeneutics of, 19; thesis on writing, 122*n*24
boundaries: being/nonbeing's disrespect for, 10; defiance of, 2; between life and death, 2

Christianity, 77, 126*n*14
circumcision, 86, 95, 97, 99, 100, 112; obeying the debt prior to, 95
Circumfession (Derrida), 81, 90, 99, 115
citation: debt incurred in, 44; function of, 44; ghostly double of, 44; as re-citation, 44
Cixous, Hélène, 100, 133*n*5
class membership, 12
confession: logic of, 99; what is confessed by, 99
conjuration: as act of obedience, 91; and belief in ghosts, 5; competing affiliations with magic and testimony, 55; connection with swearing, 43; *différance* and, 113; ending in perjury, 93; existence, 94, 95; as faith, 61; of the ghost, 15; as ghost risen from encryption in writing, 20; of ghosts to converse with, 4; gift of, 96; injustice and, 96; iteration of signifier by, 17; *jure* in, 96; and the law, 43; lies, 120*n*3; need for magic in, 5; need for writing for a record of, 5; performative, 47, 90; perjury by, 95; proof of, 43; recurrent, 16; by specters, 94; teaching art and performance of, 53; trickery and, 5; writing, 25; in writing, 120*n*3
conscience, 130*n*16; ability to produce trembling, 38; bad, 99; and death, 38, 96; as death's voice, 38; discourse of, 37–38; expression of, 96; spectral properties of, 38
consciousness: conceived as vehicle for articulation of contaminated phonic material, 107; deconstructive, 110; deferred obedience and, 21; denial of law of inheritance by, 46; ethical, 130*n*16; extending unconscious into, 36; focal, 113; insecurity with, 21; neonatal, 86; non-intentional, 56; presence and, 7; repressions and, 36; *revenant and*, 19; secret, 58; as wound inherited from birth, 52

Dasein, 30, 37, 53, 72; appropriation of self by, 132*n*17; and death, 33, 72, 73; existence of, 8; impossibility of, 10, 132*n*17; voice of, 39; worldly orientation of, 39
death, 2; of another, 74; aporia of, 60, 75; conjuring away, 114; conscience of, 38, 96; as conversation with immortals, 64; of the dead, 20; defeat of, 26; deferment of, 24; denial of, 78; deterioration of, 75; as dreamless sleep, 64; drive, 45, 91, 92, 101, 102, 116, 126*n*20; as erasure of difference, 104; eroticism of, 116; face of the holy at, 80; fear of, 22, 24, 61; first, 73; gift of, 49, 72, 74, 117; and gift of voice, 71; grip, 39; historical experience of, 76; and hospitality, 101; image of, 80; incorporation in that of another, 73; irreducible disruption of, 75; 'little,' 75; mark of,

114; memories of, 112; of metaphysical commitment, 78; nonexperience of, 23; no substitutes in, 72; notice, 70; one's own, 72, 73; and the other, 47; politics of, 76; as possibility of impossibility of being there, 75; as possibility of the measureless impossibility of existence, 122*n22*; practice of, 23; of reading voice, 124*n18*; signifiers of, 23, 66; simulacrum of through reading and writing, 24; and spacing of ontological difference, 31; strategy to negate, 65; trace of, 71; trauma of, 91; as unlived life, 37; violent, 71, 124*n21*; voice of, 38; as witness, 26, 37

deconstruction, ix, 54, 101; ab-solving force in, 120*n6*; as aporetic experience, 121*n13*; and articulation of logic of spectrality, 123*n8*; and confusion over nihilism, 1; displacement of favored position and, x; ethics of, 110; and ghosts, 90; as justice, 119*n4*; performative, 90; teaching death in, 102; temporal alterity and, ix; undeconstructible condition of, 1

deferment: constituents of, 21, 22

Derrida, Jacques: analysis of Freud's "pleasure principle," 21; analysis of inner voice, 123*n3*; and apparations, 21; *Archive Fever*, 21; breaks with tradition, 26; chains of, 12; and circumcision, 85; *Circumfession*, 81, 90, 99, 115; conception of 'ghost,' 75; conjuring the ghost of, 5; and death, 77; deconstruction and, 54; on fables, myths, 20; on gift of death, 72; *The Gift of Death*, 96; and gift of sending, 40; on Heidegger, 30–31, 52; and implications of appropriation, 7; investigation into spectral, 29; on middle voice, 12; and negative theology, 2; and origin of the non-originary, 35; and paradox of fidelity, 14; performative intentions of, 125*n2*; *The Post Card*, 21, 22, 87; presence of the ghost and, 11, 29; primacy of the ethical of, 2; on prophecy, 18; questions of disclosure for, 2; questions on prefatory material, 15; and repetition, 16; and secret of secrecy, 59; skill at thaumaturgy, 5; *Specters of Marx*, 32, xii; *Of Spirit*, 93; test as a force outside the domain of life, 26; thought of death and, 71; trembling of, 38; trope of mimesis in, 41; voice writing in meditations on philosophical work by, 6; and work of mourning, 13, 31

Descartes, Rene, 54

Diderot, Denis, 122*n23*

différance: absence included in presence, 12; apprehension of, 100; comprehension and, 100; conjuration and, 113; difference making difference and, 98; as ethical guarantor of respect for alterity, 2; generosity and, 113; as the incomprehensible, 130*n13*; and indiscernible pairs, 120*n11*; infinite, 111; lineage of, 105; masturbatory, 106; sacrifice and, 105, 106; secret of, 113; spacing between poles, 81; the unbounded and, 105; as voice of the ghost reading, 100; as witness that never appears, 109; writing as scandal of, 24

discourse: of conscience, 37–38; emphatic, 69; eschatological, 39; exorcising fear through, 23; of ghosts, 22; infiltration by writing, 23; of inquiry, 52; inventing something impervious to mutation, 18; metonymic, 41; performative aspect of, 5; philosophical, 1, 5, 12, 17, 18, 21, 22, 23, 67;

discourse (*continued*)
  responsibility of writing to, ix; Saussurean universe of, 16; shifts in grounding of, 119*n1*; spectral, 41, 69; thematics of, 23; voice of, 109; without origin, 39
displacement: forms of, 74
dissimulation, 67

emotivism, 119*n2*
Eros, 106; function of, 112; as ghostly frequency of visitation, 113
eschatos, 37, 40
the ethical: metalanguage and, ix
ethics: classical, 110; of decision, 45; of deconstruction, 110; gift of, 113; haunt of, 87; neutering, 113; origin of, 110; respect for recursive alterity and, x; specter of, 87
existence: authentic, 33; conjuring up, 94, 95; holy in, 80; irreplaceable, 56; mystery of, 8; and reproduction, 81; *revenant* responsibility for, 94; task of, 10
experience: aporetic, 68, 69, 75, 89, 97, 121*n13*, 132*n18*; concept of, 68; inexperienceable, 76; lived, 29, 30; of materiality, 29; owning, 8; possibility of, 22, 129*n12*; of the promise, 48; and relation with a presence, 69; of the secret, 132*n20*; of self, 56; testimonial, 132*n20*

faith: as conjuration, 61; and preoccupation with self, 59
foreward: folded into the text, x; as hearsay, ix; responsibility of, x; self-expression of, x
Freud, Sigmund, 22, 89, 104, 113; concern over surrender to telepathic temptation, 29; death drive and, 91, 92, 101, 102, 116; pleasure principle and, 21, 101; and resolution of obsessive conduct, 36; on triangle of ghost/dream, death, 10

gaze: auditory, 76; averting, 76; dissymmetry in, 98; free of substantial things, 3; ghostly, 75; of the invisible other, 59; of the other, 63; power to specify the *who*, 74; reciprocated, 98; trembling before, 59
Geist: as emblem of the spirit, 98; of the gift, 53; haunted by its *Geist*, 78; relation to ghost, 30; spectral work as supplement to, 35; wish to remain separate from the ghost, 31
the Ghost: acoustical, 28; admission of, 10; appearance in writing bearing witness to death, 26; apprehended identity of, 15; arrival in concatenation, 35; begetting ghost, 94; belief in, 2, 89; conception of, 93; conceptual debt to the living, 45; conditional, 83; as conjuration of father's voice in writing, 22; as creatures of an impasse, 89; defining, 2; derivative meaning of, 13; desire of to return to the conjuration, 32; discourse of, 22; of disjunction, 51; dispatching for last time, 36; as edge of terror, 80; escape from reality by, 2; essence of, 20; as figment of imagination, 38; found where there is freedom, 93; freeing, 89; future, 83; going first, followed by life, 13; held in reserve, 83; heteronomy of, 91; immunity of, 62; indeterminate identity of, 15; infiltration of living time by, 19; lack of ancestry, 124*n17*; lack of reflection of, 43; in the land of the dead, 10; lineage of, 106; materiality of voice of, 29; of meaning, 29; meditation on, 37; memorialization of, 14; metaphysical, 54; mother's, 102, 103; obedience to, 109; of one not born, 83; of oneself, 83; origin of, 12, 37; as Orphic figure, 20; part played in putting the work in

writing, 5; place frequented by, 28; plurality of, 32; possibility of, 108; potency of, 32; presence of, 29; proper work of, 18; recall of, 36; relation of *Geist to*, 30; relation to voice, 13; of the repressed, 90, 91; return as conjuration of voice reading, 20; return of, 13, 18, 43, 87; *revenant*, 3, 36; scholarship and, 4; seeing without being seen, 74; as shield against strength of nothing, 93; signifying of, 67; sounds of, 122*n*21; speaking to, 4; of spirit, 31; summoning, 25; surviving voice of, 82; susceptibility to through heavy reading, 29; of this life, 78; as the trace, 80, 83; of truth, 102; of the undecidable, 40; unshackled from living time, 36; visor effect and, 74, 125*n*9; in voice, 29, 51

gift: of avowal, 117; of conjuration, 96; of death, 49, 72, 74, 117; of a name, 32; of repetition, 16; of responsibility, 69; secret, 100; that cannot be given, 96; of the voice reading, 26

Gift of Death, The (Derrida), 96

Graham's Law, 35

guilt: articulation of, 87; of the circumcised, 99; infinite, 104; return of, 19; supply of appeasement for repression, 99; traumatic, 19; uncontested, 87

Hegel, G.W.F., 6, 8, 22, 48, 54, 71, 85, 88, 89, 98, 101, 104, 124*n*18, 126*n*14

Heidegger, Martin, 6, 8, 11, 22, 30–31, 40, 52, 54, 62, 68, 73, 85, 88, 89, 104, 110, 114; on apprehension of the future, 37; and authentic existence, 33; avoidance of 'spirit,' 53, 93; *Being and Time*, 31, 39, 40, 54; on birth, 93; and *Dasein*, 72; and death, 73, 77; delineation of the ontological difference, 30; discourse of conscience of, 37–38; *Es gibt* of, 32; estrangement of voice and, 39; immutability for, 18; *Introduction to Metaphysics*, 52; phantomization of the wound and, 52; *physis* of, 26; *revenant* of, 52; *Seinfrage*, 100; seizing the possibility and, 8; and task of existence, 10; thought of death and, 71; and transcendental knowledge, 9; worldliness of the world of, 30

heteronomy, 72, 73, 74, 91

Hitler, Adolf, 52

hospitality, 106, 114, 116; radical, 101, 117

Husserl, Edmund, 29

"I": as function or phantom, 55; identity of, 8, 10, 74; integrity of, 12; noncoincidence of, 21; as part of spectacle and audience, 55; that is gifted, 59; trembling of, 8, 40, 59; wakefulness in, 79; in writing, 78

identity: absence of, 46; and *aporia*, 8; authentication of, 7; as essence of being, 7; of the "I," 74; indeterminate, 15; of indiscernibles, 8, 120*n*11; personal, 11; presence and, 7; of reading voice, 46; of the *revenant*, 36; scar of, 112; self, 11, 72; of the *who*, 74; of who is writing, 7, 8; of writer, 7

image: audio/visual, 48; of death, 80; mirror, 28

imaginary, 30

imagination: ghost as figment of, 38; philosophical, 62; reproductive, 47; transcendental, 101; truth of, 102

imagination, transcendental, 3, 78, 101, 111, 112, 129*n*12, 133*n*2; examination of, 80; in study of ghost, 80

immortality, 116; concept of, 115; and the gift of the voice reading, 26; guarantee of, 6; personal, 4; of the soul, 23
inheritance, 91; basis in genetics, 45; debts of, 85; of debt through course of repression, 91; in discourse of inquiry, 52; gift of reading as, 28; law of, 46, 82; politics of, 3, 84; of repression, 91, 93; from source text, 44; of wounded thought, 53
injustice, 80; conjuration and, 96
Introduction to Metaphysics (Heidegger), 52
intuition: acoustic, 15
invisibility: of the acoustical, 28
Islam, 77
iterability: and ghostliness, 44; and God, 123*n*2; idealization of ideality as effect of, 123*n*8
iteration: as fidelity, 82; of the holy, 80; performance of, 80; service of delimiting the possibility of survival, 81; as time's tremble, 81; of the trace, 82

Jemeinigkeit, 72
Judaism, 52, 77, 97, 100
justice, 83; deconstruction as, 119*n*4; demand for, 81; fidelity and, 82, 109; future, 83; of giving voice to the other, 84; hypothesis of, 79; and memory, 82; owed to ghosts, 82; philosophy restored to, 131*n*3; possibility of, 83; quest for, 63; and recognition of the third, 49; reparation of debt and, 49; as responsibility, 2, 79; survival of, 79; tribunal of, 87; as undeconstructible subject, 3; voice of, 49

Kant, Immanuel, 18, 32, 62, 129*n*12; antimonies of reason and, 18; memory and, 48; possibility belonging to the transcendental of, 9; and reason, 2; reproductive imagination of, 47; transcendental illusion of, 111
Kierkegaard, Søren, 6, 62, 106, 108, 117; concept of the religous, 70; and death, 77; dialectical wavering of, 79; idea of faith, 59; understanding of the ethical, 128*n*7
knowledge: absolute, 101; aporia of, 50; of being, 35; as best of all medicines, 22; of "between the two's," 3; mimed by writing, 35; philosophy's access to, 1; possibility of, 45; of reality, 47; reductive distortion of, 102; secreting, 91; serving ideology, 102; survival of, 2; transcendental, 9; transmission and, 2

language: duality of, 108; ghost, 41; joints of, 51; 'living,' 41; meant to keep the secret secret, 112; ordinary, 41; phantom that frequents, 113; possibility of, 44; private, 8; promise of, 49; of repression, 95; safeguards transcendental life, 65; technology of, 40; undecidability and, 40; wounded, 99, 114, 116
laws: of alterity, 91; of canonical logic, 43; of contamination, 5, 12; copyright, 7; domain of, 43; Graham's, 35; heteronomous, 85, 128*n*1; of inheritance, 46, 82; just, 85; of physical universe, 43; of repetition, 22; of returning, 43; of the singular, 43; of supplementation, 12
learning: learning the lesson of, 50; to live, xii, 2, 46, 49, 52, 77; to live *with* ghosts, 3; from whom, 57; to write, 77
Lecercle, Jean-Jacques, 39
Leibniz, Gottfried Wilhelm, 8, 120*n*11
Levinas, Emmanuel, x, 39, 66, 72, 74, 89, 108, 111; and death, 75; and

epoch of being, 53; *il y a* of, 11; insomnia of, 100; primacy of the ethical of, 2; psychism of, 84; on readers, 1; thought of death and, 71; on transcendence, 129*n*8; works in "being-for-beyond-my-death," 4

life: beyond of, 46; consumed by survivor, 82; debts of, 46; disruption in sacrificial constitution of, 75; exceeding the limits of, 23; lesson of, 50; owned by whom, 46; phantom, 46; preservation in subvocal voice, 27; "thereness" of, 31; unlived, 46, 71, 74, 78

limits: arriving at, 11; being/nonbeing's disrespect for, 10; built-in indetermination in, 11; idea of, 6; of life, 10; meaning of, 10

"Literature and the Right to Death" (Blanchot), 10

logic: of after-the-fact, 131*n*7; based on oppositionals, 61; of the beyond, 18; canonical, 43; of confession, 99; of contamination, 59; of difference and differend, 58; of distinction, 31; excess in, 64; heteronomous, 18; of the position, 18; presumptive, 64; spectral, 18, 23, 123*n*8; stoic, 109, 112, 114, 117; traditional, 18, 48

logocentrism, 41, 61, 119*n*1

logos: as *aporia*, 22; father of, 95; haunting of, 29; and inherited debt, 49; rupture of, 130*n*13; transgression of, 52

magic: conjuration and, 55; embodied in dialectic, 63; need for in conjuration, 5; and *poesis*, 94; repressed, 63, 64; vocal, 61; and wonder, 61

Magic Writing Pad, 96, 99

Marx, Karl, 22, 85, 88, 89, 104

masturbation, 106

meaning: apparation of, 17; of class membership, 12; conjuring voice, 17; foundational, 12; ghosts of, 29; mastery of, 3; of mortality, 10; phantomization of, 29; rescue from oblivion by writing, 5; of the self, 56

memorialization, 75

memory: archival, 36; computational, 35; of the dead, 84; of death, 112; encrypted, 36; of the father, 22, 101; function of, 48, 82; and intimacy with imemoriality of the singular, 31; and justice, 82; living, 35, 36, 75, 82, 84; memorization of, 52; owed and repaid, 84; as phantomization of perception, 47; phantom of, 47; politics of, 3, 84, 103; possibility of, 36; as prime locale of ghosts, 47; pure, 35, 36; repetition in, 16; repressed, 101; and truth, 35; writing as aid to, 35

metalanguage, ix; the ethical and, ix

metaphysics, Western, 101; conjuration in, 94; counter-currents to, 112; ghosts and, 12; haunting by a beyond, 78; philosophical discourse and, 2, 21; presence and, 6, 7; substantial self and, 55; writing and, 7

mourning, 10; of absolute loss, 109; the avoidance of mourning, 86; to birth, 103; conditional replacements, 83; of the dead, 13; directed to the trace of the absent presence, 108; double, 87; of the exclusion, 108; the fact of substitution, 83; failure calling for, 84; forbidden, 85; infinite, 104; interiorization of, 89; and letting the ghost be, 36; for life surrendered, 114; linguistic form of, 110; memorialization of the father and, 22; obligatory curriculum of, 86; the other, 72; the past, 109; putting in writing, 10; as restitution by gift of a name, 32; self, 83; transcendent mode, 110; the unborn, 109; work of, 13, 22,

mourning (*continued*)
31, 32, 33, 37, 45, 51, 72, 74, 76, 98, 127*n*3; as work of remembrance, 110
muteness: of 'A,' 94; and holy speech, 81; initialization of, 107; as quarry for the breath, 81; and theme of the holy, 80; and voice of ghosts, 82
mysterium tremendum, 112, 119*n*2
myth, 20

Naming, 39, 40
National Socialism, 52
naturalism: ethical, 63
Nazism, 54
negation: radical, 2
Nietzsche, Friedrich, 22, 78, 85, 88, 92, 94, 104, 116
nihilism, 1, 57, 109
noema, 30

oath, 37, 40, 45, 49, 128*n*1; making, 43
obedience: about the 'twos,' 95; defining, 94; enforced, 118; to the ghost, 109; to the other, 81; phantom, 96; production of a spell by, 96; by putting it in writing, 86; in voice-reading, 79; willed, 97
obedience, deferred, 20, 53, 54, 90, 108, 109; by avoidance of truth, 99; conjuration and, 21; debt of, 93; final grounds of, 126*n*16; owed to, 117; phantomization of wound and, 52; question of immobilization of intention, 92; secrecy and, 91
object: fictive, 30; reality of, 29
objectivity: phantomatic, 29
obsession, 36
occultism, 21, 53
Of Spirit (Derrida), 93
onto-theology, 76, 77, 93, 94; sacrifice of, 74

opposition: movement of, 17; positing 'self,' 56; signification of, 56
the Other: absolute, 73, 97; alone before, 73; call to, 90; gaze of, 63; giving voice to, 84, 86; involuntary submission to, 86; memorialization of, 74; obedience to, 79, 81, 90; otherness of, 82; passage to the time of, 4; phantom, 3; raised to eminence, 53; reader as, 1; recognition of, 48; respect for, 109; responsibility to, 2; as signifier without meaning, 113; spectral time as, 37; as trace of a trace, 79; what is owed to through teaching, 3

Patocka, Jan, 96, 97, 98, 112
perjury: conjuration ending in, 93; by conjuring, 95
phantom: already an apparation of the dead, 36–37; appearance in guise of apprehension, 19; arrival as coming-back, 19; of breath, 54; life, 46; of memory, 47; need for prior life in order to return, 45; 'noumenal,' 29; obedience, 96; past tense of, 28; re-cognition of, 44; of recurrence, 16
phantomization, 31
phenomenality, 30
phenomenology, 68; possibility of, 32; spectrality and, 32
philosophy: access to secret knowledge by, 1; commitment to reason, 1; double restitution of, 131*n*3; empiricism and, 53; end of, 49, 54, 85; incorporation of Apollonian mission of Socrates into, 61; magisterial purpose of, 1; offering reassurance to children through, 22; responsibility of writing to, ix; restored to justice, 131*n*3; role of, 1; sinned against, 87; of testimony, 53; transcendental, 12; twice renewed, 62; as voice

addressed to an other, 1; as Western metaphysics, 2
plagiarism, 7, 44
Plato, 26, 41, 61, 62, 68, 87, 98, 113; on origin of *Arche*, 35; practice of death of, 23; preparation for death and, 3
poetry, 61, 62
politics: of death, 13, 76; of ghosts in life, 104; of inheritance, 3, 84; of memory, 3, 84, 103; of the polis, 82; of self-presence, 8; of virtue, 58
possibility: of appropriation, 9, 10; derivation of actual from, 30; empty, 122n22; existence of, 9; of experience, 22, 129n12; of the ghost, 108; of hearing the reading voice, 51; of impossibility, 45; of the impossibility of *Dasein*, 10; of justice, 83; of knowledge, 45; of language, 44; of memory, 36; of presence, 12; as pre-stage of actuality, 9; of redemption, 30, 101; of relating to the possible, 73; of singularity, 9; of the specter, 39, 46; of survival, 81; of survival of justice, 79; of transcendental visititation, 18
Post Card, The (Derrida), 21, 22, 87
prayer, 69; terror as object of, 79
presence: and absence, 12; apparition and, 21; and consciousness, 7; *différance and*, 12; experience and, 69; fractured, 86; as ghost of absence, 12; of ghosts, 29; of the I, 8; identity and, 7; insecurity with, 21; lost, 10; in metaphysics, 6, 7; possibility of, 12; of the present, 9, 47, 65; reduced to echo, 31; rejection of, 37; as rupture, 52; self, 18, 35, 96; self-contained, 12; void of, 69; of the *who*, 8
prophecy, 18
psychoanalysis, 46

readers: as the Other, 1; response when text bears ghost of meaning in the voice, 28; role in giving voice to writing, 28
reading: conjured to voice of writing, 19–20, 27; credulity in, 27; ghost-voice of, 13, 38; giving voice to the voice of the writer, 9; possibility of, 7; silent, 81; superficial, 2; voice, 43, 46, 58, 67, 69, 71, 76, 80, 85, 99, 102, 121n16, 123n5, 125n7; voicification engaged in, 7
reality: alternative, 102; determinate, 98; digression in, 6; escape from plane of, 2; foundational, 2; knowledge of, 47; of the object, 29; re-conjuring, 23; rubbing out of, 98; semblance of, 96
reason: antimonies of, 18; commitment of philosophy to, 1; divine, 107; Kant and, 2; objective, 107; practical, 2; pure, 2; voice of, 107
reflection, 28
repetition: first and, 39; gift of, 16; law of, 22; in memory, 16; and possibility of survival, 81; of presence of the present, 65; trace of, 16; truth and, 16
replication: support for conjuration of the ghost and, 15
repression, 36; archived data from site of, 21; of the demonic, 38, 96; dynamics of, 92; inheritance of, 91, 93; language of, 95; logic and, 64; magic and, 64; of memories, 101; persistence of, 64; of Platonic psyche, 98; recognizing, 90; release of by death, 114–115; of repression, 97; serenity of, 90; of thaumaturgy, 65; time's synchrony as by-product of, 63
responsibility: absolute, 49; appearance of, 79; arising at the aporia of the singular, 45; concept of, 69; consequence of, 129n9;

responsibility (*continued*)
constituted by act of reclusion, 76; decisions and, 62; demand for, 81; facing, 63; of forewords, x; gift of, 69; grounding, 45; and identity of the "I," 8; of justice to the other, 2; for the other before death, 74; in presence of the undecidable, 46; protocols of, 21; and respect for otherness of the other, 82; survival and, 80; victimization of, 97; of writing, ix, 82
retribution, 63
revenant: begins by coming back, 13, 19, 93; ghost as, 13, 36, 71; identity of, 36; interval of, 44; as iteration of man/work, 51; as law of returning, 43; model for, 53; requirement of living being for, 45; responsible for existence, 94; as restructured Kierkegaardian spirit, 19; returned from the repressed, 21; secret self and, 58; as sublimated spectrality, 31; time of, 63
Ronse, Henri, 95

sacrifice, 73; absolute loss and, 106; aporia as, 104; and *différance*, 105, 106; and economy of exchange, 106
Saussure, Ferdinand de, 123*n*7; account of meaning, 108; strategy of meaning conjuring voice and, 17; theory of language, 107
secret: consciousness, 58; experience of, 132*n*20; to living, 59; owner of, 58; secrecy of, 2, 59, 80, 98, 106; self, 57, 58; separateness and, 59; that teaches, 58; transmission of, 57, 58
self: abuse, 88; awareness, 99; effacement, 12; experience of, 56; faith and, 59; identity, 11, 72; irreplaceable, 72; in itself, 56; mourning, 83; presence, 7, 8, 18, 31, 35, 96; pretension to, 58; secret, 55, 56, 57, 58; substantial, 55, 56; trembling before the other, 73; tremulation of, 8
selfhood: mark of, 9
sexuality: infantile, 101, 106; primitive, 106
signification: phonic operation of, 80
the Signified: former life of, 16–17; return to haunt the signifier, 16; transcendental, 108
signifiers: of death, 23; performative, 17; phantom, 21; presentation in need of to be an identity, 17; substitution for signified, 65; system of, 67
Socrates, 17, 26, 38, 47, 49, 50, 57, 76, 87; Apollonian mission of, 61; *daemonium* of, 61, 62; intellectualism of, 64
specters: acoustics of, 27; bringing forth the repetition of voice, 27; as carnal apparition of spirit, 30; conjuring by, 94; disruptive tremor of, 39; of ethics, 87; as frequency of visibility, 30; grip on vocality by, 128*n*13; inheritance from life for, 45; location in the past, 3; phenomenology of, 126*n*14; possibility of, 39, 46; put in writing, 10; roots of in the future, 3; sensuous materiality of, 29; as spirit deferred out of deference to death, 30
Specters of Marx (Derrida), xii, 32
spectrality: as domain within discourse of the end, 37; and duality of language, 108; infrastructure of indebtedness in, 45; logic of, 123*n*8; muted with respect to being, 38; performance of, 58; and possibility of phenomenology, 32; quotation marks and, 44
Spinoza, Baruch, 82; meditation on life and, 3
spirit: association with fire, 97; blinding, 98; cleansed of demonology, 97; connection to trope of

festering, 98; contamination of by specter, 126*n*16; free, 78; of iteration, 53; phenomenology of, 126*n*14; rejection of, 54; repression of direction of return and, 98; returns in its own time, 31; as spectrality sublimated, 31
subconsciousness, 58
supplementarity, 12
suppression: caution in speaking of, 62
survival: and continuation/consumption, 82; impulse, 103; and voice heard by another, 115; and writing, 26
Symposium (Plato), 61

temporality, 80
terror: to be regarded as such, 79; fear unto, 79; as object of prayer, 79; as supplement, 98
text: alignment with author/reader prior to transmission, 1; cited, 44; commencing, 6; ghost, 89; manifold digressions within as spacings of the ghost, 44; performative, 78; situated in "night," 11; source, 44; spectral haunting of, 11; spectral prodigality of, 26; survivors written into, 115; truth of, 25; vocality of, 22; voice incorporation into, 21
thaumaturgy, 17, 61, 63, 64, 93; repressed, 67, 68
Thoth, 98
time: asynchronous, 3, 19; first, 35, 36; ghost, 19, 31; last, 38; 'out of joint,' 40, 63; primordial condition of, 37; of the *revenant*, 63; spectral, 37; of spirit, 31; synchronous, 28, 63, 92; world, 38
trace: acoustical primary of, 100, 128*n*1; of audibility, 69; of awareness of being seen, 69; of death, 71; determination of possibility of displacement by, 81; disruption by, 79; ghost as, 80; iteration of, 79, 82; of the last repetition, 16; obedience to, 92; secret of, 80; of a survivor, 80; of a trace, 79; work of, 80
tragedy, 52
transcendental: condition of phenomena, 30; ego, 32, 53, 55; imagination, 3; knowledge, 9; philosophy, 12; possibility and, 9; reduction, 30; value, 57; visitation, 18
transcendentalism: ethical, 63
traumatism, 67, 131*n*13; madness and, 90; return of, 19
trembling: as dialectical wavering, 59; of the "I," 8, 40; in identity of the "I," 10; implications of, 121*n*18; as initializing of difference, 81; produced by conscience, 38; of sensation, 79; symptomatology of, 79
Tremendum, 73, 74, 75
tremor: of the *mysterium*, 9; personal identity and, 11; of the specter, 39
truth: amnanmnesic movement of, 16; of the aporetic, 9; apparitions of, 29; avoidance of, 99; criteria of, 55; crossings of, 76; of delusion, 102; disclosure of, 39, 57; ghost of, 102; of haunting, 17; and illusion, 2; of imagination, 102; impure, 78; limits of, 76; living, 17; markings of, 16; and memory, 35; and metaphor, 3; repetition and, 16; repressed, 102; of speech, 24; of the text, 25; unattainable, 91; unveiling of the *eidos* by, 16

the uncanny, 9, 30; entrance of from nowhere, 9; impropriety of, 39; susceptibility to, 29; voice of, 48; and the voice reading, 18

violence, 49, 69, xii; of being, 52; of the nominative, 56; retaking of, 57; state-sponsored, 102; wounds of, 53; writing and, 97

virtuality, 101
visibility: proper to the possibility of actual beings, 30; of specter, 30
visor effect, 74, 125n9
voice: of absence, 65; acoustic signature of, 21; alien, 39, 128n13; always ready, 19; animal, 124n21, 128n13; auto-production of, 36; borrowed, 44; of the dead, 65; of discourse, 109; estrangement of, 39; of the father, 22; of the ghost, 16, 51, 71, 82, 124n21; ghost as non-acoustical replication of, 13; the haunted in, 25; immanence of, 56; inarticulate, 27; incorporated into text, 21; of justice, 49; literal, 27; magical effects of, 61; meaning conjuring, 17; modulation of, 28; morphability of, 27; muted, 43, 128n1; natural, 38, 128n13; not one's own, 28; patrimony of, 109; pure, 66; put into writing, 20; reading, 13, 20, 43, 46, 58, 67, 69, 71, 76, 80, 85, 99, 102, 121n16, 123n5, 125n7; of reason, 107; recalling the spectral, 44; reintroduced in writing, 13; and the sigh, 65; spectral, 32, 69; as supplementation to writing, 7; transmuted, 28; of the uncanny, 48; without breath, 65, 69; work coordinate of, 22; writing, 85, 121n16

war, 53
work: coordinate of voice, 22; difference between man and, 51; of the ghost, 18; of mourning, 13, 22, 31, 32, 33, 37, 45, 51, 98; of remembrance, 86; spectral, 35; of the trace, 80
writing: as aid for memory, 35; archive and, 21; authentication of, 7, 8; autobiographical, 132n19; to avoid avoidance, 86; avowal and, 5; barrenness of, 26; commemorative, 33; concept of replication and, 15; confessional, 120n4; as conjuration to end violence, 97; conjuring, 25, 120n3; as cure for fear of dying, 24; as dangerous supplement, 86; in the dark, 10, 122n23; death's, 38; debt to the dead in, 84; detour in, 6; ghost, 7, 44, 87; as heir to demand for reparation, 49; the "I" in, 78; importation of secret life in, 27; inclusion of what cannot be uttered, 25; invention of, 98; lack of immortality in, 26; to the last, 85; limits of debt and, 87; metaphysical nature of, 7; miming knowledge, 35; misunderstanding and, 10; as moral compensation, 87; for others, 123n5; outliving the writer, 6; part of ghost in putting works in, 5; performative, 25, 78, 102, 119n1, 123n10, 125n1; plagiarism and, 7; prefaces, 123n1; production of a haunting in, 26; putting mourning in, 10; putting the ghost in, 20; relation of new chapter to previous one, 15; rescues meaning from oblivion, 5; responsibility in, ix, 82; as restitution of restitutions, 23; retention of presence of writer in, 6; to root out sin, 84; as scandal of *différance*, 24; and sin, 85; special potency of, 120n3; supplementation and, 26; and survival, 26; uncertainty and, 10; *up* to the end, 88; usury of, 85; visitation as inherent trait of, 17; voice, 13, 85, 121n16